"HARDSHIP POSTING"

True tales of expat misadventure in Asia.

Volume 1.

Compiled and edited by
Stuart Lloyd

Chrome Pole Press

ii

All reference and likeness to persons living or dead is purely intentional.

Published by Captions of Industry Pty Ltd.
ACN 089 800 304
PO Box 350, Pymble, NSW, 2073, Australia.
Fax: 612-9499-5908
Email: **hardship_posting@hotmail.com**

Check out **www.hardshipposting.com/hp** for more misadventure with Col.Ken.

National Library of Australia Cataloguing-in-Publication:
"Hardship Posting" True Tales of Expat Misadventure in Asia
ISBN 0646 37883X (V.1)
1. Business people - Asia anecdotes. 2. Aliens - Asia anecdotes.
3. Employment in foreign countries - anecdotes.
4. Employment in foreign countries - anecdotes - humor.
5. Asia - Social life and customs - humor
(1) Lloyd, Stuart, 1962- (II) Ken, Colonel
950 00424

Cover design Stuart Lloyd and Shrimp Studios, Thailand
Photography by Shrimp Studios, Thailand.

Printed in Thailand

10 9 8 7 6 5 4 3

To The Daves. Growing old disgracefully.

"Those who leave their native lands are like a river - never stopping, always rushing, day and night." Confucius iv

Contents

Foreword by Stuart Lloyd

Foreplay by Colonel Ken Oathe

v

Foreword

This Australian guy was running the Bangkok office of an international firm. He had a new boss, stationed in the New York headquarters, who was doing his first familiarisation tour through Asia.

The country manager dreaded these things, but prepared a great presentation, covering an overview of the country, the marketplace, the competitors, the company in Thailand, the key personnel, etc. Everything the Americans would want to hear.

Come the big day, and the pin-striped Captain America arrived. Very stiff. Very formal. The presentation was well-received, if very corporate and proper. He had made plans to take his boss out to a restaurant in a nearby hotel- somewhere sanitary and 'safe'. Dinner went well, but remained a little stilted (the boss still had his tie done up!). Just when he thought *Ok I'll drop my boss off at his hotel and head down for some beers with the lads down the strip* his boss uncharacteristically chirped up: "So are you going to show me some of this famous Bangkok nightlife?"

Cut to the scene a few hours later. They're in a bar in Soi Nana. The music is pumping. The stage is full of nubile girls shimmying away. The boss has his tie around his head, bandanna style. There's a now nearly-empty bottle of Jack Daniels on the table in front of them. And each has a couple of teenage sweethearts on their laps.

The manager turns to his boss and says: "I've been meaning to ask you about the increment for the Hardship Posting."

* * *

The idea for this book was hatched, not surprisingly, over a few beers. To be exact, a friend's farewell party held at a glorious tropical golf course in Johor, Malaysia. A week before my own farewell party.

The tour was coming to a close. I had been an expatriate for a full twelve and a half years and had decided to "go home". Days later, as I re-entered Sydney, the immigration officer took one look at my dog-eared passport and said, "Geez, I reckon this would have a lot of stories to tell!"

So it had to be done. Plus, I felt the need to document, if at all possible, the incredible overwhelming sensory experience of that time. *Those times.* For therapy if not for posterity.

Along the way, I encountered many great situations of my own, many shared by others, and they in turn had regaled me (as a young lad) with stories of their time in Asia. I remember one friend telling me about the time he had just arrived in Singapore. His friend was saying, "You should go to Bangkok, you'll love it. But you should have been here years ago - it's all commercialised now." In 1975!

And Asia has changed. Dramatically and meteorically. Some love it - the adventure in foreign climes, the people, the money, the language, the kinetic energy- and will never leave. Whilst for others, it really is a hardship posting. A love/hate or even hate/hate proposition, counting off the days till the contract's up to return to their prospective home-lands.

Asia has become a good thing to have on your resume now. Years ago, when some of its cities or countries were regarded as commercial back-waters and tin-pot banana republics, it was seen as a sideways or back-ward step. I remember in the late 80's being asked several times, "What are you hiding from?" Being an expat in Asia was seen as being akin to Ronald Biggs in Brazil. (And perhaps for good reason in some cases!)

For many in 'the real world,' their knowledge of Asia extended to the Vietnam War and Nixon giving pandas to China.

Whereas now, countless people have traveled through these once-frontier terrains in their business and leisure travels and got an inkling of what Asia is about. And many of these markets have become key strategic targets for multinational operations; and so more expats, with more responsibility.

But it is true to say that being an expatriate is a different state of mind. In many cases, it could be likened to a never-ending rugby tour. A state of suspended responsibility, and extended adolescence. Where longevity is worn as some kind of crumpled and dusty badge of honour.

And from this has sprung much misadventure - some of it intentional, some of it accidental- in any case, the stuff of legend. But it has been largely unspoken outside of expatriate country clubs and the gin joints of Asia. Hong Kong expats talk of the "Kai Tak Accord," implying that what goes on tour, stays on tour. Till now!

That code of silence, tantamount to parliamentary privilege, has been well and truly shattered with this book. So many thanks to all those who gallantly accepted the challenge to come forward and willingly tell their side of the story. (And like good fishing stories, some of these have no doubt grown with each successive retelling.)

To protect the 'guilty', all stories are unattributed to individual contributors, and names have been deleted or changed so we could get absolutely the best stories published without fear of retribution or incrimination from authorities, employers or spouses (especially spouses!).

To our gracious hosts in all Asian countries - thank you for sharing your countries with us, and allowing us to enjoy the Asian experience together. No disrespect is intended, and none of this should detract from what is largely a harmonious and productive co-existence. I have made this deliberately non-judgmental, and in many cases it's the expats that lose face or come out second best.

To quote and paraphrase Somerset Maugham, he said the vast majority of expats he came across were, "Ordinary people ordinarily satisfied with their station in life". He also said, "They were good, decent, normal people," he respected and admired - but not the sort of people he could write stories about. Amen.

Whilst I don't condone *all* of the behaviour contained herein, you have to agree it's bloody good for a laugh - meant solely for the purpose of entertainment.

And political incorrectitude is a necessity to convey the full colour of the Asian experience, for which I offer no apology.

Many people asked, "Are you in there?" Yes, I'm in here. I never kept journals of my time in Asia, and it has been wonderfully cathartic and nostalgic to compile these anecdotes, with a million scraps of paper, beermat scrawlings, emails and faxes littering my study as I write this.

I found it was really only once I had left Asia that the full extent of that halcyonic weird and wonderful existence hit me. All five senses. Maybe even six. Many guys I know lead very extreme lifestyles in Asia, and when contacted for this book said, "I can't really think of anything. I lead a pretty straightforward life." To them, incredulously, maybe.

The monstrous has become mundane. The exotic has become indigenous.

There's the analogy of putting a frog in a pot of cold water on the stove. If you gradually turn up the heat, the frog doesn't sense the gradual increases, until such time as the water actually gets to boiling point and the frog is cooked to death, without ever realising that the water changed temperature. Try it if you don't believe me.

In Asia that's called "Being in the sun too long" or "Gone Troppo!" Speaking of which, I am pleased to say my erstwhile friend and noted philanthropist, Colonel Ken Oathe, agreed to not only write the foreword to this book, but also to introduce each chapter. In fact, once he started I just couldn't shut him up!

I leave you in his good (though slightly delirium tremens-affected) hands.

As they say on TV: "Don't try this at home!"

Cheers,

Stuart Lloyd,
Sydney, September '99.

xi

Acknowledgements

We canvassed not just Caucasian expats - *gweilos, angmohs, gaijin, matsallehs, bule, and farang*- but also Asian expats living in other Asian countries.

I want to thank all those contributors that have shared their stories and bared their souls (and occasionally other body parts) to make this a great collection of colourful tales. We have lawyers, marketers, managing directors, IT specialists, advertising types, executive recruitment specialists, engineers, all types of folks in here. All highly paid, mostly mild-mannered white-collar professionals in prominent positions, which makes the stories even more "out there" as a result.

To Larry Feign, who was the only person capable of doing this concept justice with his cartoons. I'd like to say we spent long nights draining bottles of red wine thinking of these ideas together, but it was all done, incredibly, via e-mail and internet. Great work, Larry!

To Patrick Gauvain, the legendary Shrimp, for so keenly embracing the assignment to shoot the cover. Col. Ken's not the easiest guy to work with, and some of the shots we *didn't* use for the cover were even better (say no more!)

To Chris Destrieux, the flying French-South African-Kiwi-Tahitian-Singaporean-Australian for being the sounding board and sub-editor.

To all others who played a part in encouraging me, putting me in touch with others who could help, rendering assistance and just being inspirational with your involvement or feedback along the way: Mike Carlson, John Ellsmore, Fern Farida, Rachel Farnay, Lena Frew, Paul Grezoux, Mark Kovalevsky, Gerrie Lim, Bruce Lloyd, Jackie McGrath, Susie Ngamsuwan, Phat Sarapa, Barry Smit, Nury Vittachi, and of course my wife, Michelle, for all those cups of coffee and my son Justin for allowing Daddy to use the computer to type this when you wanted to play on the internet instead. And to Rosemount Estate's Shiraz Cabernet for its sterling support role in the writing of this book - several good ideas in every bottle!

Contributors to Hardship Posting, Volume 1:

Nick Arnold
Chris Batson
Al Boyden
Val Boyden
Dominque Butler
Celevel Butler
Blair Currie
Chris Delaney
Chris Destrieux
Chris Fong
Fiona Fowles
Patrick Gauvain
Guy Gostling
Paul Grezoux
Caroline Halbroth
Thierry Halbroth
Mark Ingall
Mark Ingrouille
Andrew Kefford
Russell Kelly
Mark Kovalevsky

Chris Kyme
Stuart Lloyd
Gill Martin
Cass Meyers
Ian Noakes
Chris Nolan
Doug Palmer
Michael Polin
Brian Pollard
George Reinhart
Jim Reinnoldt
Barry Smit
Iwan Soebardi
Rob Speechley
Scott Terrey
Neil Thomason
Graham Warner
Andrew Way
Peter West
Reg Worthington
Greg Wright

Many thanks to the above for your contributions. We encourage everyone to come out of the woodwork with their side of the story for Volume 2. (See back page for contributor guidelines.)

Foreplay by Colonel Ken

Bastards. Go and ruin a perfectly good afternoon nap by calling to see if I'm interested in helping out with their wretched book. And then, to make matters worse, they cheapen the whole thing by involving money. What do they think I am? Some bloody $2 floozy? Heaven's above, I'm Asia's foremost freelance philanthropist. (Try saying *that* after a dozen gin and tonics, as I often have to.)

Anyway, after I managed to get them up quite substantially on their initial offer, here I am...finally putting pen to paper on something they think I know a little about...expat misadventure in Asia.

Well, let me put it this way: I remember Asia when the *water* was dangerous and the *sex* was safe!

So without further doggie-do, let's get into it then. Expats. Yes, a funny word for an even funnier bunch of people. And guess what? I found the word 'Expatriate' right there between "Expansion of gases" and "Experiment Station". Well, that'd be right. Expansion of gases is something I'm no stranger to...especially after a good curry in Hollywood Rd, Hong Kong or Race Course Rd in Singapore. Oh yes, Mrs Col. Ken could tell you all about that - singed her eyebrows quite a few a few times. I'll give her one thing...she's a brave woman sharing a bed with me after a nice leisurely session on the old Vindaloo and Tigers.

Now the thing about this encyclopedia is next to *Expat* it said: "See exile." More like *sexile*, but don't tell the old bag. Mind you, she always says I'm a philanderer not a philanthropist. As long as she's got money for her shopping and mahjong games, the old handbrake's OK.

Next, I turned to the Webster Comprehensive - sounds like a sophisticated BBQ if you ask me - and next to *expatriate* it says: "To drive a person from his native land, exile, banish. Or to withdraw one's self from one's native land." Now this may be true in some cases. I know my dear friend Pete the Pony-tailed Portrait Photographer was probably banished from England at some point. But that definition sounds a bit too negative; a bit more push than pull if you ask me (and I prefer a bit more pull where I can get it).

A chap I've leaned on very heavily here is my dear friend, Dave the airline man, procurer of cheap deals to the gentry. What he doesn't know about Asian history isn't worth knowing - truth be known, a lot of what he *does* know about Asian history is not worth knowing! Now Dave's big theory is that today's "locals" were once the original expats. Think about it...the Chinese left China and chased dollars around other key trading ports. Hindu and Sikh merchants entered Thailand around the 3rd century BC (that's even before I was born). They even named South East Asia "*Suvvanabhumi*" meaning 'the land of gold' presumably because it was the start of many a booming souvenir empire.

Even the Chinese have been in Thailand since the 10th century. And then the Portuguese started a sailing school in the 16th century and before we know it they're all over the show in Malacca, Thailand, Sri Lanka, East Timor and Macao. And thank heavens for that...they have left us with the most beautiful and exotic Eurasian descendents. That's why whenever I meet someone from Europe I always say "thank you" just in case their great grandfather was a Portuguese seaman (and I don't mean that in the bodily fluid sense of the word) that contributed to the gene pool.

Dave reckons it was like musical chairs there for a while. The Dutch bastardised Indonesia. The French took a fancy to IndoChina. The Brits took Hong Kong and Malaya. Everyone else took a turn at the Philippines. Like tag-team colonialism.

Of course it wasn't all gin and tonic and skittles. The Poms took Mallaca from Portugal in 1795, and bits of India off France in 1757, Japan took Singapore off the Brits in 1942, and so on. A complete shitfight by the sound of it.

And the only country with its imperialism left undiluted was good old Thailand. To this day the only thing you'll find diluted in Thailand is the drinks in a Patpong bar.

So us Westerners have been at this colonial thing in Asia for nearly 200 years.

We weren't always welcome of course. Barry (my trade insurance buddy otherwise known as "the boring bastard" 'cause he always comes up with useless facts and figures) reckons it was a hard road to hoe initially. The Boxer Rebellion in China being a good example of "whites out now." And for a long time, he says, Canton province was the only place where foreign trade was permitted. Even Japan and Korea earned themselves the nicknames of the Hermit Kingdoms due to their reluctance to open up to foreign trade. But, gee they've made up for lost time, haven't they? Yip, they can smell a dollar with those little oriental proboscii of theirs.

In fact the Japs are about the biggest bunch of expats in many Asian cities now, making staple commodities like golf and hostess bars highly unaffordable for mere mortals not on company expenses, like myself.

Once again, turning to my New Standard Encyclopedia (which I have used more in the last week than in the last 15 years I've owned the blasted things) says: "Love of adventure and the desire to improve their lot induced many people to settle in colonies." It then goes on to say, "...or to furnish a place of exile, as for example a leper colony or penal colony." Now they've missed the point completely. Nowhere does it mention glorious sunshine, cheap beer and dusky maidens. Penal colony? *Penile* colony would be more like it!

Dave was reading this book, Singapore Chronicles (published by The Tatler) recently, and he came across this little gem: "Others with a desire to bring honour to their families or to seek financial advancement dared the sea voyage and the human predators to make a new life. All are exceptional for taking the challenge, facing danger and making a contribution, despite the odds that towered against their fervour." Well see, they're spot on here, but let's read between the politically-correct lines.

"Desire to bring honour to our families." Well that's just ridiculous. We all have the desire, it's just that sometimes the execution falls a little short of the game-plan. Especially when you make this game-plan before arriving in Asia. And, frankly, many are here to escape their families altogether.

"Seek financial advancement." Ok, make lots more dough than if you were stuck licking corporate crevice at home. Tick.

"Dared the sea voyage..." Perhaps the modern equivalent would be flying a Chinese domestic airline or something.

"Human predators..." that would be like copy watch sales-guys in Lucky Plaza in Singapore for instance.

"Making a contribution..." Hell, I'm a founding member of the Soi Nana Frequent Fliers Club. I've single-handedly bankrolled several small third world nations with my dedicated patronisation of bars around the region. Now that's what I call a real contribution. I have fed and clothed and schooled and housed, oh, umpteen families over the years. But it's been on a selective philanthropic basis...meaning, oh, seventeen and female basically. And do I get recognised on the Queen's New Year List - no. Do I get recognised by the World Bank? No. The only time I get recognised is when I short- change one of these birds and they see me walking down the strip.

In any case, I'm glad to be numbered in the ranks of famous expats in Asia. Lads such as Sir Stamford Raffles, Jim Thompson, Thomas Lipton, Arthur C. Clarke, Somerset Maugham, Douglas MacArthur, and Christopher Patton. Guys that probably made a contribution in their own little way, but I don't remember ever bumping into any of them in Soi Cowboy.

Cop you later.

Colonel Ken

Col. Ken Oathe; D.O.M, VD & Bar.
Koh Samui, Thailand. August 1999.

PS: Where's my cheque, you bastards?

"The fasten seatbelt sign is now on."
True tales about airports and flying.

Unless you're a bloody good swimmer, any expat's journey presumably starts with an aeroplane ride.

Now my mate Dave (bless his corporate cotton socks) is a bit of a history buff and he tells me that as early as 1909 they were doing test flights in China. Lot of bloody good it did *them*! And Philippine Airlines was the first Asian airline to kick off in 1941. But aviation apparently kicked in throughout Asia in a big way in 1947 and it changed life as we knew it. Cathay Pacific, Northwest Orient and Singapore Airlines all had their genesis then, albeit under different names and badges and colours. Why 1947? Aha. That was after the war, and the first trans-Pacific flights were now possible. This meant greater access to and from the region, and people could even 'go home' for a holiday for the first time (until then, it would've been several months by sea, thereby over-utilising your leave entitlement somewhat before you'd even got to the other side).

There were the times when "Asia" and "aeroplane" were difficult to utter in the same sentence without breaking into a cold sweat and involuntarily recounting some near death experience. Call me old fashioned, but I like an airline that has an equal amount of take-offs and landings. But these days, a lot of them have really got the hang of it. You'll notice I didn't say *all*! I'm sure many of those planes from 1909 are still in service in more remote parts of China.

And just as well. If everything went smoothly, flying would be pretty boring wouldn't it?

I hate it when some bugger next to you falls asleep, using your shoulder as some kind of convenient public pillow. Little bits of drool escaping from his mouth on to your shirt. Pinning you in that position so you can't get up and chat up the hosties or go and syphon the python. Or better still, join the old mile high club.

And uncomfortable! Who in their right mind would have a chair in their home or office as small as an economy seat in an airplane. Geez, I haven't seen a chair that flaming small since I left kindergarten. But even then I didn't have to have my knees around my chest.

Who designs these bloody things? Must be the airlines' finance departments. "Oh, come on you marketing guys, I hear what you're saying about customer satisfaction but look at all that spare space. We could fit another seat in here, here, here..."

Maybe it's just that my arse is wider than before, or maybe they really do design special seats for Asian passengers. They probably do. After all, Barry the boring bastard, tells me that IATA predicts Asia will represent 39.2% of world air traffic in the year 2000. (Use *that* at your next cocktail party and dazzle them).

If you're reading this after 2000, let me know if it was correct or not. I'd love to prove some pompous statistician wrong. By 2010 they reckon it'll be over 50%. If everyone's flying, that should keep some cars off the road at least.

However what makes flying worth every cent of the trip is that most adorable of all species...the Asian air stewardess. There goes my heart again. At least I think it's my heart. A nasty palpitation somewhere in front, in any case. Many was the time we'd go down the Hot Gossip Bar in Kowloon, telling lies to the Cathay girls there. But all they were interested in is what car we drove. When I said, "I don't drive..." they'd walk away before I could say, "...my chauffeur does." Oh well, their loss. They had their chances and I hope they're now bored housewives in some failed playboy's mansion, battling with their cellulite. Not that I take it personally of course...

But who hasn't dreamed of some horizontal turbulence and a little bit of cabin depressurization with one (or two) of those airlines girls in their little sarong kebayas. I love the way the little darlings demonstrate the blowing on the emergency whistle thing. Oh dear, talk about a bomb in an ice-cream factory.

Now flying is one thing, but of course when the aeroplane gets to the other side, you've got to disembark at an airport. Ho, ho...are you in for a treat! Singapore - fantastic. The New Hong Kong one...I can never remember the name, but it sounds like a nasty urinary tract infection...fine. New one in Kuala Lumpur - fine. Koh Samui - that major international travel hub. Even Manila has finally got a decent airport. They must've won the World Bank sweepstakes or something. But if your ticket happens to be to Saigon (Ho Chi Minh City the new lot call it) or New Delhi, then best of luck! My advice- fake an illness and get whisked through all the crowds and queues on medical evacuation before staging a remarkable and spontaneous recovery just near the limo queue.

The thing is, as an expat, you're going to be spending a lot of time in airports or flying. For business or just to get the hell out every now and again. It's like taking a bus down the road. In Asia, you think nothing of flying to Vietnam for a friend's farewell party, or flying to Perth for a round of golf (it's probably cheaper than playing in Asia, even including the airfare!).

So, fasten your seatbelts because you are in for the ride of your life (as my girlfriend always says). I'm going to have a little lie down now, and dream sweet dreams of all those little hosties that *could* have had me - if they had played their cards right.

Colonel Ke

Rubber Stamp Job

In the early 80's living in Hong Kong was great....if you didn't like bars full of bikini-clad women dancing around silver poles. To obtain your regular fix meant flying to Bangkok or Manila. Manila was closer.

Now, to get the maximum amount of Manila bar time you had to grab the last flight on a Friday night. That got you into Manila after 9.00pm.

Unfortunately, Immigration Staff stopped work about then and it was the responsibility of the airline to pay overtime if they had flights coming in late at night. Airlines are notoriously cheap so often they would get together and chip in and pay for a couple of immigration people.

So there I was, on a Friday night, at Manila airport when three flights arrived simultaneously.

There were three Immigration people and some 500 passengers. I was the last person in line 3. For some reason, the line I am in is always the slowest. After about 30 minutes I could finally see the Immigration Booth in the distance. I judged it would take at least another hour of valuable bar time before I got there.

What's a guy to do? I simply left the line, walked to the booths and strolled through an empty one, out of customs and into the night.

I thought no more about it until Sunday night when it was time to fly back to HK.

I placed my boarding pass and passport in front of the official who spent some minutes leafing through every page.

Finally he looked up and asked, "Please, Sir, when you arrive Manila?"

Looking confident I replied, "Friday night...Cathay flight from HK."

Once again furious ruffling through passport pages.

"There is no stamp"

"Really", I said...."How can that be?"

More ruffling, then a smile.

Reaching for his official stamp he slapped it down on a vacant page and scribbled some details.

"Now you in", he beamed.

Another slap of the big stamp, more writing and an even bigger smile as he handed the passport back.

"Now you out!"

Opportunity Missed

On my first visit to Vietnam I recall the complex amount of paperwork involved in securing a visa and then having to complete numerous pages of poorly printed forms at Ho Chi Min airport which seemed totally unrelated to the visa application.

After much queuing, stamping of passports and then stamping of stamps, I promptly headed for the hotel and wedged the visa documents in to my tattered leather bag, somewhere between the Rennie's, a leaking ballpoint and a pile of unattended paperwork. I thought nothing more of these papers as I tap-danced through three days of rigorous meetings closely followed by three nights of rigorous drinking with the

Vietnamese.

When I returned to the airport to catch my flight home I never even considered the prospect that my visa documents would be scrupulously inspected on the way out of the country. I'd lost them! A stoic immigration officer sent me to the side of the queue to await further instructions.

When eventually confronted by the next in charge, I played the "indignant foreigner" card, often a winner in these very public situations. He ignored me.

I then tried the "naïve foreigner" approach - a guaranteed winner; particularly with customs officials - this time he raised a brief cynical smurk and then ignored me.

Final tactic - the "begging, whining, diabetic without his insulin" approach - never fails!

Five minutes later I was not on the plane but before the Chief Officer in a dull, monochrome office as he pondered my predicament.

After a while he looked up from my passport and said without emotion:

"Mister - we have a problem and perhaps you can help us?"

"Oh of course - I understand," I responded reaching for my wallet.

"No!" He snapped and raised himself abruptly from his torn vinyl desk chair.

"Good God!" I thought "they're honest and now they'll most certainly shoot me!"

He grabbed me by the elbow and directed me down a hallway. At this stage I expected a bamboo cage to be waiting behind the steel door at the end of the corridor - probably submerged to 89% in rat infested sewerage.

He kicked the door open and we were greeted by a rather bright and bustling warehouse full of paint tins, cut plywood and local signwriters joyfully singing western pop songs and painting generic airport signs in English like "Green Lake" and "Nothing To Despair"

My captor steered me to a young attractive artist - she was half way through pencilling a sign to be painted which read,

"Foreigners wittout visas - please shit until nomber called"

He looked at me sternly and said, "Correct English or not?"

I took her pencil and wrote on a piece of newspaper under the sign: "Foreigners, without visas - please sit until number called"

He looked at it carefully for a few seconds, then turned to me and smiled warmly: "Okay - you go catch flight now!"

Thirty minutes later at 30,000 feet and with one or two double scotches under my belt, I kicked myself for being so blatantly honest. What kind of chore would lay ahead for the airport janitors had I given the original sign the all clear!

Air pollution

A friend was flying on a Chinese airline and requested to be seated in the non-smoking section. Soon after taking off, his fellow passengers next to him, behind him and in front of him started lighting up.

My friend pushed the flight attendant call button and asked to be seated in a non-smoking seat. The flight attendant looked around him at the smokers, looked at my friend and said, " You are right. You cannot smoke while seated in that seat".

Airsick

A friend of mine had to fly back to New Zealand from Hong Kong. Only economy seats were available, so he pulled out a really good medical excuse about his leg rehabilitating from (a non-existent) injury so he couldn't possibly stay in a cramped economy seat for that long, etc etc, and argued the case passionately.

Eventually, the call came back that he was OK'd for Business Class. Unfortunately the excuse worked too well- they met him at check-in with a wheelchair, so he was forced to go through with the charade and was wheeled onto the plane, and off at the other end too.

By the book

Twenty years ago we were flying Jakarta to Solo, Central Java in a small Merpati plane. We were sitting in the front row (no economy) and the two 'men' crew kept the door to the cockpit open throughout the flight. I say 'men' as the two of them looked as though they were just into their teens. They kept the instruction book open and had to do everything step by step from the manual. You could even see how excited they were when they saw Solo airport!

Upon landing, really scary, I reflected how pleased I was that they were actually using the manual so dedicatedly, and not pissed off that they had to use the manual at all. I realised I had been flying local airlines for too long.

They all look the same

I was flying to a conference from Singapore via Tokyo then to Los Angeles. I had changed enough money into US Greenbacks in Singapore to take care of things till we arrived.

Waiting at Tokyo, I offered my colleagues a coffee. Three coffees (beautifully presented in polystyrene cups) came to US$10.33. No, that's not the punchline! I turned on all my charm, threw in the 2 or 3 Japanese words I knew for added benefit, and got the charming Japanese lass to agree to a flat US$10. With many thank-yous, smiles and much bowing I went back to the group, pleased with my little fiscal victory.

Halfway to LA, I was checking my passport, ticket, etc and thought "where are all my US dollars?" It turned out I'd given them US$100 for the coffees.

Looking up old friends

This film director had been on an arduous shoot in Thailand for 3 weeks. Shooting days running at least 12 to 14 hours a day. Then of course some serious partying most nights.

On the flight back to Sydney, he thought he'd better take a super-strength sleeping pill (or two) to ensure a good sleep so he was vaguely functional to start the post production work the next day.

Next thing he knew, he was lying prostrate with his arse in the air on a stainless steel table in Sydney, with a Customs officer putting on the rubber gloves for a full-body search. They were convinced as they couldn't wake him on landing, he must be a drug courier with burst balloons in his stomach!

He no longer takes sleeping pills on flights.

Pulp Friction

This guy had lived in Bangkok for a while, had come off another long, boring and tiring flight and was not in a good mood basically. This English wide-boy backpacker and his girlfriend banged his leg with their trolley, but didn't apologise. In fact the wide-boy got a little antagonistic in the *what's it to you then* school of macho-aggro behaviour.

My friend said: "Sorry mate, you picked the wrong town and the wrong guy. I could pay 1000Baht to the guys outside and they'd beat you to a f***ing pulp." And he meant it.

The backpacker's girlfriend quickly whisked him in the other direction.

Starry starry flight

I was flying from Hong Kong to Singapore, waiting at the gate to board the plane. There was a Chinese girl right in front of me, with an older Caucasian guy. Dirty (but lucky) man, I thought. She was beautiful, even in her jeans and mohair sweater without any make-up.

We got on the plane, and I still couldn't resist admiring her simple beauty, and I could've swore she looked at me and smiled once. Honestly. Let me believe it.

Upon landing at Singapore, we went to the baggage claim area, where a person came up to her and put a garland of orchids round her neck. Then, when she went out into the Arrivals area, people pushed and screamed, a million flashes went off, and she disappeared into the adoring throng.

The next morning, there she was on the front page of The Straits Times. Joan Chen comes to town!

Caveat emptor

We were heading up to Bangkok again from Singapore. Seated in Business Class (of course) one enjoyed the first of many Gin and Tonics and scoured the cabin to see who else was heading to the City of Angels. After years of flying and many hours spent in airports the name of the game was to spy out the people and imagine what they were doing and where they were going.

Among my fellow travellers were the usual assortment of American financial types - your young, well-dressed suits with the volume control permanently on "max"; an elegant elder Thai couple, he reading the financial pages of the Straits Times, she with jet-black tied-back hair well decorated with fine jewellery and the usual assortment of tanned Europeans winging their way around the good-value holiday spots of South East Asia.

But along, beyond the middle row of seats on the far side of the cabin I spotted an increasingly (after each G and T) pretty young Thai girl in her early twenties. Yuck, I thought, how could she be with that old dude in the window seat beside her. He looked a bit like a secondary school teacher. Formal trousers and a tee-shirt covered his gaunt middle-aged frame. He was topped by a bad comb-over, glasses and overall a dorky look. She smiled. I coolly responded. I glanced over a few minutes later and she smiled again. It was all on. I motioned a silent *wai*, lip synching '*sawasdee khub*' just to indicate that I knew my way around these parts. She demurely responded with a *wai*. I was in like a robber's dog I thought. Perhaps the old fart was not travelling with her, I hoped.

Countless G and Ts later we prepared to disembark. I followed behind her out the air-bridge. Frankly a very fine arse, I thought as I mentally plotted out the possibilities that awaited me if I played my cards right.

We arrived in the crowded customs hall. She was in the line beside me. The dork was in front of her. I pretended not to notice she was looking at me. She smiled. I smiled.

Then, as we waited by the carousels it happened. She nudged closer to me and the reality, far more real than I could have imagined, was exposed.

"Where you stay?" "she" asked me in a voice barely an octave higher than Chris Rhea's. I sobered up and the fantasies of the flight rapidly left my mind.

My first experience of a Thai transvestite and a very serious lesson that in Asia things are rarely as they seem from the outside.

Flying Jew East

I was sitting next to this guy in the plane who looked like your stereotypical Jewish Rabbi, but a little younger. Long beard. Large hook nose. And every so often on this long flight he would put on his yamulca and pray.

Come lunchtime, the stewardess came down the aisle obviously looking for a specific row number. She looked and me, then at him and asked: "Who's having the kosher meal?"

Non-upright citizen

Returning on CAAC from Beijing to Hong Kong, my colleague decided to get a bit of work done on the flight. She reclined her seat, put the tray down to put her papers on, kicked off her shoes and unfastened her seatbelt.

After a while, she simply fell asleep.

When it came time to land, all the various announcements were made in preparation for landing. I thought I should wake her (she was sitting a few seats away), but saw the officious hostess coming down the aisle towards her. Sure enough, the stewardess stopped, looked at her, thought about waking her, but ultimately decided my colleague looked too comfortable and content. So she returned to her crew seat, and strapped herself in for landing—my colleague still fast asleep - chair back, tray down and no seatbelt on.

Absolutely routed

Good news. I'm invited to attend a conference with my client in Hawaii. Bad news, it's now changed to Kansas City, Missouri. OK, but I'll stop in Hawaii on the way back for a break anyway. We fly Singapore to Tokyo. Tokyo to Seattle. Seattle to Minneapolis (I carry my clients shopping bags for her round Mall of America like a sycophantic so-and-so). Then Minneapolis to Kansas. With each flight the planes get smaller. We eventually arrive after nearly 24 hours of travelling.

Final day of the conference, I win the "most jetlagged" award, and we celebrate a truly unproductive session with way too much tequila. Now the next morning, I'm supposed to be up at 5am for the return flight. I get back to my room and find a message saying change of itinerary, I'm now going back via Memphis instead. Need to wake at 4am (it's already past 2!).

No sooner do I crash out, than the alarm clock goes off. I am feeling like shit. We get to Memphis and all hell breaks loose. The electrical storm from hell. Further delays and planes grounded as we watch this storm wreak havoc.

Eventually get onto the plane, bound for Los Angeles. Am informed by cabin staff, "don't worry you've missed your connecting flight but you'll be met at the airport and taken care of." Great. We land. Not only is there no one to meet us, but they've never even heard of me!

I decide to buy a ticket on the next plane to Hawaii. The one-way ticket is $400, and the return is $268. Huh? I buy the return. We then get onto the plane- it's TWA. Now, didn't these guys go out of business in the 70's or something? I'm sitting in this museum-piece plane just behind the wing. I see footprints all over the part of the wing which says "do not step over this line," the engine backfires and belches a huge black cloud as we taxi off. I have never prayed so hard in my life. Or to as many Gods, simultaneously.

Amazingly we get airborne. The stewardess comes around. Would I like to watch the movie? Yes. That'll be $2 for the headsets. Forget it- give me a beer. That'll be $2. Lord get me out of this nightmare. Somebody slap me!

We land uneventfully in Honolulu, a great time is had by all. Now, time to fly back to Asia. I'm upgraded to First Class. Yes! The gate number is 13! Aaargh.

I still have an unused ticket portion from Hawaii to LA on TWA if anyone's interested.

The Mad Mexican

Flying back as usual after a day trip from Kuala Lumpur to Singapore, Singapore Airlines. Just after take-off, the captain comes on and in a distinctive Mexican accent says, "This is your Captain Roberto..." and goes through the usual formalities.

I summon the stewardess and ask for a pen and paper. I then scribble a note and ask her to pass it on to the pilot please. She gives me a quizzical look. This is only a week after a hijacking on Singapore Airlines so they're probably a little touchy about this.

The note said: "Hey Roberto, where are the parachutes back here? If I knew it was you flying this plane I would've caught the next one!"

We often played volleyball together and he was a complete party animal. Great guy to drink with, but you wouldn't necessarily want him at the front of the bus!

Boss takes the backseat

This company introduced a policy which dictated that all employees flew in economy for all flights. This friend of mine was a largish bloke, and probably thought he deserved better than economy anyway, so came up with an ideal loophole.

As he travelled several times a month from Singapore (where he was based) to KL, he worked out you could buy the Business Class return ticket in Malaysia cheaper than economy from Singapore.

This worked really well for him, and the company was within budget. Then one day, he and the big boss had to fly up to KL for a joint presentation. He headed straight for the Business Class check-in as usual. His boss said: "where are you going?" He said, "To check in and get a ticket for the lounge." It then dawned on him - his boss was flying economy and he was up the front in Business. Oops!

"How's your coffee?" he called back to his cramped boss, as he sipped his chilled champagne in spacious splendour at the front.

Saucy stuff

Lunch had just been served in Business Class...a rather delicious but dry looking meal of meatballs. Just then, the Singapore Airlines stewardess came by with a gravy boat, and innocently asked: "Would you like some sauce on your balls?"

I wonder what they were having in First Class?!?

Freudian slip

The sweet Chinese stewardess comes on the intercom to make the official announcements: "Ladies and Gentlemen welcome aboard. Our *fright* time to Hong Kong today is 3 hours and 30 minutes." You have been warned!

Crash Landing

Just about to land in Jakarta, the American guy I was sitting next to said; "Bet you $5 we do a Garuda landing."

"What do mean?" I reply, naively.

Just then we hit the tarmac.Drinks, jugs and utensils came flying out of their stow compartments, and crashed all over the floor.

"Told ya," he smiled smugly.

Going nowhere.

It had been a great break in Manila. Full on. Now it was time to reluctantly return to reality -Hong Kong. It was a Sunday lunchtime, and the sun was beating down, which didn't help the king-sized hangover one bit. We then got into the plane and strapped in for take-off.

We seemed to be sitting for quite a while, with nothing happening. Then the pilot (an Australian) came onto the intercom. "Ladies and gentlemen, errr, we're just waiting for a plane to be removed from the runway before we get cleared for take off. Apologies, it shouldn't take too long."

I looked out the window. Sure enough, there was a small dark plane, at an odd angle.

Another 15 minutes passed. "Ladies and Gentlemen, errr," our laconic captain said, "a Japanese airforce plane has apparently lost a wheel on landing. Air control has not taken kindly to our suggestion to remove it from the runway. Under military regulations it is not permissible to remove it from the runway...it must move under its own steam. We'll be a while longer."

Another half hour or so. "Ladies and Gentlemen, put your hands up if you'd like us to start the refreshment service - yes, I thought so," he added without waiting for a response. At which ice cold beers started flowing freely.

Another hour or so later. "Ladies and Gentlemen. Now the problem is that they need to locate a tire and a jack. Once these two very sophisticated pieces of equipment are found and brought together in the same place at the same time, we should be underway."

More beer. More increasingly sarcastic announcements, which I don't remember because I got too pissed. Eventually 5 hours later we took off to much cheering and hooting and hollering...back to Hong Kong, a one hour flight.

Throw down your gum

Returning from Sydney to Singapore after a Christmas holiday on

Qantas, the Steward got up to make the arrival announcements before landing.

Apart from the usual "the airport is this far the city" announcements, he also mentioned "warning, severe penalties for drug offences and chewing gum."

As he walked down the aisle, I said: "Good one about the chewing gum! Very funny."

"No, that's for real," he explained. And that's how I found out about Singapore "banning" chewing gum.

Making herself heard

M, J and T were on another business trip in Bangkok, and took the opportunity for a bit of evening entertainment in the bars, as one does. Turned out J's particular girl of choice for the evening was a deaf/mute, making conversation a little difficult. Perfect!

A few days later they were on the plane, sitting three abreast, when suddenly J announced he was experiencing symptoms of 'a dose' as a result of his liaison the earlier night.

"The mute speaks," said the quiet and laconic T.

Honour amongst thieves

We had just arrived in Manila airport, which was bedlam. People everywhere, and soon the group was split up.

We decided to go ahead without the others and got our hotel car. Driving down the highway, we passed a cab, and who should be in it but our friend we lost back at the airport.

We pulled over to collect him. He was distraught - he'd lost his watch, a family heirloom.

We decided it must have been the kids at the airport who rush out and pretend to help you with your luggage, etc. So we went back to the airport, he identified the kids and I approached them.

"We want our friend's watch back," I said in no uncertain terms. Sure enough, and much to their credit, they returned the watch - only, with its strap cleanly cut through.

Basic extinct

Going for a family holiday in Phuket, we arrived at the airport with all our luggage, and my 5 year old son carrying his favourite toy/security blanket, a T-Rex stuffed toy from the Jurassic park movie merchandise.

This thing is ugly and hellishly realistic, and often draws a second look from people.

At the luggage x-ray machine, the officer inspected it a little nervously before realising it was a harmless stuffed toy. Grabbing it, he lobbed it grenade-style over the machine to where a woman officer was intensely studying the x-ray monitor.

This dinosaur landed just in front of her and she jumped out of her skin, shrieking. All the officials and onlookers killed themselves laughing, but it was a while before *she* saw the funny side.

From another planet

I was in Tokyo airport café, when I spied her. Walking to the table with a tray of coffee and snacks. The most divine creature ever to walk this earth. The body was just perfect in her stewardess uniform. The hair. The smile. Just everything. And when she sat down, her derriere jutted out like a perfectly ripe pear. Well, you get the idea.

Summoning up all of my courage (and probably a bit more) I went across to talk to her. In my finest broken Japanese-English I told her she was the most divine creature in the world, I'd like to have her children, and that as a professional photographer (which I wasn't really, but hey) she should let me photograph her for some potential modelling assignments.

All this, while she said not a word. But looked at me like I was from another planet.

It was then that I spied her name badge. "Annie Wong. Northwest Airlines." She was Chinese, not Japanese.

Needless to say, we didn't get married.

A close call

LG and wife (from Jakarta) arranged to meet me for a drink in Singapore - I was flying late afternoon and they were on a later evening flight from Jakarta.

Arriving at Jakarta airport I discovered a Qantas flight was leaving around the same time as my booked SilkAir flight. As I had an unused Qantas ticket (Jakarta-S'pore) that was soon to expire, I changed my flight over to them. No problems with the flight, I arrived home and fell asleep, awaking 2 hours after the time I was supposed to meet my friends for the drink.

I called the hotel they were in and the wife answered the phone. In typical fashion I put on a stupid voice - she worked out it was me - but her tone seemed strange. She was crying. She said: "Is that you? You're alive!"

The husband took the phone off her and told me my booked flight had crashed, with no survivors.

Late arrival

When I was working at the airport, there was a passenger trying to find his way onto a flight to Oakland (via San Francisco). Due to a comedy of errors, he was put on a flight to Auckland, New Zealand. The best part was when the captain radioed back (from 33,000 feet) asking if someone could call his wife to tell her he would be three days late!

Very frequent flyer

A passenger bound from New York to Hong Kong via Japan got off at the Tokyo airport to make his connection. Due to language problems, he was put back on the flight to New York and then had to make his way back to Tokyo (three, 12-hour flights later) only to be accidently put on a flight to Seoul! We wonder if he received frequent flyer miles?

If you have a good story about aeroplanes or airports in Asia, let us know. Email us at **hardship_posting@hotmail.com** *or fax The Editor at 612-9499-5908.*

"You buy me drink!"
True tales from bars, restaurants, nightclubs and karaoke joints.

I know this is not the place for dispensing medical wisdom, but I've outlived the last 3 doctors that have told me my lifestyle's crap and I was heading for an early grave.

My health tip: line your stomach with a few beers in case you'll be eating later on. And if you want to live past 50 like me, you should do the same. In fact, I plan to live to a ripe old ninety nine, only to be killed by a jealous husband.

Now this may surprise you, but I believe in giving life a bit of a shot. I can get all the rest I need when I go to meet my manufacturer. But one thing's for sure...I hope he's got no Filipino bands in heaven playing Hotel California. Because that means I must've taken the 'down' elevator instead.

But anyway, we're getting sidetracked here from the deliriously uplifting topic at hand. Eating, drinking and being Mary.

Now you may have the impression that expats drink more than the locals. That's only because it's true. Barry, my fountain of useless information, tells me that in Australia we drink about 92 litres per head each year - OK, hands up, which of you wimps is bringing down the average? By comparison, Asia's biggest beer drinkers are the Taiwanese (well, they're not that big - around 5 foot 6 on average) and they sip a modest 23 litres per head. This is followed by China at 15 litres, Thailand at 14 and Malaysia bringing up the rear (sorry, Mr Anwar, I'll rephrase that) with 7. But you should see them nail the hard stuff!

As an expat, bars and restaurants are really where you're gonna interface with the locals most, unless you're one of those fancy wankers that just fraternises at Ye Olde Country Clubbe. Get a life! And you haven't lived until you've been thrown out of at least two of the following establishments in the same night: The Wanch, Top 10, O'Kims, Juliana's, Harry's, JJ O'Mahoney's, Joe Bananas and The Tanamoor. I had heard much about Tanamoor in Indonesia as a sacred ground where regular worshipping rituals are undertaken...it turned out I was mistaking it for Tanah Lot in Bali. But I have seen a lot of people brought to their knees there.

And, according to research (well, my last Mastercard statement actually) this is where you will spend at least a third of your monthly stipend. Then several years later you'll wake up and think: "Who is this man in the mirror that looks like me but is wearing Pavarotti's stomach?" But be proud of it. A lot of effort goes into cultivating a fine beer gut. If it were that easy, hell, everyone would have one. You've got to stand up for it. And if I could stand most nights, I would.

Best of all, the Asians have this wonderful euphemism for fat pr*cks like me. It's called 'prosperous,' based on the assumption that if you can eat so much rice that you can get that fat you must be hellishly rich. I don't disabuse them of the notion.

Anyway, this gin and tonic diet seems to be working. I've only been on it 3 weeks and I've already lost 4 days.

On the downside, we can blame the Japanese for bringing Karaoke into this world, and encouraging millions of talentless wannabes with enough Dutch (Japanese?) courage to actually believe they are Tom Jones or Frank Sinatra re-incarnated. The fact that those two are still living doesn't seem to matter...sorry, what's that? Oh, I've just been informed that Frank Sinatra is dead. Oh well, maybe now one of you out there will actually become him after all. "Micalaphone to taber seven prease!"

Anyway, I've got a question for you: Have you ever seen a fortune cookie in Asia? Me neither.

Then there's the concept of *heating* and *cooling* foods. I can never remember what is what, but it's really interesting...something to do with yin and yang. In fact I used to date a couple of Chinese twins called Yin and Yang - identical, apart from their faces. But what I did learn is never to eat durian and drink beer at the same time. This can apparently kill you, according to my good friend, and king of the underworld, Pete the

HARDSHIP POSTING

Pony-tailed Portrait Photographer (he hates it when I call him that). In fact, I believe just eating durian on its own is likely to kill you. I must say, I could never believe that anything which smells that bad could taste any good (I'm talking about the durian here, by the way, not the twins).

Then in the Philippines, you have all sorts of quaint customs like if you really really like the food that has been served up to you, make sure you leave some on the plate to show you've had plenty. This, from the nation that also brings you signs such as "Please check your gun at the door" and gun racks outside. Who said Cowboy town?

But be prepared to have your mind expanded with the items available on the menu in Asia. Not only can you not pronounce many of them, but a qualified neurosurgeon would have trouble locating the exact part of the body many of these so called delicacies come from. Apart from the self-explanatory "Monkey's brain". I believe people ate this in the belief it would increase their IQ and it did...to the level of monkeys.

Then there's the cut snakes in Shanghai, and the drunken prawns. What a way to go!

As my good friend, His Excellency P.J. O'Rourke, says in his literary masterpiece, Holidays in Hell: "Hark to the cry of the tourist in the East: "Is it dead or is it dinner?" (I thought the gratuitous grovel was worth it as I know he has a much larger expense account than these miserable publishers have given me.) Oops, I didn't mean to say that...never mind, it won't get printed. (Note to editor: please delete remark about miserable publishers. Thank you).

Be prepared to not flinch when you hear a 2 metre long noodle being vacuumed up millimetre by millimetre, with all the reverberant accompanying noises of the Electrolux test centre, only to turn round and find it's the elegant young lass you eyed when she walked into the restaurant. Elegance and refinement go out the window the minute noodles are involved.

Oh yeah...and you'll need to master chopsticks. The acid test, or rather the oil test, is trying to pick up those slippery suckers otherwise known as peanuts they serve in Chinese restaurants. I don't know how Chinese culture beat the rest of the world to civilisation by thousands of years, but failed to detect that a spoon and fork was, all things considered, perhaps the best way to go. Probably the result of a budget cut in the Ming Dynasty R&D department. To cut it short, you won't find better food anywhere in the world. In Asia it's always chow time right around the clock. With interesting concepts like the Hobbit House in Manila (the place with the midget servers...I always ask them if they've got younger sisters - just the right height). And that place in Bangkok where the waiters and waitresses get around on rollerblades. It's effing huge). Then there are all those exotic, quixotic and erotic "hands-free" establishments where the delightful lasses spoon-feed you. Like a dress rehearsal for the nursing home years. Now that's what I like - a bit of respect for their elders.

Goodness, got to go. It's 11:30am already and I'm late for drinks down the Koh Samui Rugby Club.

Colonel Ke

Does not compute

It was lunchtime. It was Hong Kong. I really wanted fish and chips. The local food court featured it on the light-box menu. But the chips looked really disgusting.

"I'll just have fish please."

"We only have fish and chips."

"Yeah, but I don't want the chips."

"No, you can only have fish *and* chips."

"Never mind, I'll still pay full-price. But I don't want any chips."

"Cannot..."

"But the cook has to put fish on plate, then chips on plate, right."

"Yes."

"So, just put the fish on and don't put the chips on. Or put the chips on, then take them off."

"Cannot...must be fish *and* chips."

"Aaaaarggggh!"

www.hardshipposting.com

Chipping in for an old mate

The lads were in Manila having a huge weekend. For some strange reason, they decided to eat, and found a suitable restaurant/café. Isn't eatin' cheatin' ?

Orders were placed, mostly of the greasy American meal type...huge dishes of burgers and fries, fish and chips, etc. which the guys wolfed down voraciously.

Halfway through the meal, one of the guys in the group went into a real seizure.

While others panicked and rushed to his aid, the bloke next to him leaned across and asked, casually and conspiratorially: "Hey, John. If you die, can I have your chips?"

Cherries and cream

It was J's birthday so naturally the lads wanted to have a long lunch. Actually the lads didn't normally need a reason, but if they had one *then* the justification for staying out all afternoon took on an air of legitimacy.

So, there we were, some 30 or so guys in the famous Roberto's Italian restaurant (in the heart of Patpong), in a private room, all seated at a table which must have stretched for some 5 meters.

As the wine flowed and the afternoon wore on, the telling of one urban legend lead to the next, the jokes got worse and the noise level increased.

Then there was silence.

Not instantaneous silence, but the sort of silence that slowly works its way around the room as different people suddenly realize the atmosphere has changed.

And the reason for this change was an attractive young lady, standing at one end of the long table, wearing not a stitch, but with her breasts, navel and pubic hair covered in whipped cream.

As we all watched she was helped up onto the table, and she slowly, sexily walked down its length, around coffee cups, wine glasses and ashtrays and sat herself demurely in the birthday boy's lap.

Still there was silence.

It was finally broken when one wit whose plaintive voice asked: "Hey J, can we watch while you open your present?" Which he proceeded to do right there on the table, with much encouragement from the lads.

Sign your life away

It was always amusing and sometimes a little scary - whenever CM would pay his bill by credit card, they would come back with the card and the slip to sign. He would pick up the card, hold it up to study the signature, then slavishly copy it as he signed on the slip.

The waitresses always found this amusing, but he could've got away with murder if he'd wanted to.

I often signed slips as Bozo the Clown and Ronald Reagan, and it was still accepted!

He was framed

For some strange reason Thai ladies-of-the-night do not like men of the Arab persuasion.

Now, our old friend DB is not an Arab but with his beard, swarthy complexion (after countless hours of sailing under the tropical sun), he can, when the light is right, pass for one of our Eastern Brothers.

So when his birthday came around, some of his friends chipped in, took a photo of DB down to an artist in Pattaya, and commissioned a portrait. The picture was to be of DB in full Arab gear.

It looked great, and was hung with great ceremony on the Wall of Fame in Goldfingers Bar just in time for DB's birthday bash. Randy, bar owner and consummate host, put it right at the top, "in honour of DB" but in reality, well out of DB's reach (height is not one of DB's long suits!).

The party went really well. Lots of mates turned up, lots of LBFM's and lots of fun.

Towards the end of the evening, DB was standing next to Randy near the Wall of Fame, when he happened to glance up and spy the picture at the top.

"Tell me Randy", he asked bemusedly, "why do you have a picture of an Arab on your wall?"

Randy didn't miss a beat: "Because today's his birthday."

Silence....and then the penny dropped!

Snake in the glass

After only a few weeks in Kuala Lumpur, a couple of the local

Chinese lads at work decided I was fair game. I duly received an invitation for dinner - at that city's famous snake restaurant.

I had eaten crocodile, kangaroo and other exotic species in Australia so what would be the problem with a snake or two?

We arrived in a dank and dingy premises somewhere in Chinatown and walked in to be greeted with the sight of dozens of live snakes behind the lunch counter writhing and wriggling on metal hooks, obviously pretty pissed off that they were on the menu.

The idea was you informed the proprietor of the snake of your choice and it would be lovingly prepared for you. I asked for Kentucky Fried Cobra but they didn't seem to appreciate the joke. My companions chose their snakes, which were then slit up the middle and the blood and gizzards drained into a glass underneath. This they duly drank for virility. (Why is it that every second Chinese medical concoction is for virility? It probably explains why there's more than a billion Chinese on the planet.)

I passed on the snake's blood cocktail (almost passed out in fact) much to the amusement of the local throng. They then threw all the snakes on the BBQ, and they actually tasted OK. I was informed of an old Cantonese saying which, loosely translated, says: "When the Chinese spot a snake in the grass, they immediately think of ways to cook it."

Burst your bubble

We were all having a great time in one of those raunchy upstairs bars in Patpong, and the usual sideshows were in progress...the ping-pong balls, the razor blades, and so on. Then came 'the balloon show'.

One of the girls came up to my friend and asked him to hold up this balloon, which the girl in the middle of the platform was going to shoot down with a needle shot from between her legs. Yes, really.

With a bit of a build up, the needle was fired...it sailed right across the room...and straight into my friend's hand! The girls roared with laughter as he winced, the balloon still intact.

"Ha, ha, Aids, Aids," said one of laughing bar-girls pointing at his hand. That rather put a dampener on the rest of his evening.

Flat out

It had been a big night. We were already smashed by the time we got to Top 10. One of the group was a member there, and had a bottle of gin behind the bar. Now I am actually allergic to gin, but somehow I managed to drain about half the bottle on my own.

When the bar closed, we headed across the road to Denny's for the obligatory Grilled Chicken sandwich at 3am.

Next thing I knew, I was being shaken awake, with voices saying: "Hello, hello. Better get up now." I looked up to see two police officers. Worse still, I was face down in the bathroom. They escorted me down the spiral staircase to the entrance. They then they asked where I was staying.

"What city is this?" I asked.

"Singapore," they replied.

"Oh I live here," I said.

"Well, better get a taxi home," they instructed while assisting me out the door. As luck would have it, a cab was parked right outside Denny's door, so I opened the back door and hopped in. Next thing, the door was opened.

"No, Sir, that is *our* car. The taxi stand is over the road."

I had hopped into the back of the police car, mistaking the lights and sign for a cab!

I then got into a cab, told him my address and passed out. A little while later, the cabbie woke me and said: "We're here, sir." I opened my eyes, opened the left side door, threw up, paid him, and exited by the right hand door.

Organ grinder

A hawker near where I lived in Singapore was in trouble for not only concocting a soup from goats penises, but proudly proclaiming the fact on a large sign (which the tourists loved - the sign, not the soup!).

He was subsequently allowed to continue his soup making, but was forced to change the sign to simply read "Organ Soup".

Learning Curve

I had just moved to Hong Kong, and the company had put me up in an apartment just behind the Nathan Rd tourist strip. On my first weekend we all went out on a junk trip, and get merrily sloshed. I thought *I'm gonna like this place.*

Walking back to my apartment afterwards, this guy called out from an alleyway, "Hey Joe, wanna beer?"

I thought I might as well - seemed silly to walk past a pub and not stop. I entered. It was dimly lit, and I was the only customer. The woman behind the counter wore no top (unfortunately she had lousy tits!). I sat at the counter and she brought a beer. After a while she said, "You want to go to lounge?" Sure, why not?

I was ushered to the salubrious lounge...vinyl sofas, etc and sit in the corner. No-one but me. Next thing 2 rather lithesome ladies shuffled in, said hello and sat either side of me, treating me like I was Mel Gibson, and rubbing my thighs. I thought *I like these Hong Kong pubs!*

A couple of drinks later (the ladies each had a couple of "brandies") I thought I should take my leave. So I asked for the bill. The original old guy from the door came through with the bill...HK$2800 (nearly US$300) !!! I said "Excuse me, captain, I think you've given me the wrong bill." Not likely in an empty pub. I protested that I'd only had 3 beers, and a couple of drinks for the ladies.

"Yes, but I only charge you for *one* lady. Special deal," he said.

"I didn't order any ladies," I naively retorted. "They just came and sat with me. Where does it say I have to pay for ladies?" He pointed to a blackboard behind my head.

"Well I don't have $2800 on me." As I said this, I suddenly recalled all those scenes from kung-fu movies coming to life right there. *I was too young to die.*

I took the diplomatic approach (much against my nature), we settled on $1450 (after turning my wallet upside down and shaking it) and I exited swiftly.

Welcome to Hong Kong, sucker.

Who custard tarted?

The rugby tour through China was in full swing, and a special dinner was laid on for the group at the Peace Hotel in Shanghai. The specially printed menus proudly stated "Lugby Dinner" on the front cover, and inside one of the special dishes was "Egg Custard Fart". Funnily enough, the roast duck and pork chops were more popular.

Contemplating your naval

The US Navy was in town. Something like 14,000 marines swarming all over Wanchai. The place was humming, the bars were packed. Needless to say, the Shore Patrol (SP) guys were also out in force to keep them in line.

Our good friend was a mild mannered internal auditor with an international bank by day, with short-cropped hair and pin-striped suits, but enjoyed a couple of toots down at the Makati Inn at night. Well, this particular night he had overdone it and eventually went head-down on the bar counter where he was sitting.

The SP's came in to do their rounds, saw this guy passed out and assumed he was a drunk and disorderly sailor. Next thing he knew, they muscled him out, down the street and he ended up in HMS Tamar, the naval docking facility. They asked him for name, rank, serial number, which boat he was off, etc, and he vehemently denied everything, which only made things worse.

Come morning, he was allowed to call his office (the Bank) who vouched for him, and he was let go amidst much "Terribly sorry, Sir" sort of sentiments.

Dress Rules

We had been to lunch, and stayed out. As usual we ended up at Joe Bananas in Hong Kong about 3pm, notorious for the world's most stringent dress code for a pub, and lacking in sense of humour with it.

We then continued with a barrage of B52's and all manner of spirits all afternoon.

Eventually it was dark and the after work crowd shuffled in. I went up to get the next round and they refused me service. "Sorry, we can't serve people after 7 o'clock without collars."

"But..." No use. I went back to the group and explained the predicament. "That's f***ing ridiculous," said one of the guys. "Tell you what, why don't you put on my shirt, and I'll whip home and get another."

With that, he stood up (and we're talking a man of major intestinal substance here), took off his collared shirt, and walked bare-chested with sweaty beer-belly glistening, through the amused crowd and out the door.

I put his shirt on over my t-shirt and was served another round as if nothing happened.

Standing at attention

It was Hong Kong, late eighties. A venerable lunch group met once a month for a bit of fine wining and dining, and getting up to a bit of mischief, in a swanky establishment.

Part of this was to have a girl "on duty" beneath the table. She would move around and administer anonymous oral gratifications at random.

The game was that at any stage, if the gents suspected one of them was on the receiving end at that particular moment, they had to point to that person and say: "J'accuse" (literally, I accuse you).

The accused would then have to immediately stand, revealing a state of full dress or - if unlucky- an undone fly and a standing member.

Boss in fishnets

We had this guy (technically my boss) come up from New Zealand to help on a particular assignment in Hong Kong.

R was a typical Kiwi...nice natured and friendly (ok, maybe that's not typical!). We decided to take him out to the Lamma Hilton on Lamma Island for some seafood.

As usual, we hooked into a million beers on the junk on the way over, and several more at the restaurant. This brought R out of his shell a little, shall we say, and my lingering memory is of this guy with a huge cigar sticking out the side of his mouth, slacks rolled up to the knee, wading through the live seafood tanks with a fish net whilst a little old Chinese lady scolded him in Cantonese and banged on his back to stop.

Bjorn Again

There was an ABBA-revival band playing at a club. My friend and I decided to go and see (er, it made sense at the time!).

Arriving at the club, we were informed of the hefty entry prices. "Or," the dainty little waitress advised," if you buy a bottle for $125 you can have free entry as long as you have the bottle on the shelf here."

Sensing good long-term value, we went for the "bottle" option. A bottle of vodka in this case. By 11pm, the bottle of vodka was demolished between the two of us, and a few more drinks were ordered. The blonde bird in the band with the beard was brilliant, and a good night was had by all.

I suggested to my friend that he stay at my place in Orchard rather than go all the way back to Sembawang on the far end of the island where he lived. We got home, I told him to crash out in the spare bed in my son's room.

Next thing I heard blood curdling screams - male *and* female!

He'd taken his clothes off and collapsed in the spare bed on top of my maid who had decided to sleep there that night whilst caring for my son. Order was soon restored and peace fell on the household once again.

Shrewd Bar-stard

In the heyday of Pattaya in Thailand, there were actually way too many bars, and this particular bar owner was going out of business fast. So he hatched this great plan to sell it to some (any!) undiscerning Arab visitor who would like a piece of the action (er, the business that is). So he passed the word around to all his friends that for a week they could drink "at cost" in his bar.

Needless to say, word got around, the bar was packed, and the joint was jumpin'. When an Arab approached him and said "Great bar you have here," he pounced. "It's for sale- you wanna buy it?" The Arab couldn't believe his luck. Contracts were signed, money was exchanged, and both parties were ecstatic.

The day after the sale, the pub was empty - all the freeloading friends disappeared!

Chicken feed

Years ago, when I was fresh off the plane from Europe, I visited a remote island in the Philippines for a short break.

Tired of the resort's food after a few days, we went wandering down along the beach to see what else was on offer. We went from restaurant to restaurant, and each place we stopped at to check the blackboard menu had the same words written up:

"Today's special: chicken."

Whether it was fried chicken, chicken adobo, or whatever, they were all serving the same special that day. Chicken, chicken or chicken.

Taking a seat at about the 5th place we came across, the cheerful proprietor took our drinks orders. We inquired whether it was usual that every restaurant along the beach would be offering the same menu every day.

After a moment's thought, the proprietor responded; "Today Monday. Yesterday cock-fighting day."

Heady times

The upstairs bar in Patpong known as the Kangaroo Bar was once wonderfully described as "A sea of bobbing heads."

His name's Bill.

In the good old days of Singapore when Brannigan's was about the only bar in town, everyone who was anyone amongst the expats was there. And you knew most of the faces.

It was common practice in places like that to hand over your credit card and ask them to hold it with your bill behind the bar until the end of the evening.

We (no names mentioned) used to have a great time seeing who was there that we didn't particularly like, ordering drinks and saying "My name's Jones (or whoever was there), my card's behind the bar." Excellent way to get free drinks, and of course the other guy was always too pissed to notice.

Flaming mad

There's a bar owner in Ho Chi Minh that's famous for his flaming zambuccas...with a twist. He puts the glasses up one end of the bar counter, then lays a trail of lighter fluid all the way down the counter, round any glasses or bottles that might be in the way, round ashtrays and even handbags till the trail reaches the far side of the counter.

Then with the flick of the Zippo - woof! Flaming zambuccas all round. Maybe they should get this guy to light the next Olympic torch.

Excuse du jour

We had this hotel round the corner from our office, so it became the unofficial canteen for lunches. One of the items on their menu was Gula Malaka...basically a sickly sweet flavoured syrup coating on a base of crushed ice.

I ordered this one day. The waitress came back a few minutes later with the news, "Sorry sir, sold out of Gula Malaka today." So I ordered something else. A week later, different waitress: "Sorry, Gula Malaka finished already, Sir."

I suspected it didn't really exist, so this became the running joke for nearly 3 years, through countless new batches of waiters and waitresses. We'd order the Gula Malaka, they'd earnestly go off to the kitchen, only to return with the expected flimsy excuse.

And they never quite understood why we would piss ourselves laughing every time they reported they were out of Gula Malaka.

Finger lickin' gross

I took one of my Chinese clients to lunch. He recommended the restaurant...one of the best Chinese cuisine places in Singapore. We had a nice time, good food, etc. At the end, we decided there was still room for dessert.

I went the ubiquitous mango pudding way. He ordered frog saliva soup! When it arrived, all hot and steaming, I damn near threw up - especially as he went on and on about its therapeutic value.

Name games

It was a high level regional directors conference...all the Managing Directors from Asia Pacific, plus the worldwide number 1 and number 2 had flown into Manila for this session.

Unlikely as it seemed, we ended up having a few drinks that evening. It then progressed to the 'harder' end of town...the 'real' Manila bars.

A couple of guys in the group had grabbed a table at the back, sunk a few, and were joined by the usual friendly and chatty local 'waitresses'.

"What's your names?" Lolita asked.

"I'm Jack, and this is Harry," said one of the guys, using the names of our worldwide honchos as convenient aliases.

A little later, the door opened, and who walked in but the real worldwide honchos. They go up to the guys at the table to say 'Hi.'

"What's your names?" enquired Lolita of the newcomers.

"Jack and Harry," the Chairman replied honestly.

"Oh, all the same names!" says Lolita.

The guys saw their careers flash before their eyes.

Mistaken identity

A guy in our social lunch group had managed to score some membership cards to one of the more popular late night establishments in Singapore. These personalised and embossed plastic cards were prized possessions, as it saved a fortune in door charges, and you could also ponce about in the members section of the club.

One of the more gregarious members of our group had just been transferred to KL, and I was new so hadn't got on the list in time to qualify for a card.

Being the opportunist, I said, "I'll take Johnno's card."

A few nights later, I confidently walked in to the club, nonchalantly flashed 'my' membership card, and was ushered up to the members section. I ordered a round of drinks. The girl behind the counter asked to see my membership card. I paid by Visa, and whilst processing it, she noticed the name on the 2 cards did not match. She asked why this was, and I gave her a very swerving response, of which many politicans would have been proud.

Moments later, the manager arrived and asked to see my membership card.

"You're not JP", she said. "He's very well known to us!" And I was duly escorted from the premises.

Rear view dinner

As was the tradition in our company, each Chinese New Year we would have an all-staff celebration at a fancy Chinese restaurant. I left the local committee in charge of all the arrangements, menus, etc - it was their day, basically.

One year, it seemed every item ordered was a whole animal, still with limbs and heads and tails intact. We had chickens, fish, octopus, the works, all staring up at us from the middle of the table.

But the piece de resistance was the pig. This bugger was staring straight at me, with an apple in his mouth, and cute little deep-fried ears poking up. It was more than I could stomach (pardon the pun) so I asked someone to move it. They spun the 'lazy Suzan' round and then I found myself staring at the arse end of this damn pig.

"Actually, on second thoughts I think it was better the other way round," I said.

Truth in advertising

A group of us had flown to Seattle in the States for a conference. On the last night, after the formalities, I decided to hit the town with my good friend, LW, a very un-Chinese guy who ran our China operation. He was a hard-core party animal, capable of sniffing out the sleaziest establishments in any city in the world.

We took a cab downtown, and saw a place which said, "We have 50 pretty girls and 3 ugly ones" in four foot neon-pink letters on the side of the building. Had to go there!

"Let's check this place out," said LW. "Looks quite interesting."

As we entered what was basically a strip joint- the manager turned to my friend and said "Ah, nice to see you again, Mr W!". Turns out he'd been there the night before.

As it happened, I think all the pretty girls were on leave the night we visited, but they did have a celebrity stripper who was introduced with much Hollywood-style fanfare as having been the star of "Buttslammers 9." Her mother must be very proud of her.

Hair job

I'd never been to Korea before, but as I was going to Seoul on business a friend gave me a good briefing on what to expect. Amongst the crucial business survival tips, he also pointed me in the direction of what he considered the finest "hairdressing salon" in the whole of non-communist South Korea.

("Hair-dressing salon" is the front used by massage parlours there).

He gave me specific info...go to this hotel, walk through the back exit, cross the street and on the left, you can't miss it. Actually there were dozens of similar establishments, but one bigger and brighter than the rest.

I walked up to the entrance, greeted by a pleasant Korean lady. "Yes?"

"I'd like a...um, haircut please."

She ushered me into the seat, put the aprons on me, and proceeded to cut my hair as requested. I was thinking this is a very elaborate front that they have here, and a hell of a rigmarole to go through just to get a massage. Just then I spotted girls in the salon that didn't look like they were qualified hairdressers, sitting off to one corner. I also noticed what looked like concealed doorways.

I expected any moment the mamasan would say, "And would you by any slim chance be interested in a massage or something like that," but she never said anything. No glimmer of invitation. No nudges or winks.

My haircut finished, I got up, paid and walked out into the cold Seoul night, puzzled. To this day, they must still laugh about that white guy that came in and asked for a *haircut*!

Ducking hell

On business in the Philippines, I was keen to make a good impression on the locals, and probably vice versa. Overall, I loved their food - couldn't get enough of it. Then one of the guys said we should get some 'balut'. "Duck's egg," they said. "National delicacy of the Philippines". Harmless enough, I thought.

These eggs arrived, and everyone started peeling one, so I followed suit. What they hadn't told me was that it was duck's egg *with the duck still inside*!

There was no mistaking that crunchiness in the middle of the soft boiled outer. I wish they had offered me 'bilat' instead. Ask any Filipino guy what this is...but let me assure you it tastes a darn side better.

Waxing the bikini line

A cab driver had talked a group of us into going to a bar very much off the beaten track, but somewhere near the Mabini strip of old in Manila.

It was, perhaps not surprisingly, pretty ordinary. But the quality of the dancers was great, and they'd come out one by one and do the slow striptease thing. With each song another garment would be peeled off.

One bird was stunning...a Filipino Audrey Hepburn. Statuesque. Great smile, great presence. Great body. Skin like fine Italian marble. The small talk seemed to dry up round the bar, and there was a palpable sense of expectation for the final item (some really nice white lacy knickers in case you want your own mental picture completed) to be discarded.

In due course, the knickers came off, and she turned around to reveal what can only be described as an explosion of thick black pubic hair. It was like she had a large black cat strapped to her pelvis.

"Bad hair day," said one of the lads, echoing our disappointment and bemusement.

Head office job

JC loved those business trips to Bangkok and took every opportunity to visit the girlie bars. On one particularly outstanding evening he found himself in a passionate kissing embrace with one of the striking dancers.

He was accompanied by two Bangkok expats who knew most of the girls by their first names. They also knew that JC was necking with a *gatoy* - in other words a male transsexual. They kept that as their secret to relish the next time JC was standing before them in some boardroom making a pitch.

Get forked

I used to work in a pub in Hong Kong, which was a regular "on-on" venue for one of the local Hash running clubs.

Preparing for another regular onslaught, I remember our owner saying : "Hide the cutlery, girls, the Hash will be coming in tonight!"

Something special on the side

In a Taiyuan bar:

"Special cocktails for the ladies with nuts."

Indian giver

In the early 70's Hong Kong's first "first class" Indian Restaurant, The Bombay, opened on Upper Wyndham Street.

It is perhaps worth explaining at this point that most local Chinese were very chauvinistic, and narrow-minded, about food and perhaps Indians in general. It was rare to see local people in any restaurant except a Cantonese restaurant.

At the time, neither my Chinese girlfriend nor I had ever tried Indian food but, eager for a new experience, we went to The Bombay within the first few days of its opening.

The menu was as bit of a puzzle and, after studying it for a while, we decided to ask a waiter for some recommendations. We called a waiter over - a young Chinese guy in his early twenties - and my girlfriend asked him, in Cantonese, "What's good here?"

The waiter leant towards my girlfriend and in a hushed, conspiring tone said to her: *"Nothing's* good here; it's all Indian food you know!"

If you have a good story about bars and restaurants in Asia, let us know. Email us at **hardship_posting@hotmail.com** *or fax The Editor at 612-9499-5908.*

3

"Snakeoil salesmen"
True tales about bribery, corruption, entrepreneurs and conmen.

Now I'm not saying that corruption is widespread, but the addresses **www.mister10percent.com** and **www.backhanders.com** were snapped up pretty early when the internet came to Asia. It's pretty safe to say money talks.

After missing out on a government contract, an old friend of mine in Sri Lanka once said, with head nodding from side to side, and hand motioning behind his back, "Now you know why they call Sri Lanka the land of the swaying palms!"

Another buddy of Barry's in Jakarta used to get a big extra sum of money each month, in used US dollar bills, which was his "tea money" so he could obtain *free* information from government departments. Obviously they've got a different definition of 'free'.

Still it's not just the locals that are looking for a bit of leverage and lubrication. God knows there's the odd expat chap that dirties his hands. And the winner isssss...unfortunately Mr Leeson couldn't be here to collect his award in person. Bleeding idiots. Then you've got those human parasites posing as stock brokers selling junk bonds in 3rd world gold mines. "Good news, your shares are now up to $12.50, but I can get you another 1,000 for only $11 each...oh, what a shame they've had a coup so I'll be keeping your money then. Thank you!" Bastards. If I ever catch them, I'll flaming have them down the mine-shaft...shaft being the operative word.

No-one, and I mean no-one, pulls one over Col. Ken and gets away with it...I've got friends in very low places, you know. You have been warned.

HARDSHIP POSTING

But they weren't the first, they weren't the last.

I was bitching about this to Dave over drinks the other night, and he reliably informs me that way back in 1743, slightly before *I* was born, a young bloke called Robert Clive went to India as a clerk in the Dutch East India Company. Apart from shuffling papers, he was obviously fairly good with the blunderbuss and sword as well, because he defeated a French army of 64,000 in Plessey, India. And there were only about 3,000 blokes on his team when he started. Head office would've been proud of him. In fact they were...they made him Baron Clive of Plessey. I would've taken the opportunity to change my *whole* name if I were him. What kind of name is Clive, anyway? Especially for a friggin' war hero.

Anyway, our hero Clive had a little fall from grace (I've always been a little nervous of dating girls called Grace, just in case). The Pommie parliament turned him upside down on charges of corruption in India. Yes he did accept valuable gifts from Indian rulers but was not seen to have been actually dishonest. Where's Phil Coles from the Sydney Olympic Committee when you need him? Sadly, the bugger committed suicide shortly afterwards (Clive, not Phil).

Then a little later, Dave says, another Pom called Warren Hastings had a go. He was the Governor-General of India from 1773 to 1785 (pay attention, students- this will be in the exam) and was also an employee of the East India Company at the same time. Two pay checks - excellent! And a real recipe for scamming, I reckon. Sure enough, young Warren was accused of corruption and tyranny, despite an outstanding record. His trial before the House of Lords ended in acquittal. Sounds like the lawyers were the only real winners there.

Well, that joke's really gonna stand me in good stead down the Cricket Club tonight, I can see. Since when did a lawyer buy me a drink anyway?

So all in all, it's on for young and old. But I'll leave you with a little tip: always take a can of WD-40 with you...because you never know when the wheels are going to need greasing.

Colonel Ke

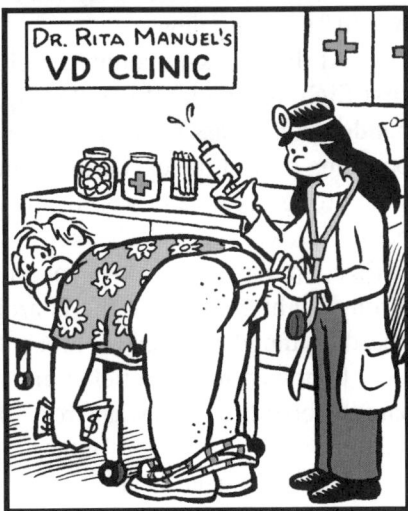

www.hardshipposting.com

3-in-1

I must admire the entrepreneurial spirit of this guy in Kalibo, a one-horse town in the southern Philippines. He was Doctor someone-or-another.

On the main street, was his medical clinic. Behind his clinic, was another building in which was his bar- fully stocked with liquor and dancing girls, including his daughter. On the other side of the quadrangle was his flophouse. It wasn't exactly the Grand Hyatt, but it was reasonable overnight accommodation, with short-time rates as well.

It struck me as the perfect vertically integrated business - go to the bar, take a girl to the flophouse and collect your clap medicine at the front on your way out.

Business should be that easy!

Pay now, fly later

I was at the airport in Ambon on my way to the Banda Islands. The airport was a tiny place that probably saw about 3 or 4 flights a day. There were two scheduled flights a day from Ambon to Banda Islands, but as I was told later, rarely did more than one go and often no flights would go on any day.

At the check-in counter, a clerk gave me a boarding pass for the first flight to Banda. When the flight was called, I went to the gate and handed in my pass to an agent. It was the same guy who issued me the boarding pass at the check-in counter! He looked at my pass and said it was wrong because it was for the *next* flight to Banda. I looked at the pass. He was right. I checked my original ticket and sure enough, I realized that at the check-in counter he had taken my ticket, written the wrong flight number on the boarding pass and was now rejecting my boarding the plane because of *his* "error".

I showed him my ticket and pointed out his "error". He calmly said the boarding pass was wrong so he would not accept it and I would have to wait for the next flight.

Knowing what I had to do, but just out of curiosity, I asked him when the next flight was. The answer was no surprise- the next flight was cancelled for that day. I paid my bribe and shook my head thinking how much easier it would have been for him to ask in the first place.

Who's wallet is this anyway?

He was desperate to impress head office and prove that behind the expense chits from Tanamoor was a bloke achieving the contracts his company had sent him to Jakarta to win.

The High Commission warned him the Minister he was visiting was not above the odd fiscal lubrication. He could become rather co-operative if there were a personal incentive, they had said. But of course nothing should be said of corruption.

The meeting was arranged.

He was ushered into the grand office—lots of space, secretaries a gogo, and a comfortable corner with deep couches and a coffee table. Without being asked, the black espresso coffee sipper he was, was brought a cup of white coffee. He had remembered the orientation week and patiently waited for his host to motion to him he could drink his coffee. Yarghhhhhh, not only did it have milk but it also appeared to have a tonne of sugar in it.

As the meeting closed, he remembered to deftly put his hand into his trouser pocket and quietly leave on the couch the new wallet he had bought and stuffed with the 5 Million rupiah for the "envelope".

The Minister escorted them to the front door. Smiles, polite thank yous and warm goodbyes were said as they waited for the driver to be paged on the intercom. He was happy, the meeting appeared to have gone well and the wallet would see to it the deal was sealed.

As our man stepped into his car, one of the Minister's men came racing out the front door. " Mistah, mistah," he cried out. "This is your wallet."

"Oh, no, I believe that wallet belongs to the Minister," our man said a tad puzzled.

"No pak," replied the Minister's man insistently. "The minister's wallet has 10 Million rupiah in it."

Aha ! Our man now knew the going rate.

Burning money

Coming back from Cebu once, we arrived at the airport to get a flight back to Manila. As we had changed our plans we had no ticket, let alone a confirmed flight.

The terminal was a shitfight. Obviously there had been a bunch of delayed or cancelled flights, and the place was overflowing.

My Filipina girlfriend went to check out the situation. "Next available flight to Manila is 2:45 this afternoon,"she said. I said no way would I wait in this hot smelly terminal for like 5 hours more.

I broached the subject of "surely money talks" so we went to the counter together to try again. The officer repeated the situation: *sorry sir, the flights are full, there is a long long waitlist, people have confirmed tickets, etc etc.* No way, Jose.

I waved a wad of Pesos in front of him.

"Smoking or non-smoking, sir?"

Greasing the wheels

You have to picture Indonesia in 1978, the old Jakarta airport and even older planes, systems airport control and so on.

I was at the Garuda airline counter with no booking no ticket and needed to fly to Unjung Pandang in South Sulawesi. I calmly approached one of the airline baggage handlers and explained quietly where I wanted to go and when. "Next flight that looks like taking off please". I also politely asked him in Bahasa how many children he had and he was rewarded a few rupees per child. *'Ini untuk anak anak .....bisa deatur kippu untuk Unjung Pandang?'* Basically I asked again for a ticket for Unjung Pandang. Without too much fuss, no loud words but a few more rupees, plus some extra for the aisle seat I was on the flight.

Just as I was departing to go through the noisy, milling crowd of would be travellers, I heard a loud American voice shouting his displeasure at hearing he could not fly on the flight today as it was over-booked. "God dammit! I was booked and confirmed on this flight only yesterday! See here on my ticket! How can you do this? I have to be in Unjung Pandang today!"

The middle-aged American was obviously new to Indonesia! Red-faced and really pissed off as nobody was listening to him. Not wishing to interfere, but also not happy to see a fellow *"orang putih"* in such a predicament, I quietly offered to assist him. I explained there may have been a mistake - the ticket just needed a little "lubrication" and I had my new friend the baggage handler assist again. The children needed some more help!

As we finally boarded the flight, some four hours late, I had a chance to discuss the various techniques, merits and challenges of travelling in Indonesia. We had a few 'bir bintangs' on the three hour flight and on arrival at Unjung Pandang we were close mates.

Small change

Our office in Taiwan had a good thing going. As the advertising agency for several leading global brands, we would purchase air time on the three state-owned television stations from local production companies. Our media staff would negotiate deep discounts for large up-front commitments.

The opportunity for increased wealth was, in keeping with the amount of the actual discounts, a closely guarded secret.

Once a month, a man from the production companies would deliver a bag full of cash to the agency's accounting department to be divided up by the agency's insiders. For the record, I never got a dime. (yeah sure! - ed.)

To allay any suspicions, the agency would pass on discounts to the client and explain that the discount rate was fixed at some low rate - chump change compared to the real discounts, but every client was so happy to see their rebate check that they never challenged the amount.

I happened on this scheme by chance. The president of one of our large clients asked if his company was paying commission on the rebate and I went in pursuit of the answer.

Seemed easy enough. Go to the billing department and inquire if the agency's commission was charged on net or gross media costs. They hemmed and hawed, and used language as a convenient excuse for claiming not to understand my question. They thought I was asking about the amounts received from the production companies. Soon the Managing Director, who was Taiwanese, got involved and told me this was not something I should spend my valuable time doing. I smelled a rat.

I had long wondered how the media director who was divorced and came from humble beginnings managed to send her daughter to an exclusive boarding school in England on her relatively low salary. And, how the accounting department head could contemplate the purchase of a home worth US$500,000.

After an investigation it was estimated that the media director alone had managed to siphon off US$3 million over the previous 10 years.

Fortunately, she had the foresight to invest in real estate and she didn't really need the job anymore.

Join the club

My friend was once coming through customs in Taipei. He had a suitcase full of computer components, samples, etc. The customs guy stopped him, checked his passport, asked purpose of visit in Taiwan, etc. All seemed in order.

As he was going in for a Friday meeting with a client who loved golf, he took his clubs - a set of Wilsons- planning to stay the weekend to get a round in.

The officer spotted these slung across his back, and all of sudden, he developed a mysterious "import duty" problem on the computer parts. What business was he in, did he have a proper letter to conduct business while he was there, and so on.

My friend was a bit puzzled, then belligerent, and saw this going nowhere till the officer said "Oh you like to play golf? Nice clubs." Then he knew what his game was. "I enjoy golf, too," the officer said, just to make sure they were on the same wavelength.

He reluctantly handed the clubs over, papers were stamped and he was through.

Little did the customs officer know- my friend used left-handed clubs that would be of absolutely no use to the customs guy at all! That softened the blow somewhat.

Magical disappearing act

My new posting was Bangkok. After six years in Singapore, I was looking forward to a bit of a change and I already had some good friends living there. The one problem was the job: my US-based company was in a joint venture with a Thai partner, who owned 50% of the business and had been running the operation (at a loss) on his own for three years. He had been the managing director, I would replace him and he would be elevated to Chairman.

Initially he was very nice to me, but became evasive every time I asked to see *all* the books, not just the top-line summaries I'd been getting. Another thing bugged me; we were paying salaries for 72 staff, but at most I could only count 47, and some of those seemed to be part time.

It came to a head when my Thai partner, KP, was on a trip to Japan for a week. I had to sign off the car insurance premiums for our company cars. The docket indicated that we had seven company cars, but I thought that we had three. Where were the other four? Then we had a delivery of three sets of golf clubs. I was told by my partner's secretary that they were his personal purchase, yet the company was billed. Then I visited one of our clients for a meeting. It was a major European multinational company, and according to their Amsterdam HQ, they should have been spending much more money with us, but in fact were spending less than half their budget.

The Thai marketing director sat at his desk opposite to me, "But we do spend all of our budget with you", he said, "and KP is always very generous to me personally, you know you have some very sexy girls working for you who he sends to take me out for a drink and some fun, if you know what I mean. We spend half our budget with your company directly and the other half with KP's other company."

I was gob-smacked. Not only was my partner supposed to work full time for our company, it appeared that he was creaming off from our worldwide clients for his own company. And providing some kind of pimping service. I called in the auditors, our legal people and people from our New York HQ.

This is what was finally discovered: Nine cars had been purchased by the company, but only three were recognised. Seven of them were still registered and finally traced to relatives of KP. The Golf Clubs (which still sit in the office today) were purchased as bribes. Several of the staff were working a half-day at our JV company and a half day at our partner's other company, other staff members were actually working for the other company, but being paid for by us, and that two of the staff there were fashion models on retainer, but we were paying all of their salaries! Two staff members just did not exist, but the money was being paid into bank accounts being accessed by other people.

Driving me round the bend

Having lived in Hong Kong for 5 years without a car, I finally decided to get a small one. I decided to aim for a Mazda 121 funtop,

3 years old.

One came up, but at HK$ 38,000 was way over its fair price. Next day it was advertised again for 32,500. "Perfect Condition" the advert said. I reckoned if I could get it down to 30,000 it would be just the job.

I spoke to the seller over the phone and arranged to see the car the same morning. It was in a car park just a few minutes from my office and coincidentally above the offices of the Independent Commission Against Corruption (ICAC), a good omen I assumed.

The bodywork was indeed in perfect condition. I started the engine and asked if I could have a test drive. The seller advised me that the road tax had just run out, so I couldn't go out on the road but I could drive it round the car park. This I did - round and round in left hand circles - and all seemed satisfactory. There was a "mini car-vac" in the back, which I could keep too. I would have liked to get a professional inspection, but just then another potential buyer called and I realised there was no time for any inspection - the car would be sold before I could organise it.

I asked about the maintenance history, and was told that it was maintained by a company in Causeway Bay and their computer had the record. Can't argue with that, I thought.

The chap had an honest face and friendly demeanour, and we agreed a price of 31,000 on the spot. The chap selling it to me told me he was selling it on behalf of a colleague of his who had been relocated back to the UK. The owner had signed the transfer form, so we could reregister it in my name right away.

We began the new owner registration procedure, and I was mightily grateful for the fellow to take me through the steps. He literally stayed by my side as we bought car insurance (through a broker he knew about), we bought road tax and then completed the re-registration. He assured me that if there were any outstanding convictions or fine payable on the car the re-registration would not go through, so I had nothing to worry about. All the same, since the car was not actually his to sell, I did have him write out a receipt for the cash, with his ID card number on it.

Out of the car park and along an expressway all was well. But the last part of my journey home is along a winding road, and whilst the car turned left very nicely, on turning right any faster than walking pace, it juddered violently and the tyres squealed. I was not happy. Maybe the front wheels needed retracking, or maybe there was a problem. A friend of mine suggested a friendly auto mechanic who gave me the bad news. He said the car had clearly been in an accident and I should refer back to the seller. It was not worth mending - if it could be mended at all.

So now began a process of calling up the seller to see what I could salvage. He of course at first denied any problem, but offered to exchange it for another car, a Rover. Not likely, I thought - but how come this diamond buyer seems to have plenty of cars available. And every time I called his office, he answered on a mobile phone. Very slowly it dawned on me that this chap was a professional Confidence Trickster. I was worried one day the phone line would be disconnected and I would never trace him again.

The phone calls to the seller got nowhere until I mentioned that I was about to get an independent check on the vehicle done by the local Automobile Association, and that if the car had indeed been in an accident, I would take the facts, including my receipt (thank goodness I at least got this) and the advert description to the police. He then suddenly agreed to buy the car back for 25,000. I would still be out 6,000, plus the registration fee, but I reckoned I could reclaim my insurance and cash in the road tax licence.

However when the guy inspected the car, he was another person. Angry, reluctant, aggressive. He knew that I had had enough of this car by now and just wanted shot of it. So when he saw I had removed the road tax, he screamed at me "how can I take this car anywhere without tax?" I let him keep it, took my money, signed the transfer document and the re-registration document as seller, and left. As I went, he already had the mini car-vac out and was busy preparing for the next victim.

I had lost close to US$2,500 and incurred very unwanted hassles, but to show how systematic this con man was - I discovered that he even got a 15% commission on the insurance!

If you have a good story about bribery, corruption or conmen in Asia, let us know. Email us at hardship_posting@hotmail.com or fax The Editor at 612-9499-5908.

4

"Chop Suey...a bit of everything thrown in"

*True tales of interesting characters, events,
goings-on and all kinds of other stuff.*

"May you live in interesting times," said Confucius, and his wish was definitely granted. For better or for worse, each and every day that dawns in Asia is "interesting". Exciting, enervating, dynamic, kinetic, frustrating, and often a complete shitfight. But you wouldn't be anywhere else in the world for quids. I love Asia!

For many, though, it's love and hate. Mind you, I don't remember falling in hate too often. But I do fall in love, and we're talking deep-seated true love here, about...oh, 25 times a day on average. Don't tell Mrs Col. Ken though. The old trout, she thinks I only have eyes for her. Truth be known, that's about as far as it gets just between these four walls.

Anyway, there is a lot of "only in Asia" stuff. Down the road from my place, for instance, is the Samui Yacht Club. But anyone going there in the hope of seeing anything remotely resembling a yacht would be sorely disappointed. "We just liked the name," says the cheery duty manager of the hotel.

And I've always loved the fact that the Vietnamese currency is called The Dong. After all, that's what it's mainly spent on.

The other noticeable thing about Asia is space. Or lack of it. Now a guy like me not only likes my personal space, but also needs it for this not insignificant girth of mine. But in places like Hong Kong, with its 14,000 people per square kilometre, your personal space is invaded several times a minute. The alarm goes off - perimeter security has been breached. Old lady on sidewalk has veered straight into your path and is not giving way. Bang, you bounce off each other with nary a Sorry, Oops or Good Day To You, Ma'am. In fact, you're lucky if the old dragon hasn't put her bony elbows deliberately into your kidneys. Oh, they're crafty like that.

And the MTR is worse. Just the like the Tokyo underground. Or a Calcutta bus. The only way to create a little temporary personal space is to let one fly after a good curry lunch. A little botty burp. Research has shown that this buys you about 15 quality seconds in the more developed countries, about 8.9 seconds in the secondary markets, and...it has no effect at all in Calcutta. You're just one of the crowd.

And being just one of the crowd is an important part of Asian life. The desire to blend in and not ruffle any feathers. Put community and society ahead of your individuality. Barry tells me that in a recent poll, 87% of Japanese wanted to look like everyone else. Presumably the other 13% wanted to die their hair blue, put on leopardskin rockabilly suits and go dancing at Shinjuku Street on a Sunday.

Non-stop mayhem. That's what I like about this place. Not knowing what's around the next corner. Anyway, time for my blue pills and a little lie down now. Hammock or sofa? Hammock or sofa? I hate hard decisions.

Colonel Ke——

Cunning stunt

Our client, a major French shipping company, was approached to sponsor a French Festival. We were told the organisers had a unique concept and event that was perfect for us.

It turned out we were to meet with two French guys: one was a motorbike stunt rider who was going to ride a flaming motorcycle across a tightrope over the Singapore River up one of the tallest buildings on the other side. The other guy built paper boats.

Come meeting day, these guys are ushered into the room. One is a rough looking guy, with leather jacket and scars all over his face. I say to him: "Bonjour, you must be Pierre the stunt rider?" He says: "No, I am Guy the paper boat builder."

HARDSHIP POSTING

I hear voices

Let's call him Terry. He came to Hong Kong in the late '80s to fill a copywriting post in a large international agency. Much was expected of him. Terry was a black Londoner. A sort of advertising Sol Campbell (though, as you'll see, without quite the staying power). When he first arrived, he bubbled onto the scene, all full of hope and optimism for making his mark (as you do), and within a few months, had certainly achieved that.

But then he did something which, how shall we say, put the locals out a bit. He started putting up a little series of stories on the agency notice board, which basically poked what he thought was just a bit of harmless fun at the locals, and their social habits. Which, if you know the sensitivity of the Hong Kong Chinese when it comes to 'face', was, well, a wrong move. To put it lightly.

Then Terry began acting a bit strange. I received a weird phone call from him one morning at the office, claiming he'd been arrested in the night and spent the night at the police station. How he got there, and what he did, was somewhat vague. Although he seemed to be mumbling something about being 'set up'.

After this, he began acting jumpy around the office. Wandering in looking over both shoulders muttering things like, "They're out to get me man. I know it." The story of the arrest seemed to suggest that his drink had been spiked at the hotel he was staying in, and he ended up in an argument with a taxi driver, which led to a fight on the way to the police station. (Why he was in a taxi, when he was already drinking in his hotel, was unclear.)

His actions got worse, and we concluded that he was acting like someone indulging in serious drugs. Paranoid. Mumbling about rubbish. And it was seriously affecting his work. Which led to his boss having no choice than to inform him that he was sending him back to London. It got worse. Terry had decided that he liked Hong Kong. And was staying. His behaviour became weirder and more erratic. He'd turn up on my doorstep, like someone on the run from secret forces. Everyone was out to get him. He was off his rocker.

The next thing we knew, he turned up in the Chinese press. There were pictures of him being arrested after a chase with the police.

Apparently he jumped off a footbridge to escape them, and was under arrest in a hospital. Some of us went to see him. He was chained to a bed. Of course, being an ex-colleague, our human emotions got the better of us. So we grouped together and put him up in an inexpensive private hospital, so he could recover. Unfortunately for us, Terry liked the hospital, and decided that he'd like to stay there a bit. Suddenly it all reached a bit of a head, not to mention a hospital bill the size of Chris Patton's lunch budget. Terry, to be brutal, simply had to go.

How it all ended, was that his sister had to fly out and literally drag him back to London. There was some mention of extensive drug use. What drugs, we were never quite sure. Or were his drinks being spiked?

First name basis

This list of real-life Hong Kong persons' names was collected over several years by a Hong Kong engineer :

ACNE Chan - a female bank clerk
ARSENIC Lo - an unemployed male
BEATLES Lau - a male garment quality inspector
BELLWIND Lau - a male music teacher
BELLY Leung - a bartender
BIONIC Yip - a female knitwear merchandiser
BRUNHILDE Ng - a female chiropodist
CANINE Poo - a waitress
CEMENT Cheung - a male security consultant
FOREVER Yung - a male graphic designer
GIPSY Lee - a female at Hong Kong Arts Centre
HANDY Kam - a salesman
HERNIA Kong - a female railway worker
HUCKLEBERRY Pin - a policeman
IRON TIT Ng - a male cook
MARMALADE Tin - a female student
MORNING Sun - a female student
MOTOR Fan - a male electrical engineer
PENGUIN Chang - a male McDonald's employee
PERPETULAR Lee - a female bank manager
PIANO Chow - a female shop assistant

HARDSHIP POSTING

POTATO Pun - a policeman
PRICK Chan - a male driver (fortunately)
SCARLETT Pong - a female working for Estee Lauder
SILICON Cheng - a female at Hongkong Telecom
SNAKE Fang - a female lawyer
TACO Pang - a male trading company boss
and the list goes on...

A small problem

Myself and an English friend of mine had gone to this function in Singapore. On of the organisers/hosts of the function came across to introduce himself.

"Hi, I'm Wee Wang," he said.

"I'm terribly sorry to hear that," said my friend, drily.

Mud wrestling

I could never forget the Mud Olympics at the Frog & Toad pub on Lantau Island in Hong Kong. Hundreds of mad *gweilos* would make the annual ferry pilgrimage to the hallowed mud pit, which was a couple of football fields big, and drink a shitload of beer and participate in various childish games and sports before the whole thing descended into an absolute bloody mess.

At the end of the day, all you could see of people was little eyes peering through the mud. And you'd be digging mud out of your belly button and other orifices and crevices for months afterwards. God knows what the locals made of all of this!

Gang etiquette

Singapore in the early Eighties was still a little on the wild side. I remember walking out of the Cathay Cinema at Bras Basah, and as we came round the corner, a Chinese gang fight in full swing with these 2 sides beating the shit out of each other.

As we rounded the corner, they immediately stopped. We nervously walked through the space between the warring factions with nods of "good evening" As soon as we passed, they went back to flailing the hell out of each other. Very weird.

Great expectorations

One of the more endearing (not!) characteristics of the Hongkies is their ability to develop industrial amounts of phlegm, and rid their bodies of it at astounding decibel levels. Anytime, anyplace. It apparently has something to do with expelling the devil or bad energy from your body, so it's undertaken with gusto and not the slightest amount of discreetness.

One morning, walking through the Tsim Tsa Tsui tunnel (sounds like a phlegmatic expulsion in its own right), I heard someone behind me exorcising the devil. And it built up, and kept on building and building until the person was on the verge of turning inside out. I thought this has to be my Kiwi colleague GH, who often caught the same train as me. He was obviously having me on, so ridiculous was this de-phlegming process.

So I turned around and said: " Nice one, mate!" only to be confronted by this little old Chinese guy hoiking for all he was worth. The "phlegm thrower" from hell. I lost my appetite for breakfast.

Global village

I was holidaying in Tokyo, and went to visit the temples in Nikko. Whilst checking out the temples, I couldn't help but notice a couple of rather shapely blonde girls also wandering around.

Naturally I contrived to bump into them and strike up a conversation. It turned out they were airhostesses for Lufthansa (immediately dispelling many myths I had about German girls!)

The coversation continued. It turned out they had been backpacking around China, and had studied Chinese in Guangzhou for a few months. "Oh, I had a friend that did that too," I said, keeping the conversation going. "Vot voz heez naam?" one of the German blondes asked. "Richard...," I said and she completed the surname for me. They had backpacked around China for 6 months with my good buddy from Sydney.

Amazing! What are the chances of an Australian bumping into two German girls outside Tokyo who had met your good buddy from Australia in China? Any statisticians care to work that one out?

HARDSHIP POSTING

Singapore...Boy?

The trap was set. One of our good buddies was having his buck's night, and we were going to set him up a beauty.

The plan was to get him totally trashed and drive him out to Changi airport, dress him in a Singapore Airlines hostess outfit, and leave him sleeping on a bench inside the airport.

This was doubly funny as S, the victim, was 6'2 and blonde!

Unfortunately, our plan was a little derailed because at one of the pubs we went to was the ex-boyfriend of the bride to be. And his gang of friends. He was still feeling jilted, and couldn't resist making a scene.

Soon, it was on for young and old - a big fight, and our original game plan had to be abandoned.

High times

It took us all by surprise when C announced he was getting married, so of course we had to prepare a memorable buck's for him.

The night started out at Chico and Charlie's Restaurant in Singapore, where major amounts of margueritas were consumed. The plan was to slip some Capto's into his drink (Captogons are a rather lethal little speed amphetamine tablet), and various people were given tablets to slip into his drinks, in case one of the others didn't get a chance.

After dinner, we swapped notes - *all* of us had managed to slip one into his drink, so he'd had about 4 or 5 tabs. We all pissed ourselves laughing as C's eyes grew wider and wider, and he started talking non-stop.

Then we ended up at Club 392, (a bar in the infamous Four Floors of Whores complex on Orchard road) where he continued to be lively and loud whilst the rest of us were falling apart. Then E started rounding up the ugliest tarts in the place...the older, the uglier, the more disfigured the better...and he would bring them to our table one by one and introduce them personally to us. They were flattered; we were hysterical.

C later reported he couldn't sleep for 3 whole nights after we spiked him.

Keep the change

The Hong Kong Rugby 7's is an institution. A weekend of complete body and brain abuse. One particular day, I was so messed up from the night before, I couldn't bear the thought of another beer. My head was throbbing. I was not far from clinical death. Fans yelling and screaming didn't exactly help, and nor did having to pass jug after jug of beer down the rows (as is the custom at The 7's). You also passed down the money (HK100 and the girl normally kept the tip).

Around 3pm, I felt that perhaps I was ready for my first beer after all. I signalled the Beer Girl, decked out in her tight blue and yellow spandex Fosters outfit (desperately attractive if I remember correctly) and a jug of beer came my way. I opened my wallet and only had a HK1000 (US$125) note, which I passed down.

I enjoyed the beer, the rugby got better, I got better. Then I turned to my friend and said, "Where's my change?" "I said to the girl keep the change." "You asshole, that was $1000!"

The rest of the weekend, I was continually swarmed by beautiful Beer Girls hoping to cash in on me. Good for the ego, bad for the bank balance!

Time warp

Sunday morning, second day of a particularly arduous Sevens weekend. We're all feeling completely f***ed as a result of 2 horrendous days and nights of alcohol abuse. However, we want to get good seats, so get to the football ground in Happy Valley around 7:30 am.

We immediately got into the jugs of beer. It was Finals day after all. After a few beers, we decide it's time for breakfast. Hmmm, MacDonalds.

So we were already pissed again, and chomping egg burgers when my friend turned to me and said: " I can't believe this. It's 9 o'clock in the morning and I'm pissed and eating hamburgers."

I said: "Don't be too hard on yourself. You're from Tokyo, right? It's already 10 o'clock there. Or to put it another way, it's 9pm on Saturday night in New York so party on." Which we did. Relentlessly.

HARDSHIP POSTING

Information service

I had had a big night. I eventually staggered into the Shangri-La hotel in Hong Kong at 6:15am. I had a breakfast appointment lined up, which meant I had to be up at 7am to get ready.

I buzzed the operator and requested a wake up call "for sheven pleashh." "Is that a.m or p.m., Sir?" she politely enquired. "Whatever it ish, er, 45 minutsh from now," I shaid, er, said. "That's a.m.,Sir."

No sooner had my head hit the pillow, than the phone rings. "Good morning, Mr L, this is your wake-up call. It's 7am and you might like to know that today will be 18 degrees so you might like to take a sweater."

At my breakfast meeting, I was saying to my counterpart how impressed I was with the wake-up call...the simple but useful touch of telling you the weather and how to dress in a climate you're not used to.

"It's better than that," he said. "They give you three useful bits of information...the time, the weather, but most useful of all... your *name!*"

A real dog

I had been out driving and had my Dalmatian in the car with me, when I decided to go to a "curtain hotel" in Bangkok, one of those short-time establishments where you park your car outside and they pull the canvas curtain across to ensure your visit is discreet.

Having "done the business", the attendant opened the curtain on the driveway and I was waiting forever for a gap in the traffic to edge out into the traffic again. It then struck me that people driving by were staring very curiously...

Here is this guy coming out of this brothel with a Dalmatian, lovingly poised in the front seat next to him!

If you have a good story about any general stuff and goings in Asia, let us know. Email us at **hardship_posting@hotmail.com** *or fax The Editor at 612-9499-5908.*

"Sharing your home with strangers"
True tales about Drivers and Maids.

As my dear old mate, Sir Les Patterson, so eloquently puts it: when you leave Asia, you won't miss the maid and the driver. Because the missus will be the maid, and you'll be the driver!

If maids and drivers could talk, my guess is that none of us could ever run for public office. Thank God for that. Because they see a very private side of us, not just the veneer that the adoring public sees...all scrubbed and shiny and smiley. And from what I hear, some maids see an extremely private side of us...the side our mummy probably hasn't seen since we graduated from kindergarten. Just hearsay, of course.

Here's a double-edged pork sword if ever I saw one. Don't get me wrong, it's terrific that we get to subsidise third world economies in yet another way, but sometimes you just wish you could walk into the lounge room in your droopy old white cotton Jockey undies, and have a good old scratch whilst reading the Sunday Bugle. Or have it away on the dining room table like you used to. But with servants around, you can't. And with the missus around, you certainly can't.

But they do have their good sides (er, maids that is). Sometimes they do become a part of the family. An indispensable appendage. Breastfeed the kids, even. And get taken on exotic holidays to England in the winter to wipe the runny noses of their master's spoiled little brats.

Some of these little Dorises are prime material for a quick tune on the old pork flute. Fresh from the provinces. A chance to flirt with a dashing Sean-Connory type like myself. It's stuff their kid sisters back home could only dream of. Stuff that I could only dream of. Still, eh. Yip, Pete reckons she'll press your trousers while you're still wearing them.

Thing is, they earn more money scrubbing my dunny than they do as civil engineers back home! And as they're engineers, may as well do an on-site inspection of the erection while they're at it.

But the down side is some of them can be butt-ugly. And who wants *another* older butt-ugly woman under their roof? The trouble and strife, of course. Because she knows what's going through your testosterone-powered, hormonally-misted mind.

There you are at the Maid Agency, flipping through the bios and stopping at all the 16 year olds with puppy dog eyes, gold lame jeans and a t-shirt barely containing those nubile buds of hers. Your missus on the other hand is stopping at all the ugly photos saying, "This one looks good...hmmm, cooked for an expat family before, has 6 kids of her own so she must be good with them..." And, of course, she always wins.

The uglier they are though, the less other problems you'll have - like a life of her own, for instance. Because if they're even half-way attractive they'll attract the men folk from miles around. Old Dave just caught his maid shagging a local bloke. "Oh, found a chink in your amah, did you?" I said. Couldn't resist it.

But take a stroll around Statue Square in Hong Kong or Lucky Plaza in Singapore on a Sunday, and it's an absolute *adobo* smorgasbord. The maids are in their Sunday finest, literally - enough lipstick and cheap perfume to keep a major cosmetics house in business into the next millenium. And boots. Why do they all wear those ridiculous platformed lace-up pointy boots - is it some kind of latent Tina Turner fixation? Great if they could look like Tina Turner...one of very few non-Orientals that actually gets ole' Colonel Ken standing to attention, along with Pocohontas. When is Disney gonna bring out the Pocahontas inflatable doll as part of their merchandise? What a winner that would be and whatsername...Anna Pornikova. Dear me, I'll need to have these trousers dry-cleaned...a one-man Exxon Valdez yoghurt tanker disaster.

Take your ear-muffs, though. Tagalog can sound like an AK-47 at point blank range when they all get together to tell of rumour, scandal and intrigue after a week or more without seeing their friends. After all, a week's along time in toilet cleaning.

And then there's the drivers. They drive your car. Badly.

Lolita, my slippers please. Sir's written almost 2 pages today, and I'm going to have a little lie down now.

Colonel Ke

Key to success

The first evening our new maid was with us, I handed her the key for the car for her to clean it in the morning. The next day, she proudly gave me the clean and polished key - probably thinking I was a real idiot!

© Captions of Industry Pty Ltd.   **www.hardshipposting.com**

A real puzzle

My girlfriend stayed up to 4 in the morning to finish a 5,000 piece jigsaw which she had been working on for a week. Next morning we find the jigsaw neatly packed back in the box. My friend was mad as hell and went off to work telling me to sort it out.

I told the maid she was in trouble and she'd better fix the puzzle. When we returned, a third of the puzzle had been completed - but with all the wrong pieces being forced together, completely destroying the cardboard pieces. That maid didn't last long!

Ironic

Our new maid had arrived at Changi Airport; we duly set off to the agency to claim her and bring her home. Her name was Rebecca, from the Philippines; she was 19 years old.

Rebecca was keen to get started in her new job. Spying a large pile of laundered clothes in the spare room, she asked whether we would like her to do the ironing. Off she went, closing the door to the spare room. We returned about seven hours later.

I heard a wailing noise coming from the spare room. I went in to see what was going on and saw Rebecca, a tiny pile of badly ironed clothes on one side and a huge pile of un-ironed clothes on the other. She was sobbing, "I can't do it, Sir, I can't do it." She continued, "Your iron no good. I try and try and try, but your iron no good".

I looked around, saw the iron (a brand new Philips) and asked her, "Why?"

"No heat, Sir"

Then it dawned on me. I pointed to the electric cable and said "Where did you put that, Rebecca?" She looked totally mystified. I picked up the plug and put it in the socket.

Rebecca had spent all day trying to iron clothes, but had not plugged in the iron.

Slippery customer

SC had heard of the possible temptations of maids, so when he arrived in Singapore, he decided to hire the ugliest maid he could find. The logic being that not only would she be unlikely to have boyfriends around his apartment when he was out, he himself would not be tempted on those occasional evenings when he returned home pissed out of his brain.

The new maid turned up. And she was ugly. The Singapore Rugby team was better looking.

But she did her work, mixing a mean G&T and keeping the fridge stocked with beer. So off SC went on a business trip to Hong Kong for four days. But as business finished early, so he returned a day early.

On returning home, he noticed a strange pick-up truck in the drive. Lights were on in the front room. He made some noise going in the front door with his keys, and was just opening the door when he was knocked aside by a man "of Indian origin", rushing past naked - apart from some clothes held covering his cock. The Indian jumped into the pick-up truck and zoomed off.

By this time, SC was inside calling for the maid. He looked everywhere, and finally in his master bedroom. What a mess! There was the maid in a corner, hurriedly dressed, looking guilty. His sheets were all over the place and smeared all over with something. And around the bed, in a regular pattern were placed eight large jars of Vaseline.

SC was cool. He told the maid that he would be in the living room, that she should clear up and come to see him. But instead, she went to her room, packed her things and climbed out of the window, never to be seen again. Costing SC his $5,000 security deposit.

His next maid was very pretty.

Back seat driver

I once had a driver who, in typical Jakarta heavy traffic, turned to me and said that he was very stressed! He then got out of the car and walked off, leaving me sitting in the back seat.

Dead funny

A Kiwi friend of mine, Kevin, lived in a small house on an island called Cheung Chau, near Hong Kong Island. Kevin was originally from the South Island and had never travelled outside his home country (before Hong Kong). His family was parochial New Zealand, unseasoned in travel.

Kevin had lived in his house on sleepy Cheung Chau for five years. Over the five years his maid Gloria had become very attached to him as so many do and, being somewhat older, treated Kevin in a motherly kind of way.

One day, Kevin's dad made a surprise visit. It was so much of a surprise that he wasn't home. It was a Saturday and Kevin hadn't made it home from Friday night because he'd been on the piss in Lan Kwai

Fong, a popular party area, and had missed the last ferry back. So he decided to party on. Kevin's dad, armed only with his postal address, was completely unaware that he'd have to get a taxi to Hong Kong Island, then a ferry from Blake's Pier out to Cheung Chau. Consequently, he arrived at Kevin's house disoriented, frustrated, and in no mood for any more difficult conversations with the locals.

Kevin's dad is a typical country man from New Zealand with a low tolerance for idiots and a rich Kiwi accent, which doesn't help matters if you're travelling in the wilds of Hong Kong.

With his bag over his shoulder and drowning with sweat in the 90 percent humidity, Kevin's dad eventually finds his house and knocks loudly on the door. Gloria, worried that Kevin hasn't returned home, is sure that it's Kevin having lost his key - again. She rushes to the door and is mystified by the stranger. In her wonderful Tagalog accent, Gloria says: "Yes Sor, can I help you?", to which Kevin's dad simply announces himself in a loud, confident voice rich with a Kiwi accent:

"Kev's Dad!".

Gloria is stopped in her tracks! She squints her eyes, strains her ears: "Pardon, Sor?"

"Kev's dad!" he repeats a little louder and more forcefully.

It would not be Gloria's way to question a European man, and as the words slowly sink in she begins to cry and scream at the top of her voice in a high-pitched squeal. She elbows past Kevin's dad and rushes down the road waving her arms screaming, "Kev's Dead! Kev's Dead, Kev's Dead!"

Kevin's dad watches her disappear in a frenzy, wondering what on earth Kevin told her about him that would scare her in such a way. Nonetheless he was convinced now he had the right house so he let himself in and made himself a cup of tea.

An hour and a half later a disheveled Kevin returned home to find his dad sitting supping tea. They greeted, exchanged pleasantries and Kevin's dad explained what happened. Ten minutes after that Gloria walked in flooding with tears on the arms of two Filipina friends consoling her for her loss. They walked in, took one look at Kevin and then all three screamed at the tops of their voices and repeated the whole process again!

Any port in a storm

RHT got his prescription for Viagra, and went home to get ready for his wife's arrival, planning a vigorous surprise for her. The doctor's instructions were to wait an hour for best effect. He called her and she said she would be home "in an hour." Perfect, he thought, and proceeded to pop his Viagra.

An hour went by and the Viagra was making its presence felt. But no wife. He called her on the mobile again and she said, "The traffic is terrible, I'm still on the other side of town, maybe another hour and a half."

Shit! He called his doctor.

"What should I do?" he asks the friendly and understanding doc.

"It would be a shame to waste it," the doctor says. "Do you have a maid around?" he added, half joking.

"Yes, but with her I don't need the Viagra!" said RHT.

Creative licence

My friend Cedric in Hong Kong had employed a driver. An Indian lad who was hard-working, enthusiastic and dutiful. He was also a few screws loose on top when it came to, well, common sense matters.

First of all there was the interview stage. Which was, by all accounts, thorough and lengthy. An hour or so briefing and question session, which covered off all aspects of the job. And then touched on issues such as dedication, ambition, character. And so on. All the pre-requirements you would expect when employing someone to drive you around in a Japanese hatchback.

It was only after having passed all this with flying colours, and having eased into the job with the first number of trips already under his belt, that it emerged that our friend the driver neglected to mention that he didn't actually have a driving license as such. A small oversight.

There was more. Upon having been instructed by Mr Cedric (for Cedric had now become Mr Cedric) to "go to meet my wife outside Lane Crawford", the driver arrived at exactly the right time, all keen and smiling and ready to where Mrs Cedric (for theoretically, she was) wanted to go. Minus, however, the car. "But Mr Cedric asked me to go and meet you. He didn't mention anything about bringing the car."

HARDSHIP POSTING

Needless to say, the employment period was short and sweet.

At arms length

When my friend, JG, arrived in Bangkok from the USA a few years back I had my driver, Khun Ram, pick up at the airport.

As John came out of immigration, Ram extended his hand to help with his bag. John grabbed his hand and started shaking it "pleased to meet you! My Name is John! What is your name?" Obviously pleased with this reaction, Khun Ram could not stop smiling and laughing all the way to the hotel. In fact, he still asks, "When Khun John come back? I like him!"

A good start

On the first day on the job, my part-time maid flooded the apartment and burnt a shirt, but didn't tell me so I only found out once I returned home.

"Why didn't you call me?" I asked incredulously.

"I can't use the telephone, Sir," she explained.

I've since given up trying to teach her to use the washing machine. In fact nowadays to avoid me she turns up late and leaves before I come back so I can't even fire her.

Jet brag

In 1985 Pan Am returned to Bangkok and we were tasked with setting up the staffing etc and making the promotional rounds. Pan Am had a Captain of Chinese descent. His family emigrated to the US about 100 years ago to work on the transcontinental railroads. His family was from the mid-west and, aside from being ethnically Chinese, he was as far removed from China as one could get.

Captain Lee was also an expert on "jet lag". At the time , Pan Am was operating long haul non stop flights from New York to Tokyo and San Francisco to Hong Kong so jet lag was affecting many passengers and Captain Lee gave talks on it.

We had set him up to address the American Chamber of Commerce in Bangkok and before the talk, we took him to meet the US Ambassador at the US Embassy for a photo op. Captain Lee was in his Pan Am

Captains uniform with the four stripes, scrambled eggs on the hat and everything.

After the photo shoot, we were offered a ride to the Chamber of Commerce meeting venue and Captain Lee (and about 4 of us) were waiting by the Ambassador's car in the Embassy compound. A lady comes rushing out and sees him and runs up and asks -in that loud, slow English that Americans use when talking to Asians- "Are you the Ambassador's driver?"

Captain Lee was gracious. "Yes, when he drives to Washington, I drive him".

If you have a good story about drivers or maids in Asia, let us know. Email us at **hardship_posting@hotmail.com** *or fax The Editor at 612-9499-5908.*

6

"Hang on to your balls"
*True tales about golf, dragon-boating,
hash running and other sports.*

It won't surprise you that a fine physical specimen like myself is an all-round sports fanatic with a rigorous discipline and training programme. Not a day goes by that I'm not watching some game of rugby, cricket, Thai kick-boxing, tennis, golf, snooker or whatsoever on Star Sports. The discipline is all about controlling the mind - of the others in the room. My wife and servants know they must be absa-bloody-lutely quiet, except in the commercial breaks. And training...they know that as soon as my drink gets to 1/3 from the end, to bring another one.

And whilst Asia is a lot about work, it's also about sport in some ways. The locals are now making up for all the time they spent in the office building their countries up, by getting out and playing golf. Mind you, they'll take their mobile phone, their pagers, and everything so it's not like you're actually getting away from anything. I wouldn't be surprised if some bugger brings his computer and laptop to the course one day. By laptop, I mean secretary.

Years ago, the Japanese looked down on anyone with a darker skin. Obviously a peasant that spent his days toiling in the sun. But now, a tan is a status symbol - you can obviously afford to play golf, or at least vacation in Hawaii or Bali.

It may amaze you as much as it amazed me to know that there were 7,463,542 golf courses under construction when the Asian crisis hit. Er, approximately, according to Barry. These are now slated for use as all-purpose public tai-chee parks.

Of course, where I live in Koh Samui, Thailand there is not a single golf course and not even a driving range. So it's surprising that my game is as good as it is...I shot a 74 the other day. The *second* nine wasn't quite as good though so we headed off to the 19th hole to avoid any further embarrassment (unsuccessfully, as it turns out).

But sport is not just confined to golfing endeavours. One of the world's most venerable institutions, the Hash House Harriers, has its roots in Asia. And I do mean roots. The HHH is basically a drinking club with a running problem. Dave tells me it was started in Malaysia in 1938 by a bunch of bored expats that invented their own game based on the English schoolboy game of "Hare and Hounds." They used to meet at a restaurant/bar called "The Hash House" in Kuala Lumpur after each run. And so, The Hash, was born.

The name has nothing to do with the obvious drug-related connotations. Speaking of names, each hasher will be given a hash-name after he's completed a certain amount of runs based on some spurious incident or attribute. Hence you have fine fellows with names like Flatulent Ferret, Duke of Puke, Pumpkin Head, Grateful Douche, Pole Pounder, Scud Stud and Fanny Sniffer, running around the jungles of Asia with terrorising calls of "on, on!"

As for me, I'm what's known as a SCB or a BWB...a Short-Cutting Bastard or a Back-Walking Bastard. But that's just strategy...that's where the birds are!

Cricket is played in all the ex-British colonies as well. (Another game the Brits invented and can't really compete in anymore). Instead we have countries like India, Pakistan and Sri Lanka near the top of world competitions, and in Singapore and Malaysia, well it's more an expat game plus the odd Indian here and there. Some of them very odd.

At least Singapore is on the world map for rugby. For one of the biggest thrashings ever (by one of those renowned rugby nations like Malaysia or Thailand).

But nothing beats the sheer spectacle of the Hong Kong Rugby Sevens. I've been to every single one, and I still don't know who has won each year until I read the paper the next day - or two days later - when I finally awaken from a beer-induced slumber. Of course I'm yelling for Australia or Thailand and it turns out that it's bloody New Zealand and Fiji in the final. Oh, yes, my fair-weather friends - The Sevens is the mother of all weekends.

Expats have a bit of fun with dragon-boating, too. Some buggers call them long boats or even swan boats, but they're the same thing. Load up 20 odd guys in a boat and paddle like hell till your pacemaker explodes or you pass the finishing line, whichever comes first. Then drink yourself to death. Simple stuff. I like sports like that. The race is about 2 minutes long, then you spend the next 7 or 8 hours talking everybody through it and replenishing those vital lost body fluids.

Its popularity has rippled outward from Asia to become a truly global sport according to some rag I was reading recently. For about 2000 years they tootled about with dragon-boats in China, but it was really Hong Kong that put the sport on the map with its International festivals since 1976. Now in Sweden alone you'll find 1200 teams! And Paddler magazine calls it the 2nd most popular sport in the world. I can't believe that...maybe they mean is it's the second most popular sport *amongst rowers*?!?

Still, can't knock it. I've got more medals from dragon-boating than I ever got from fighting for my country. Glory days! And the birds love to play with my medals.

Anyway, all this talk of physical exertion is wearing me out. Might just have a cheeky little Gin and Isotonic to keep my fluid levels up. Dashed tropics, really takes it out of you.

Colonel Ken

A beautiful course

Some of the nicest courses in Asia are in Thailand, and the Thais are the nicest and most gentle people I have met (outside a kick boxing ring).

As I was being driven into Blue Canyon Golf Club in Phuket, I noticed a huge crowd on one of the greens. I thought the group must have had a bit of a gallery.

After giving my clubs to the caddy master and signing in, I proceeded to the 1st tee where I was confronted with a gorgeous caddy carrying my clubs, another with an umbrella to keep the sun off, and another carrying a stool for me to sit on.

The crowd was now easily explained. Wait till I tell the boys at The Grange GC in Adelaide about this.

www.hardshipposting.com

Hole in the pocket

Playing golf in Singapore can be dreadfully expensive. Club memberships are bought and range from S$30,000 to S$250,000, indeed they are listed like shares and rise and fall along with the stock exchange and the housing market. Not what I was accustomed to. In Australia I had paid A$1200 for my membership. It was at Singapore Island Country Club (the most expensive club in Singapore) where I was invited as a guest on a couple of occasions by a colleague that my most expensive game of golf took place.

One day he informed me it was becoming difficult for him to put "Mr Smith" on his expense sheet to recoup green fees and would I mind paying for today's game. Being a golf desperado and suffering withdrawal not having played for a month, I agreed. I forked out S$247.00 and headed for the 1st tee.

The sky was heavy, not unusual for Singapore. After 3 holes it started to drizzle and as we approached the 4th, the skies opened and the storm hit with lightning and thunder. The siren went and we headed for shelter.

They eventually closed the course and, returning to the club house, my host duly went to retrieve my green fees and was told they had a "no rain check" policy.

At A$60.00 per hole it was the dearest game I ever played.

Metal Birdie

Having learnt how expensive Singapore golf could be it wasn't long before a group of us expats discovered the more economical courses of Malaysia. A short drive over the Causeway into Johor Bahru were a myriad of golf courses to test our skills. One favourite was Tanjong Puteri Golf and Country Club.

Hosted by a member, our green fees on a weekend were reduced to approximately US$45.00 including an electric cart .

One Saturday morning our flite was coming down the 9th fairway when a helicopter landed on the driving range. A dignitary and his entourage emerged. As we headed for the 10th, a "security" man asked us to wait so a Sultan and his group could play through. A bit rough, I thought, and not good etiquette. My host then informed me it was public knowledge this Sultan had a temper and in fact allegedly got upset with a caddy once - swinging a 5 iron at him, killing him. We duly stepped aside.

After waiting for 20 minutes for them to get out of sight and getting the go ahead by security, we proceeded up the 10th. As we were putting out, we saw the "royal" crew make their way down the 12th and "his royalness" seemed to be in some difficulty under some trees. Thinking nothing of it, but having a quiet chuckle about his misfortune, we were once more told to wait as the Sultan wanted to start his round again. It seemed he was not satisfied with the score.

The 11th was a par 3 and now we waited while he completed the10th and moved onto the 11th tee. The Sultan hit off and landed on the green some 40ft from the pin. To my complete surprise, the other members in the group agreed it was a "gimme" and off they went to the next tee. That was how he kept his handicap down to 3.

Out of bounds

The lads had a good thing going. Being married, their only vaguely plausible excuse for a weekend getaway was a golf trip, which they did on a regular basis.

Koh Samui in Thailand became their favourite spot. So every month or so, D, would dutifully pack his golf bag for the 'golf trip' to Samui. This went on for a few months, almost becoming a routine.

Then one day his wife was reading a travel article that said something like: "the amazing thing about Samui is that it is almost the only place in the whole of Asia that doesn't have a golf course or even a driving range..."

Oops! His travelling activities were somewhat curtailed thereafter.

Big name players

My mate Ed was keen on his golf, and played often at the Nongsa course in Batam, Indonesia. He had a pretty good grasp of the local lingo, having lived there for several years.

Whenever he played an 'almost good' shot, or the ball nearly went down the hole, the Indonesian caddies would exclaim "sidikit", meaning almost, nearly, close, a little off, whatever.

He now addresses all his caddies as "Sir Dickhead," much to the mirth of the other caddies.

A bit off colour

We were all set for a game in KL once, joined by some guys from our other Asian offices.

As one of the group emerged to take his first tee shot, a club official walked across and stopped him.

"Sorry, Sir, we can't let you play in that shirt," he said.

"What do you mean? It's a proper golf shirt," my friend remonstrated.

"No, Sir. It is yellow, the royal colour...only the royal family can wear yellow."

He was offered a selection of other coloured shirts to wear, and packed his own yellow shirt away.

Beating around the bush

The Yongsan Hash House Harriers, located in Seoul, Korea, was (and is probably still) a notorious group for naming hashers who have completed their 6th Hash Run.

As in most hashes, the group would excuse the "unnamed" hasher and then the other Hash members would try to collect as much "evidence" to find the appropriate name.

In one particular case, the "unnamed" hasher was dating a local Korean girl who owned a souvenir shop in the local Itaewon Shopping district. The name of her shop was "The White House." During this time period, Mr. Bush was the U.S. President.

The creative (and of course dirty) minds put these facts together and the name "Bush Banger" was this hasher's name forever.

Handy excuse

A group of Hong Kong-based financiers had a ritual which involved regular sessions around a hotel swimming pool, drinking with golf gloves on...thereby cultivating the appearance of being serious golfers due to the distinctive 'golf tan' they sported. Without ever playing a shot!

Losing the plot

After a long, hard, and treacherous Inter Hash Run in Phuket, two hardcore Hashers wanted to enjoy the Pattaya Full Moon Hash—one of the "unique" Males Only runs.

A quick dart to the Phuket airport got them to Bangkok and a search for a forwarding flight to Pattaya. To their dismay, they were forced to seek other transport. All flights were booked. Their final option to make the late afternoon "event" was to trust the local taxi man to make the two hour trip in speedy time. A taxi was chosen at random - the driver appeared to understand where the hashers wanted to go - and they set off on another Hash "journey".

Departure from Bangkok was a relief as the traffic and smog were overwhelming. The taxi riders became thirsty as they left the big city. They sated their thirst with the local Singha brew. Feeling some compassion for the driver they also passed a bottle forward and the journey continued.

During the trip, the driver appeared a tad disoriented many times and was forced to ask directions. The Thai road signs seemed to be unreliable. (Oh so true!) After another beer stop, the driver seemed to also be wavering in his driving ability and at one point he was cut off abruptly- Not a happy camper now!

Hashers being Hashers, they went with the flow and enjoyed the local spirits, scenery, and good hash stories. The two hour trip was extended to a four hour "'sploring" trek and the hashers arrived thirty minutes late for the ON ON! As they bellied up to the local Hash House bar and ordered another local brew, they reflected on the past few hours and drank a toast to poor, misguided Thai taxi drivers and their good fortune to have arrived in the Hash House Haven alive and with all limbs intact.

TV dinners

Years ago, before cable tv and live sports broadcasts were an option in Singapore, we had an annual ritual - a party to show the Grand Finals of the VFL football from Melbourne. "Live by satellite!!!"

Someone would tape it in Australia, and get it to us on a plane the next day. People naively assumed it to be a live broadcast, although some would say, "Wasn't this held yesterday?" But of course we'd disabuse them of that notion.

The real trick to receiving this illegal satellite broadcast was to hook the antenna wires to a good old Chinese wok, and put this out on the balcony while I adjusted the wok for the optimal picture clarity. A bit left, a bit right, etc. (Behind the scenes, someone was playing with the tuning of the VCR player until we got it 'right'.)

And the 'live' broadcast would commence. To make it authentically Australian, we'd also serve up meat pies and sauce. Depending on how much beer you brought, you were seated either in the Members area (downstairs) or in the Outer (raised level behind). Farting contests also added an air (pardon the pun) of real Antipodean maleness to the event.

But the most fun was throwing meat pies at the ceiling fan - this was an art, nay a science, of precision judgement to get them through the blades as it spun without being hit. Of course, we often messed up, and a splattering of meat pie and sauce would go everywhere! This resulted in the maid quitting one year.

To this day, I sometimes pick up books from the shelf and find traces of 10-year-old meat pie in them.

If you have a good story about golf, hash or other sport in Asia, let us know. Email us at **hardship_posting@hotmail.com** *or fax The Editor at 612-9499-5908.*

"Gunboat diplomacy."
True tales about embassy life and lowering the tone of highbrow functions.

There was a good one about this American tourist coming off his cruise ship in Manila Bay. As he was walking down the gangplank, the usual gaggle of hawkers and riff-raff were spruiking every product and service under the sun.

"Would you like a lady?" asked the pimp.

"No, nothing for me," said the tourist who walked on.

"Very pretty young girl, perhaps," said the pimp.

"No thanks," said the American.

"Hmmm, maybe you are interested in boys instead?" the pimp changed his angle.

"No girls, no boys," said the annoyed American.

"Aha, you are interested in animals. Maybe you like a donkey?" the quick-thinking pimp asked.

"No girls, no boys, no animals. I just need the American ambassador," grumbled the tourist.

"No promises, Sir. I'll try to get him, but that'll cost you a bit more," the pimp said.

Oh shit, there goes my chance at a multiple re-entry visa for The States. Anyway, I'd much rather go for a rear-entry than a re-entry any day. Especially at my age. Don't these frisky maidens realise that sometimes a man just wants to be cuddled? And, besides, I need to be emotionally prepared. Because I'm a ...what's the fancy term?...sensitive new age dirty old man! SNADOM for short.

Now what was my point. The point? The point. Oh yes.

The point is that as an expat you gain access to that wonderful netherworld otherwise known as "the embassy". Now the embassy actually becomes some kind of social fulcrum for many when they are behind enemy lines. There's regular piss-ups masquerading as important networking sessions. Networked as a newt, the expression goes, I believe.

But there's also the chance to bond with your fellow countrymen and discuss all the reasons why either you're happy to be away from wherever you came from or you can discuss how much you miss wherever you came from. Whilst drinking at taxpayers' expense. Geez I love it! In fact the more tax you pay back home, the better the beer tastes at the embassy. I reckon I single-handedly clawed back most of what the government had taken away in taxes before I left home - by my calculation I'm probably in a healthy profit situation by now.

In fact, if anyone important is reading this...it'll be cheaper for the taxpayers back home if the government pays me a regular sum to stay away from the free piss at the embassy. So how about chipping in, eh? That's a good cause. Just send me a monthly cheque and I promise not to drain the ambassador's fridge. That should sort out the national deficit problem. I shouldn't be too hard on them, but I've always wondered what some of these clowns do. Probably more than me!

I remember once meeting the Chilean ambassador. Excuse me? That cannot be a full day's work in Asia. But he did make up for it by working really late - I mean this guy would attend the opening of a roll of toilet paper in a public loo. And his main duty seemed to be promoting Chilean wines, which I believe are the worst wines in the world, but somehow quite light and fruity by the time you get to 11pm. With a subtle aftertaste like Marcelo Rios' socks after a Wimbledon final.

(There go my chances of a knighthood in Chile. And Australia. And America. And...)

Stuff them, if the pompous gits can't take a joke. As far as I'm concerned, ever since George Bush threw up all over the Japanese Prime Minister at dinner, everything's fair game.

That's my own personal high-water mark to emulate. Mind you, old Slick Willy Clinton's another role model hero of mine. Now, if we can just get him to improve his taste in women.

Dash it...got to run. Another wine-tasting at the Chilean embassy to attend. I've always liked that chap tremendously - did I mention that already?

Colonel Ke

Friends in high places

This British guy in Bangkok thought he'd have a bit of fun, and had business cards made up, complete with the name and contact details of the current British High Commissioner.

Whenever he met a girl, or was doing the rounds of the bars, he'd pass out these cards. Obviously some of the girls, keen to become the next Mrs High Commissioner, would be calling day and night following up on their lustful meetings and lavish promises.

Much to the surprise, annoyance and confusion of the *real* High Commissioner!

He obviously put his best men on it (maybe the MI5?) and soon enough the imposter had an "invitation" to explain his case to the British authorities.

He turned up to the High Commission, was ushered through and

given a very stern and severe dressing down. But right at the end, the Commissioner gave him a wink and said, "Jolly good fun, what. But don't do it again, old chap."

Backing the wrong whores

It had been a long lunch (again) and the lads still had a bucks party that evening to look forward to at the Singapore Polo Club.

One of them decided that they should spice up the evening and invite a couple of hookers. A quick flick through the phone book, and it was sorted. 2 girls for 8:30. Polo Club.

After going home and smartening up, they head for the Polo Club. Horror of horrors, it's a very polite party, and *mixed*. Whoever heard of women at a bucks party? Anyway, the lads soon got in the swing of it, whilst M kept an eye on the door for the 'company' to arrive.

Just after 8pm, a couple of likely looking local lasses turned up. He darted across to brief them. "Just make yourselves at home," he said, "mingle and try to fit in as best as possible. We'll let you know if there's anything *special* required a bit later on." They drifted into the party, a bit bemused, and were soon mingling all too well.

Right on 8:30, the door opened and the *real* hookers arrived. M did a double take. "Shit!" The ladies he had briefed were good friends of the bride-to-be!

Multi tusking

I remember a New Year's Eve party at The Regent in Bangkok several years ago. It was very refined, with a mini orchestra playing upstairs, everyone dressed in their finery.

Gradually things began to get out of hand as the night wore on, and all I remember was being dressed in a tuxedo and monkey mask, picking the ivory tusks out of 4' carved elephants on the balcony and throwing them down at the General Manager and his guests downstairs.

Fortunately I knew him, and he seemed to find it equally amusing, otherwise I probably would have been in deep shit.

Durian surprise

My wife and I were invited to the Brazilian ambassador's house one evening for a pre-Christmas gathering. It was quite a formal affair and the guests, numbering close to one hundred, were all decked out in their seasonal best. Although the apartment was quite large, it wouldn't accommodate everyone for a sit-down dinner, so a variety of exotic dishes were served throughout the evening by several hostesses milling through the guests.

It was nearing the end of the night when the ambassador announced a special treat for dessert. Since he had invited a handful of Singaporean dignitaries, he decided to go with a local favorite, but neglected to tell us what it was. I was never a huge dessert fan. I passed when offered one of the little glass bowls containing what looked to me like cream custard, opting instead for another glass of champagne.

As I was merrily sipping on my bubbly and chatting with a friend, I began to notice a strange thing occurring around the room. Some distinguished guests were spitting the first mouthful of dessert back into the dish. Others were trying to swallow it gracefully, but the look on their faces was one of sheer horror. Still others were bravely attempting to get the whole thing down as quickly as possible, moving toward the bar as they ate. But the best one was a guy who nonchalantly guided his wife over towards a big pot plant and, with a quick flick of the wrists while still talking and laughing, they both emptied their Durian Crème Brule straight into the pot!

Needless to say, for the ambassador and his honored guests, the evening ended on somewhat of a 'sour' note.

Happy New Yard

It was a great New Year's Eve party...a mix of old and new friends in a nice big black and white bungalow in Singapore. Mainly European guys and their very attractive local girlfriends/partners/wives. Then at some point late in the evening, the girls threw down the gauntlet.

"We bet you five guys don't have 3 feet of cock between you."

Being absolutely smashed, we took up the challenge - the prize being that if we won, the girls would all have to strip and dance in front of us. It was then decided that we would individually go out to a back room, one guy at a time, where the girls would then measure us with a ruler. What made it more fun was that we all went with someone else's partner to do the measuring.

Needless to say, there was a little bit of "getting ready to be measured" involved, which the girls seemed all too happy to go along with. As each of us came out of the back room, the girls would then yell out the respective measurement, to cheers or boos.

After two guys, we were right on schedule. The next guy let the side down badly...it looked like the girls could win. Then the host, a very tall Scandinavian disappeared into the backroom with the most attractive of the girls.

"11 inches!" came her triumphant call.

The guys had just scraped over the 3 foot mark by a whisker, and the girls then had to get their gear off one by one and dance in front of us. How we enjoyed that!

To this day, I still see some of these girls around in polite circles, and never quite forget that one New New Year's eve, they had measured my dick.

Hot under the collar

A fine lunch was had at The Tanglin Club, one of Singapore's Colonial vestiges. Excellent food. Wonderful wines. Good company. More wonderful wines. And even more wonderful wines.

From then on it was a little sketchy.

However, B, a member of the aforesaid establishment was summoned by the membership committee to defend his possible expulsion from the club. It was always going to be a difficult task trying to convince the stern management that wearing a 3-piece suit in the sauna at 4:30 in the afternoon was reasonable behaviour for members!

Not in tune

We had been invited to a night at the Orchestra. An evening of lavish entertainment laid on by one of our biggest clients. A black tie affair.

Much champagne was sipped and smoked salmon scoffed before we were called to go in.

Sitting in our special seats, the orchestra came out on stage and was going through their painful but necessary process of getting everyone in tune, with various screeches and twangs and thumps and blasts. This cacophony seemed to go on forever.

BG, one of the wisecracks behind me piped out: "Don't think much of this so far."

On the quiet

This Kiwi friend of mine, A, was a good bloke and threw lots of barbecues and parties. Not strictly an embassy official, he worked for a government body and travelled on a diplomatic passport.

One night, the party was in full swing, and the drunken debauchery was just getting into high gear. The music was cranked to "11". All in all, probably not a good thing to do in an apartment building.

Next thing, a knock at the door. It's the Police, investigating a noise complaint. *Damn, the party was going so well!*

Next thing, A went to his bedroom and came back to resume the discussion with the Police. He showed them his passport, they had a quick discussion... and left!

He'd pulled out his diplomatic passport and invoked "diplomatic immunity"! The party continued in full swing with no more fear of rude interruptions.

Animal instincts

One of the upscale business publications had sponsored a wine tasting evening, held at the refined Goodwood Park Hotel in Singapore.

A pleasant balmy evening, cocktails were sipped before adjourning indoors to where tables had been beautifully laid out, with name tags, and 12 glasses of wine (6 red, 6 white, partially filled) at each place.

The high-profile sommelier was duly introduced and he proceeded to take us through each individual wine in a rather serious fashion. As it happened, there were 2 seats beside me vacant...each with 12 glasses loaded and ready. Seemed a shame to waste them, so I downed them in quick succession.

The sommelier was still going on about fruity bouquet and oak aftertaste. Most of the crowd were taking it way too seriously. I was getting well hammered. Little cynical jibes about the sommelier's comments began creeping into play, but then his piece de resistance: "and with this one, the aftertaste is almost...animal."

"Yeah, mine's got a bit of donkey in it," said TP, smartarse next to me, and I hit the floor howling with laughter.

I was gone for all money. I tried to recompose myself, but everytime the sommelier would start off again, we'd all lose the plot. There were tears streaming down my face - I had to cover it with a serviette. Seeing the serious faces around the room just cracked me up even more. Truly memorable, apart from the last hour or so - I have no recollection of trying to play the grand piano in the lobby!

Cat got your tongue?

I had not been in Hong Kong long when I was invited to a cocktail function. Caught at my welcome lunch by the "chickens feet" surprise ("hmm, this is nice and crunchy, what is it?") I was pretty vigilant, nay paranoid, about what was being served up.

A plate came around, with what looked like smoked mussels. Now I've seen the state of Hong Kong harbour, and buggered if I was putting anything in my mouth from there. I declined with thanks. M, my elegant Chinese consort for the evening dived in for a few pieces, dipping them in sauce and smacking her lips in appreciation.

"Don't you like duck?" she asked.

"Oh, I thought it was mussels," I replied.

"No - duck's *tongue*," she explained.

Don't come the raw prawn

Before the elections in South Africa that would bring Mandela to power, I was required to host some meetings between the incoming non-Caucasian tourism officers and various travel and tourism parties in Singapore.

As they would make up the new South African Tourism Board, I set up a meeting with their counterparts at the Singapore Tourism Board.

We were welcomed warmly by the Singapore delegation in their very impressive headquarters, and taken through an overview of their marketing strategies and activities in a rather formal presentation.

After the obligatory video, the highest ranking of the South

Africans piped up: "I hear Singapore is a good place to come for ladies, they tell me you can find some nice girls here!" he winked and nudged. I cringed. The Singapore official deflected the comment politely and diplomatically. "Maybe I can find another wife here tonight. Where's the best place to go?" he continued. I wanted to hide, it was so inappropriate and embarrassing.

As if that wasn't enough, we then adjourned for lunch...a nice private room at a swish Chinese restaurant. Chopsticks were hurriedly abandoned and spoon and fork wheeled in for our cultured "friend". One of the dishes was prawn noodles.

"What do you call this?" the South African said, poking a prawn. He had never seen a prawn before, much less eaten one. After lunch, he excused himself and for the rest of the trip we didn't see much of him - we was on the loo nonstop, just about missing the main purpose of his visit - the press conference.

It wouldn't have been a bad thing, mind you - he was talking a lot of shit anyway.

Good face for radio

Before leaving for Australia for good, my wife needed to sort out her PR/residency papers. Even though I am Australian, and we had been married for 10 years, there was still a lot of form filling, interviews and rigmarole to go through.

The process could take up to 6 or 9 months we were told.

My wife was requested to go for an interview, and bring photos of the family travelling abroad, extra points for photos of her and my parents, etc etc as proof of our bona fide relationship.

One of the pictures she showed was us in Australia with my best mate, a radio announcer.

"Who's this guy?" the immigration officer quizzed my wife.

"That's CM, my husband's best friend," she truthfully replied.

"You're joking...he used to be the d.j. in our country town," said the officer.

Permanent Residence granted on the spot.

HARDSHIP POSTING

The great unwashed

In Hong Kong, I found the socialising tedious. Every conversation was along the lines of "...and how long have you been here?" followed by "...and who are you with?" as if the value of your entire being was which company you were working for.

Even though I worked for one of the big multinational names, I used to play my own game at parties. When the "...and who are you with?" line came up, I used to reply:

"I'm a window cleaner."

"Oh really," would be the feigned response as they would suddenly find the cheese dip on the other side of the room urgently interesting. For those that did actually hang around, I embellished the story further:

"Commercial windows, that is. Look around you...what do you see? Lots of tall office buildings. Somebody's got to clean them all. It's big business, very lucrative contracts, millions of dollars..."

No one lasted the entire explanation, as I recall. Hey it was their fault for wanting to talk about business on a Saturday night!

My friend used to hand out cards with a similar anti-sentiment saying: "No money, no MBA, no car, no condo."

Rushin' to finish

I had the dubious honour of organising a multi-government meeting with the United Nations several years ago. It was hosted by the Government of India, in New Delhi. You couldn't imagine a more frustratingly bureaucratic combination of organisations than these two. The whole episode was a nightmare, and only made bearable because of the continuous source of amusement it dished up.

Approximately 40 United Nations governments participated in the meeting at ministerial level. The evening before the meeting, the Ministry of Surface Transport together with the Federation of Indian Chambers of Commerce and Industry (FICCI), hosted a 'Welcome Dinner'. The Minister of Surface Transport was guest of honour and would give the welcome speech. As was tradition at cross-cultural State Banquets in India, alcohol was not served and in its place were fruit drinks of dubious origin each harbouring the flavour omnipresent in all things culinary in India - a kind of quinine and domestos mix.

After a very quiet and somewhat uneasy hour of stilted conversation unaided by alcohol, the Secretary General of FICCI took the podium and introduced the Secretary of Surface Transport. Mr B in turn took the podium and in his most eloquent English explained that "the Minister is most fervently apologetic but is unfortunately unable to attend this important gathering due to *a period of heavy preoccupation!*" 'Preoccupation?', I thought, as I imagined the poor Minister sat in his office with his elbow on his knee and his face resting on a fist immersed in a 'period of heavy preoccupation', "*no, no don't bother me now! I'm thinking damn it!*". An anonymous cackle simmered as the most erudite of the gathering conjured up a similar image.

The Secretary pulled a wad of Indian government foolscap out of his pocket, a sort of A4-sized shiny toilet paper, and proceeded to read the Minister's speech verbatim. After a long day, umpteen fights with bureaucracy and hours of miscommunication I was not in the mood for lengthy diatribe. Something about "India as the world's largest democracy" and "land of opportunity" was the last I heard as I faded out. After about forty-five minutes of drivel it suddenly occurred to me, and the rest of the audience, that one table of people was actually enjoying themselves and even capable of raising audible laughter in response to the Secretary's intermittent attempts at monotonic humour. The Russians!

As the speech continued into its second hour it became evident that the Russians were developing their own humour. And as often happens in these circumstances the speaker mistook the laughter as a response to his interjections so he started adlibbing - embarrassingly. The crowd responded empathetically, adding more embarrassed laughter that further encouraged the Secretary. The whole situation was becoming intolerable with the Secretary spouting forth, up on his toes, with a glint in his eye like a rabid comedian on ecstasy - the Minister's speech totally disregarded. Something had to be done.

In a break between fits of giggles I sidled up quietly to NR, a most serious individual from Moscow who no doubt once resided in a dark office in Tchazinsky Square. I asked him if everything was OK. At this moment AC, seated to his right, leans back and, dragging a spare chair from a less populated table, offers me a seat between them. I took it.

HARDSHIP POSTING

AC is was a large Chinese Russian with red bloated cheeks and rugby player's eyes! AC leaned over and, in what could only be described as Flemish, asked me if I would like a glass of 'vlwater?'. Rather naively I start to explain that it's not good to drink the water as it's in jugs and not bottles....then a hip flask the size of a hot water-bottle passes under the table from the Russian Ambassador. I've partied with these boys and they know I can't be scared by the prospect of a beverage or two. But, after a quarter of a pint of this Muscovite fire-water, the Indian Secretary was suddenly Eric Morcombe reincarnate!

After a full hour and three quarters of speaking, much of it unplanned and unwritten, a gratified and seemingly popular Secretary wound up his speech, stopping short of telling us we'd been a wonderful audience. He departed the podium to the delight of everyone in the room except for the Russian delegation and myself who, rather disappointed at his early finish, cheered and clapped him all the way back to his table.

The dinner was supposed to be followed by networking discussions in the foyer but by this stage the Russian delegation and myself had emptied the hot water-bottle and are seriously in need of replenishment. So, embarrassed, we do the 'walk of shame' through the throng of businessmen and ministers looking like we're on anti-submarine drill - zigzagging all the way to the lift, the cars and the Russian Embassy.

The party went on until the very small hours and became the talk of the town. Perhaps, not surprisingly, for the following two days the Russian tables at lunch and dinner became the most popular venues for congregation. This probably did as much for the Russian economy in consumption of vodka as did the rest of the entire meeting on infrastructure. And a great number of friends were made in the process!

Grounds for happiness

My buddy, D, and his new-found local lass, G, came out of the bar one night and were looking for a convenient location to, shall we say, consummate their relationship. She suggested the Botanical Gardens, which had large tracts of private and secluded spots. They got there, but alas the huge entry gates were locked (as you'd expect at 3am).

However, all was not lost. Driving round the back of the Gardens, the embassy district, they found the front lawn of the French ambassador's residence suited them just fine.

Bowl me over

An airline we worked with sponsored the live broadcast of the Superbowl, and marked the occasion with a fancy breakfast for key corporate customers and supporters.

There was a prize of 1st class tickets to USA for the best costume. Some turned up in grid-iron paraphernalia, but overall it was quite a reserved crowd in business attire. Then came JH...bounding in wearing a Hawaiian grass skirt. When he heard he had won the tickets, he cartwheeled down the aisle, jumped into the arms of JR, the gracious host, and knocked him flat to the floor!

JH then jumped up on a table, lifted up his grass skirt, revealing g-string underwear in the design and shape of an alligators head, with the jaws snapping up and down with each swing of his appendage!

All this at 8am on a Monday morning in one of Singapore's finest hotels.

If you have a good story about embassies or fancy functions in Asia, let us know. Email us at **hardship_posting@hotmail.com** *or fax The Editor at 612-9499-5908.*

"Holidays in paradise (with great views of Dante's Inferno on a clear day)"

True tales of vacations gone wrong, and some rent-a-shock stories as well.

It looked a little better in the brochure. For a start, there seemed to be light-bulbs that actually *worked* in the glossy picture. And those beautiful women up to their necks in soap suds in the tub...presumably that wasn't *cold* water. Or was it?

But we have been warned by none lesser than the great Mohammed himself, who said, "A journey is a fragment of hell." Quite a smart guy for a boxer.

Oh, the disappointment when paradise lets you down. Heaven goes to hell in a hand basket. Blow me down!

Dave and his family just got back from holidays and he was crying in his beer to me.

"Now let me get this straight," he said.

"I wake up at 6:30 every morning, well not awake but violently interrupted by the alarm.

I then have a cup of coffee and cornflakes while thumbing through the Asian Wall Street Journal, get in the car and c-r-a-w-l my way to the office through traffic full of guys who should have been rejected by driving schools if they ever got their license at all. Then I would have to deal with a bunch of over-demanding, over-achieving corporate wankers (sorry I believe the politically correct term is " sexually independent"), all day and often into the night and weekend. So that for a few weeks - a few rotten lousy measly weeks - a year, I can sit in a flying tin tube to paradise with screaming kids, and then...*this!*

He said the resort was worse than a Yugoslavian refugee camp. Lucky there were the encephalitic mosquitoes gnawing on his ankles to distract him, otherwise it would have been completely unbearable.

"Welcome to paradise, Sir. This is your welcoming fruit punch".

Did someone say *punch*?

Colonel Ke—

Flash in the van

We had decided to rent a jeep to get us around Bali. The guy said he had one left. He would give us a small discount because of a faulty fuse box.

"No use high beam, otherwise no problem," he warned.

A few days later we were driving up around Ubud, in the hills. After wandering around some art galleries and stopping for tea, it was getting dark so we decided to head back to Legiaan, near Kuta. We hopped in the jeep, I switched on the lights, and ...poof...they blew. Nothing.

We decided to keep driving as there was enough sun left to see, and then stop at a service station or auto mechanic. We drove all over the place, and didn't see either. By now we were well out of Ubud, and getting lost in rural back roads looking. Still nothing.

Real darkness fell. We kept going as best as we could...after all, there were no streetlights among all the rice paddies. To make it worse, we couldn't see the giant potholes. We hit every single one of them.

Then I had a brainwave. I was carrying my camera with me, which has a huge flash unit which you could activate by pressing its "test" button. Eureka!

So I grabbed it, switched it on and, feeling mightily chuffed with myself, we set off once again. Now to try out the theory - I held the unit up, pushed the button and - FLASH!!! The whole cabin flared with light, blinding me. I had to stop until normal vision returned.

I worked out it was a much better idea to roll the window down and flash out the window instead.

And we did - hundreds of times - all the way down the hills, through the windy roads, past the rice paddies. Flash, drive, flash, drive, flash, drive, till we found an auto electrician in the middle of nowhere who fixed our fuse.

We had lights once again. Well, until we were stopped by a Policeman for going one way down a two-way street (no, I didn't understand it either). Getting back into the jeep, my knee hit the "high beam" stick and we were plunged into darkness again.

Shooting through

It was my first weekend away with my boyfriend - a weekend at the Hyatt in Macau. The Grand Prix, sponsors passes all the way. By Saturday evening we were at "a la Portuguese" enjoying Mediterranean food and surprisingly cheap wine. Later we met with a group of friends in the bar of the New World Empire Hotel for a few beers. H and I chatted away with the snugness of a new-found couple. Our friends sought out a more practical solution - they went for a massage.

We left the bar, and waited outside the hotel for a taxi in a queue with the usual opportunists. Next in line, my eye was on the taxi closest to me, whilst H on my right was looking at a van obstructing the taxi. The van's engine started. There was a bang - and I thought "Macau, firecracker city...this van has back fired." Meantime H shouted something at me, and all I could think was *I am going to get this taxi before any body else does.* Meantime, the glass in the driver door shattered right beside me as it moved forward. I was still moving towards the driver door when I saw a man behind it draw his arm out of the shattered window. In his hand was a pistol. I started to run and swerve to the right - as I looked over my shoulder I saw the guy aiming towards me. Oh shit.

I felt this thing hit my leg - like the worst dead-leg my brother had ever given me - but I kept running. I threw myself on the ground behind a car, and waited, terrified, thinking the gunman would reappear. More shots were fired. Then all was quiet. H was on the other side of the car. There was a hole in my leggings, and bright red beautiful blood spurting out of it.

Then people ran screaming from the hotel. I was nearly runover by the car I was hiding behind. I remember seeing H pushing against the flow of people to get help. After the rush, another sudden silence as ambulances arrived and left. I saw bullets on the ground and finally was taken to the hospital. Next to me in the ambulance was another casualty who was squirting blood and shaking. His eyes looked dead. The ambulance took off without strapping us down and H had to hold both of us in the stretchers as we went around the corners.

Later in the hospital, I was wired up, given some shots and x-rayed. The doctor explained that they would not need to remove the bullet from my leg- he rolled my knee over and showed me the entry and then the exit of the bullet.

After that, this short, slightly balding guy in a casual jacket sat next to my bed. He looked around the room and then spoke in a low voice, out of the side of his mouth, and said: " I am going out onto the streets of Macau tonight, and I want to find the man who shot you, what did he look like?" Unbelievably, these guys really do exist.

The others were not so lucky: a triad member, apparently "the Tiger of Wanchai," and two of his friends were dead, plus a Thai girl and another guy had been seriously injured.

But I did have the best excuse for not turning up for work the following Monday: "I'm sorry I won't be in tomorrow... I've been shot".

The Chosun few

Korea in the late 1970s; the country (and the people) were so different from any other we had experienced - and any other in Asia. University girls would literally stop you in the street and ask to have lunch/dinner with you to practice their English, and it was still on a war footing!

Three stories then, arising from the security situation.

The curfew was at midnight until 0600 every night. I traveled to Seoul regularly, about twice a month. I always stayed in the only western-style hotel in town, the Chosun, in the centre of the business district.

Sometimes, we went to the bar area near the American base, Itaewan (the Sportsman being the favorite) It was at least 30 minutes away through one of the main tunnels. We used to play a game of 'chicken' and see how late we could leave the bar, negotiate a taxi and get back to the Chosun before the curfew. Quite foolish in retrospect, when the security forces would shoot first and ask questions later and took no heed that you were a foreigner!

The Koreans had an air raid warning/practice at least once a month, planned in advance, and then another which would be a surprise. I was travelling in a taxi to Kimpo airport (which was some way out of town before the city grew out to reach it!) when the air raid sirens went off. The driver stopped, grabbed me by the hand and we ran through a village and across a field to a shelter. There I was, the only foreigner in this shelter, holding hands with the taxi driver (who wouldn't let go as I was his responsibility - or he perhaps he actually fancied me), surrounded by curious Koreans, all breathing garlic from their kimchee breath - weird!

One Friday evening, I got back to the Chosun (just before curfew!), when hotel staff banged on the door and told me to stay in the room and on no account to look out of the window (where there was a growing loud grinding noise). Naturally, I looked out the window and there was a full military turn-out, including tanks as I later found out this was the evening President Park Chung Hee had been murdered by his bodyguard at dinner. Exciting stuff. Except there was a 24-hour curfew the next day and the airport was closed for two days!

Pussy vs Possee

During a 10 day trip to Boracay, that beautiful but somewhat commercialised corner of the Philippines, a friend of mine had an experience he'd probably rather forget.

Our gentleman was there with a few friends, and sans partner. Leaving him free to, well, sow a few wild grains of rice. And the occasional flirtatious eyelid flutters he was receiving from a particular student/waitress/resort assistant did nothing to discourage this. After all, in such a seductive, romantic setting, with warm tropical climate, balmy fragrance of flowers and fresh sea air all around one could get, well, seduced.

So he let the circumstances pursue their natural course. Which in this case, was winding its way right up to his chalet door. Resulting in a physical liaison quicker than you could say *chicken adobo*.

This was to be the pattern for the remainder of his stay there. The young lass was by now all smiles and bouncing around like a spring lamb on a pogo stick. There was a new-found spring in her stride, shall we say.

These antics however, did not go unnoticed among the other resort staff members - the male contingent began making snide and unsettling remarks to the young lady in question.

Come the last afternoon of the stay, the couple (for by now they were, if in its temporary form), making plans for their final, moonlit, promises of a return, cuddling and kissing, tearful farewell night under the stars.

Meanwhile, elsewhere, the local 'possee', was preparing to slaughter and roast a pig, in tribal, primeval fashion. And letting everyone else in on the tools required, by making no secret of the fact that they had a shotgun and a couple of machetes at hand.

This little scene became the focus of the afternoon's attention, to both locals and resort guests alike.

Meanwhile, our friendly neighbourhood 'Don Juan' had it in his head that the forthcoming ceremony might well involve the removal of his testicles as part of the attraction.

As the evening drew nearer, he became more and more paranoid as to the intentions of the local pig-terminating crew. After all, earlier in the week, there had already been a couple of 'shots fired into sky' incidents on the beach in the small hours of the morning. Common in such places where scare tactics were sometimes employed for either fun, or as a warning to cocky visitors as to who was boss.

All of which resulted in one extremely frightened individual spending an entire night curled up on the floor of another couple's chalet, terrified that the hit-men were planning his final reunion with an unsuspecting sow. And there he stayed until the morning sun lifted the burden from his weary shoulders.

A certain sarong and perfume-adorned island maiden spent the night on the beach wondering where her Romeo was.

Circle of life

A couple of guys I worked with had gone to Nepal for a lengthy trek. On the way back, they decided it would be great to unwind with a few days in Phuket.

One evening, P was enjoying a few sunset beers along the beach, and had a few amphetamines coursing through his veins as well, just in case.

A Thai guy approached him - would he like to go out on a jetski? The rental terms were negotiated, and P headed off into the sunset.

Literally. He had been told to stay within the bay area, but as it was such a calm beautiful evening he just kept going, enjoying the freedom of the moment.

Then disaster struck. Trying to make a sharp turn, he got thrown off the jetski. And the jetski kept going (the steering cable had broken, voiding the auto-circling mode they are supposed to go into). And going. And going...

With no other option, P started to swim back to shore...he could just make out the beach he started out from. Not the strongest or fittest guy you've ever met, he kept swimming as the sun disappeared altogether, and lights twinkled in the distance. He kept his focus on that one light that was the bar he was in a little earlier.

The water and sky were now pitch black - he felt fish and jellyfish swipe against his legs. Soon, his reserves were running out. The alcohol didn't help; the speed tabs probably gave him a little extra. But the lights weren't getting any closer.

Exhausted and afraid, he tried shouting but with the beach bars now in full swing no one could hear him. Three times he gave himself up for dead...had that "life flash before your eyes" experience. Thought *what if I just give up and go under?* But each time he found a little extra emotional and physical energy to go on. *I'm too young to die.* He also remembered re-evaluating his whole life. *If I survive this I'm going to change my lifestyle, be a nicer person, sell the sports cars*, etc etc.

Next thing he remembered being awoken on a rickety bed, surrounded by Thai faces. He had been found face down the next morning, on the edge of the sea, at a beach about half an hour's drive from where he started out!

Whiplash

I had it all planned. A company conference in Arizona, USA, then fly to New York, take the Concorde across to London where I was to be the best man at my brother's wedding, then spend perhaps a couple of weeks driving around the English countryside with my family and relatives.

Reality: deadline demands piled up, and I had to cancel the Arizona leg. Things were still looking good for completion on time to make the England wedding and holiday. But commitments continued to pile up.

Eventually, the day before I was due to fly to London, I decided I couldn't make it at all. I steeled myself to call the relatives and apologise for my no-show. "We're so looking forward to seeing you, we'll pick you up at the airport...you're going to love it here," they said, giving me no option to back out.

So we boarded the plane in Singapore about 8pm, after work on Friday. Arrived Heathrow about 6:30am Saturday morning England time, taken straight out to Berkshire, changed into my tuxedo at the hotel, walked across to the church to do the service, back to the hotel for the reception (including best man's speech and way too much champagne) and then finally collapsed about 10pm.

Woke up Sunday morning, had breakfast with my Mum, and then was driven straight out to the airport. Arrived back in Singapore about 8am Monday morning, and went straight into the office.

"How was your weekend?" a colleague casually inquired.

"Oh, just the usual," I said.

What's first prize?

Our company had a long and hard year, but made a decent profit. We decided to take the whole company on a trip to say "well done."

I'd always left the organisation up to a committee, and then rubber-stamped their proposals.

This year, the committee short-listed a resort. I was a little nervous because they didn't have a brochure. However, everyone thought this place on Tioman Island, Malaysia was where we should go.

We had so much trouble getting there. We should have taken it as an omen and turned back. First, we arrived in Mersing by bus, to be told that we'd have to wait another 5 or 6 hours because the tide was low and our boat couldn't come into the shallow waters to take us to across Tioman. To put it mildly, Mersing was a shithole with absolute nothing going on, so we lay around in the sun, waiting and waiting.

Eventually, we boarded our boat and headed off, the boat chugging off into the near darkness. Spirits were once again bouyant, our 20-odd staff joking and playing cards below deck. But as the water became choppier, diesel fumes poured into the cabin.

Suddenly rain and lightning enveloped us. We had sailed right into a storm. We lurched from side to side, up and down. A few people started vomiting. Then dozens others retched violently in sympathy. The stench triggered off all the others. Except me.

The boat slowed down. We must be at our destination. No, explains the boat hand - we are lost! Scanning the horizon for lights, we were flying blind. Below decks, we were running out of bags and buckets.

After an eternity, we made it to Tioman, thinking we had reached the promised land. Unfortunately, our holiday would only getting worse.

The place was a dump. Doors hung off their hinges of the wooden shanty rooms. There were toilets without seats. And linen seemed an optional extra.

It rained for 3 days non-stop. We were cold, wet and dispirited, and couldn't wait to get home.

On the way back, our coach from Mersing to Singapore put on a video to entertain us: "Speed," the movie about the bomb on the bus. Brilliant!

We've not had a company trip since.

What a dive

The guys were preparing for a dive trip in Malaysia, when they decided to set S up as he was new to the sport and new to the region.

"You'll need a full length wet-suit to guard against the jellyfish and rays, good quality knife, serious torch because there are lots of caves. We also suggest you get Nitrox tanks, etc etc" our briefing to him went. We said we already had all our stuff and gave him the name of a dive shop to go to get everything. He spent well over $1000 on dive gear.

At the airport, he arrived laden with all the stuff. Bags and bags of all the kit, spilling over. We told him we'd already checked our stuff in.

The next morning at the resort, we were all getting ready to go diving. S came out in his full-length wetsuit with bags of gear and tanks and equipment. We were all standing at the rental shop in our swimming trunks, t-shirts and flippers.

"Where's all your gear, guys?" he asked.

"Oh you don't need all that stuff," we said. "The water's warm as, and we just rent the tanks from the shop here."

A set-up...he was fuming!

Not a morning person

MK had been up early one morning in Phuket, and decided to take out a jetski. He whizzed the thing around the bay for the half-hour period, and returned it.

He was just about to walk away, when the rental guy called his attention to a scratch down the side of the not-exactly-new jetski.

"You make scratch, you pay me," said the operator.

"Bull-f***ing-shit," said MK, stating his position quite clearly.

The operator seemed set on extracting some extra dollars from him, and they were obviously in a stalemate. It did not seem this could be resolved through the usual diplomatic channels.

As the guy kept on harping on about the damage, MK looked up the beach, down the beach, saw the coast was clear and threw a surprise roundhouse right which felled the guy. He then walked off to have his morning coffee, leaving this guy out cold, slumped beside his jetski.

Weight of the world

BB was going back to Sydney for a break, so we thought we'd give him a rousing send off. Picking him up from his place, we started with a few beers. While B was enjoying some last minute laughs with the lads, a couple of us sneaked into his bedroom where his suitcases were waiting, fully packed.

We threw out all his clothes, and replaced them with bags of sand.

Next we were off to the airport. "No, no, let us carry those for you," we gallantly said as we loaded them into the car. He was none the wiser.

At the airport, once again we enthusiastically volunteered to carry his cases for him, straining our backs all the way to the check-in counter. After a couple more beers at the airport, it was all smiles and waves as B walked through customs and off...

Claiming his luggage in Sydney, he thought his bags were a bit on the heavy side as he struggled to lug his two suitcases through customs.

The officer asked to check his bags, and poor B had to explain exactly why 'Sir' was carrying two suitcases full of sand into Australia.

It then dawned on him what had happened.

Oasis of tranquility

DC, DH and I had gone to Vietnam, and were put into a small boutique style hotel in Hanoi. 'Boutique' meaning a five story building with 1 room per floor. I was assigned to the 'luxury penthouse' on the top floor. I was getting ready to go out when I heard an almighty crash. I looked up to see a huge, steel construction girder on a chain swinging through my window, passing through the room, slow motion in front of me, and then crashing into the opposite wall, before exiting where it came in from.

I was shocked, and lucky not to have been in it's way. I shakily called reception.

"I just had a girder in my room," I explained.

"Girl? No problem," said the receptionist.

"No, no, a girder. Come to see."

He arrived upstairs and took one look at the debris and damage to my room before exclaiming: "What you do?" I explained the whole thing to him.

We went out that night to forget the whole thing. I got home earlier than the others, but was awoken by yells of, " Hello, hello!"

Out my window, I saw DC calling to be let in, because at night all the staff (and their motorbikes) slept in the lobby area, behind a big metal shutter door at the front of the hotel.

I tip-toed through the sleeping staff to let DC in. But he said he had found an excellent underground bar (The White Bar) accessed through a trap door. I passed on the offer and went back to bed. DC went off partying again.

I had no sooner gone back to sleep when I heard an almighty bang and crash followed by screams. I went down 5 floors to investigate.

A motorbike with a sidecar somehow managed to swerve off the road straight into the iron shutter! The people were still lying on the road screaming.

Our hotel staff were still fast asleep.

Highly geared

Borocay, Philippines in the mid '80s would have been a great place for someone to "go troppo" - cash up and turn their back on the real world...or perhaps start an enterprising Bakery & Bike Rental business.

We rented a couple of bikes from the operator, an ex-British seaman. He explained the way the gears worked, etc, and we set off.

Within a kilometre, going up a hill, my gears had stripped, the chain came off, and I ended up with a tangled mess of chain, gear cogs and so on. Finding this marginally amusing (as I don't have a good track record with rental vehicles) I put the bike over my shoulder, and trudged back to the Bakery & Bike shop.

The owner took one look at it and, in his wonderful East-end accent, poetically pronounced: "The F***ing F***ers F***ed!"

"Not my problem," I said. "It obviously wasn't in good shape". With that, World War 3 broke out.

"You'll pay for this," he raged. "These are expensive imported racing bikes. This'll cost you..."

I explained that all of this wear and tear and cost of spares should be factored into his cost of rental. He wasn't having any of it:

"You've buggered me bike up. It's Ok for you lot, earning bloody US Dollars. I'm only earning f***ing pesos..."

I calmly explained to him that in a worst case scenario, I should lose my security deposit-but not a cent more- if I were liable.

Eventually we struck a compromise. We'd pay him the forfeited deposit equivalent. With that my friend went off to our resort to get some more cash. He came back, still indignant and fuming from this exchange with his fellow countrymen, and was amazed at the sight in the Bakery...

I was sitting down enjoying a cup of tea with the operator. This muscle-bound and tattooed ex-merchant navy seaman was pouring out his soul to me, and literally crying on my shoulder, tracing his whole sad life story and how he came to be running this miserable business in Borocay, and how unfair life was. My friend shot me a quizzical glance as if to say *what the f***'s going on here*?

Once he'd finished, the operator apologised profusely, and we shook hands and went off without paying him a cent. We now refer to that as

The Great Borocay Breadbin Disaster of 1987.

Trailing off

I had been warned about unscrupulous rental operators renting shoddy vehicles then holding you accountable for the damage, so I was on my guard.

This was Phuket, late 80's. I rented a 175cc trailbike for a week to get around.

One morning I decided to get off the beaten track a little and, with the previous night's bar girl in tow, headed off on some really bad gravel tracks. Soon enough, the whole back end of the motorbike fell off...mudguard, lights, and probably some part of the seat as well, because my passenger was tipped off the back.

I assembled all the parts and, using wire from the tail-lights, tied them up to the back of the bike. Back at the rental shop, I was ready for their accusations of my negligence, and expected them to hit me up for the repairs.

"It was already damaged," I ventured, handing over all the pieces. The rental guy looked at the back of the bike, ran his finger along a previously welded seem, saying; "Very bad welding job before. No good."

I was so ready for war, it took me by complete surprise.

"Never mind, Sir," he said. "We can have this repaired by tomorrow. Meantime, you choose any other bike in our shop to use."

"But, but..." It was nice to win one of these discussions without bloodshed.

Presidential suite

In 1989, my Filipina wife and I had had a great holiday in The Philippines, visiting Bagguio, Cebu and a few other places. We finished up with a stay in Manila, and checked in to one of the nicer hotels on the classy Makati side.

A couple of days later my wife said something didn't feel right. She felt some sort of weird tension in the air. We re-arranged our flights and left the next day. The very next night on the news, there was our hotel, with troops on the roof and bullets and rebels and bloodshed everywhere. Another coup was in full swing.

Sand storm

Based in Sarawak on a construction site, we used to spend a lot of time diving the area around Miri.

One day, my wife and I were out on a boat having a good day, when it began to cloud over. A storm rolled in as we headed back to port. It's a bad storm when the crew are amongst the first to start throwing up. The boat was being thrown around violently.

One wave broke over the bow, washing my glasses off my face.

Then, to make matters worse we were stuck on a sandbar near the harbour.

Once we managed to get free and get back to port, I miraculously found my glasses - they were stuck on a wire stay right at the back of the boat.

Visa problems

I was going on a lengthy holiday to Koh Samui (with a few days of fun in Bangkok en route) so was arranging my finances. I took only about US$600, and asked a friend who owed me some money to send it through to my bank in Thailand.

In Bangkok, one thing after another chiselled away at my limited finances. Still, I knew once I got to Koh Samui I could "reload" my wallet. Arriving in Samui on a Friday, I planned to go to the bank on Saturday morning. It was closed.

Come Monday, I went up to the counter to withdraw- " not enough funds" they said. Sure enough, my friend's funds hadn't arrived yet. Same on Tuesday. Same Wednesday. I called him to confirm that he'd sent the money.

"Oh, I didn't realise you needed it urgently," he said.

Meanwhile, my family and I were down to our last few dollars...living on cheap bowls of noodles, bread and cereal, and forgoing lots of pleasurable outings and activities. Of course, not many of these places accepted plastic.

Then it occurred to me - I could get a *cash advance* on my Visa card. I asked the money changer for US$1200. The machine beeped. "No good," she said. Strange. "Try US$600." The machine beeped. "No good," she said.

Now we were literally down to our last few cents. Just enough to call the Visa Card centre. I said I'd just paid a huge amount before coming away. They explained I was already over the limit taking this amount into consideration. I requested a temporary increase. Possible, but I had already used much of what she was authorised to extend the limit by. I could use the card "at retail immediately" but would have to wait a day to make a cash advance.

Such sweet words I have never heard...we immediately went out and enjoyed a slap-up feed at the nearest but nicest seafood restaurant we could find! Food never tasted so good.

Labour of love

We were on holiday in the Maldives, when I began to feel contractions (I was 7 months pregnant). The doctor diagnosed it as some sort of gastric thing, and told me to lie down and put my feet up.

Well the contractions continued, but the doctor was more interested in looking after the divers than me.

Eventually, the holiday over, we flew to Colombo, arriving on a particularly bad day - they'd had 7 bombings that day!- and the contractions got worse. A doctor gave me some Ventalin to stop it, but I knew what was coming.

"Just get me back to England, get me back to England," I said. (We were based in Borneo at the time).

We had just arrived in London and my baby was born - 2 months premature - after a total of 12 days in labour!

Long distance call

I had borrowed the car of the guy who ran our associate company in Colombo to take a week touring the idyllic isle of Sri Lanka. While I was away, HR arrived to take over management of the Hong Kong office where I was a regional account manager.

We were driving around the south coast four days into the trip when I was flagged down by the local cops who said I was needed urgently in Colombo.

It took the best part of the day to get there (not pleasant with two young kids in the back and no aircon - as the car was a 20 year old

Renault). When we returned to the office, my friend said HR had called saying it was very urgent he spoke to me, so he had used his influence to get the police to find me.

It then took another half day to get through to Hong Kong (this was in 1979 or 1980) and when I did, HR asked me when I was coming back to the office. That was all!

I said my secretary knew (she had my trip plan in the office) and HR said she had told him, but he wanted to check with me personally, thus screwing up my holiday just for that.

Now *that*'s a control freak!

Hold the bill

PQ and NM spent a month trekking the Himalayas and 'finding themselves'. What they found amazing was these little mountain villages in the middle of nowhere that accepted Visa and Mastercard.

So wherever and whenever they could, they just put it on card.

To this day, over 10 years later, they have never received a bill for any of those purchases in Nepal. Obviously the vendors hadn't undergone the full merchant training programme.

Tyre-some journey

D and L decided to go to the casino at Tagaytay, Philippines one night, so borrowed their friend's Toyota for the drive.

Halfway there, in the middle of nowhere in pitch darkness, a tyre blew out.

D got out to check the problem. All the tyres were as slick as a baby's bum, the spanner didn't fit the wheel nuts, and the spare tyre didn't fit the wheel rim. Great!

One person they flagged down assured them, saying , "Don't trust the police, they're the worst offenders out here." Just then the Police turned up and luckily helped them flag down someone with a spanner. Then the passing Fire Brigade also stopped to lend a hand.

Eventually they got going again and stopped at Burger Machine for refreshments. They noticed a long black jeep out front, with completely blacked out windows. As they went inside there were sinister-looking guys in black overalls, blacked-out faces and M16s. They checked out D and L from head to toe in sneering fashion.

Having paid for their burgers, D and L ran out of there, and drove like hell, looking over their shoulders to see if the eerie black jeep was following.

If you have a good story about holidays in hell somewhere in Asia, let us know. Email us at hardship_posting@hotmail.com *or fax The Editor at 612-9499-5908.*

9

"Home Sweet & Sour Home"
True tales about Houses, Flatmates,
Landlords and Handymen

Now, the average person always imagines that every expat lives in some kind of *Gone With The Wind* grandeur. Sometimes, this is true...think of Jim Thompson, the silk magnate. He built that beautiful place on the side of the *khlong* in Bangkok. Very Asian, very tropical. Beautiful. I saw him coming out of Burger King in Malaysia the other day, by the way. He's looking well.

The other bugger that built himself a great piece of paradise was that French bloke Count de Mauny-Talvarde (I hope I spelt his first name right...I've never seen it spelt *that* way before). Basically he's gone to visit his buddy in Sri Lanka, seen this island off the coast and said, "I'll have that." His place, Taprobane, takes up the whole of this little island just off the coast. A bitch to drive to, but that's the compromise you got to make I guess.

The French also left behind a beautiful legacy in Vietnam...all those Froggy-style homes and boulevards in Ho Chi Minh and Hanoi. Hmmm, Froggy-style? That's one I haven't tried yet. Maybe it's for guys that are hung like a tadpole. You know who you are.

Then you get those great old "black and whites" in Singapore...sprawling Tudor-ish whitewashed homes, with lawns the size of your average city's Botanical Gardens. Dave the history buff was telling me over cocktails at breakfast in The Tiffin Room that one of the most historical places in Singapore housed the British military commander of Singapore at the time when the Japs took over. Near Upper Bukit Timah, it is the highest house in Singapore, which is a shame because the Japs made him walk all the way down the hill to the Ford factory to sign the British surrender. When the ink was dry, the Jap leader then walked up the hill and that became *his* house. No lease agreement, no bond, no rent in advance. Shrewd businessmen the Japanese.

Actually the Japs made a bit of a habit of this, Dave reckons. MacArthur's penthouse in Manila was annexed by them when MacArthur moved into the fortified tunnel on Coreggidor. A very poor swap if you ask me. Unless he had a bastard of a landlord, in which case living in a rat-infested tunnel is probably a more satisfying option. Mind you, the general furnishings, lighting and décor was probably more tasteful in the tunnel. It was provided by the US Army and not the local landlord.

And the Japs must have thought it was the promised land. When you consider they were probably living in places so small back home that when you open the front door you block out the kitchen behind it. Places so small you've got to outside to change your mind. How do they ever procreate with so many generations under one roof, or even in one room? *Granma-san, preez pass the KY...me and Yoko now make sneaky night love action. Kindry rooking the other way preez.*

Don't get me started about furnished apartments and houses. *Hmmm, that blue vinyl sofa goes so well with those chocolate wall tiles...and just look how that plastic 7-tiered chandelier makes the reflected light fairly dance across the walls to the neon light in the kitchen.* Lucky I don't suffer from epilepsy, although maybe that's more enjoyable than paying a rental premium for a bunch of nasty crap that the word "kitsch" is too good for.

Then Barry was telling me you get places like Mumbai (what's wrong with Bombay, for heaven's sake?) where they can charge up to 5 years' rent in advance. Or Jakarta, where 2 years' upfront was the norm. In US dollars, mind you.

It's probably also the reason why some expats choose to live aboard boats. Just right there on their yachts. But maybe the main reason is that they don't have to put up with contractors and home handymen. Save me, Lord! By the time those bastards have finished changing your lightbulb, you've got ducting and wires and switches all over your wall, *on the outside.* Somebody please tell them that all that shit can be cunningly concealed inside a brick wall and painted over to leave a nice smooth aesthetically pleasing result.

HARDSHIP POSTING

This was not lost on my good friend Joe Conrad who wrote in Typhoon: "You can't trust the workmen nowadays. A brand new lock and it won't act at all."

And then there are the travails, or should I say the game of Russian Roulette, that is flat-sharing. Many expats do this because the good old days of money-no-object housing allowances have gone out the bedroom window. So they end up in decrepit apartments surrounded by gangsters and mahjong players, and catch the bus to work. Ah, the romance and glamour of the expat existence.

People with high-faluting social ideals often say to me, "Colonel Ken, how do you sleep at night, with that lavish mansion of yours, full of maids and man-servants, knowing that many in Asia are homeless or living five to a room?"

My answer? "In satin sheets."

Speaking of which, please turn down the bed, Lolita. I might have a little nap after that exhausting walk all the way down the driveway to the mailbox. Got to be fresh this evening, as we have Jim Thompson coming round for a game of poker.

Colonel Ken

Making a monkey out of me

In Thailand, it is common for people to have gibbons as pets. In fancy homes, these are normally kept on a perch, with a little chain round their leg to stop them straying too far.

This one particular party, way too much of everything had been consumed. One of the guys began to feel nauseous. The bathroom was occupied. He went back into the party. The nauseousness came back again. Unable to control himself, and not wanting to embarrass himself in such polite company, he reached out, grabbed this unsuspecting gibbon off its perch, and barfed into it, as if it were an airsick bag.

Feeling much better, thank you, he put the gibbon back on the perch and politely exited, wiping his mouth as he went. However, the gibbon belonged to a high-powered Thai society person, and he was physically 'done over' by the minders and ended up in hospital the next day.

Land of the Giants

Anyone who has spent time based in Jakarta will tell you the craftsmen of Java are exceptional. With hand-made tools they can build a cabinet or bed using only their instinctive knowledge of ancestral joinery processes.

When it comes to complicated instructions, however, the results may not always be what was initially expected.

We moved in to a beautiful home in the heart of Kemang - hang out for expatriates and one of the nicer suburbs in this massive metropolis of 9 million (officially!).

The house had a pool and a rather sparse tiled patio directly off it. This I promptly declared my "bar area". Off we went to a local, highly recommended carpenter called Sidik who specialised in timber and rattan.

" I want it 200 *centimeters* long and 110 *centimeters* high with three matching bar stools," I explained in my rather pathetic attempt at Bahasa Indonesian. Sidik grasped the concept quickly and showed me a thumbnail sketch of how it would look. Satisfied that the brief would be followed, we went home and thought no more about it.

A week later, I arrived home from work and was greeted at the front door by my Asian wife holding a freshly poured glass of my favourite scotch. Unusual, I thought. She's never greeted me this way before.

"What are we celebrating?" I asked curiously

"Your new bar has arrived - but I want you to down the scotch before you come in," she responded.

"Oh okay!" I said. This was obviously some sort of local ritual that I wasn't aware of - just like breaking champagne over a ship's hull - I was toasting my new bar prior to inspection!

When I stepped outside to the patio I realised why she poured me a double. Towering above me was a wall of rattan that blocked out the patio light and cast a cold dark shadow across the swimming pool...the bar! The patio ceiling fan was almost chaffing at the top right hand corner gnawing away at the rattan - and it seemed like you had to cross the street just to get around behind it. This was no bar - this was a shrine!

"What the hell happened? Why didn't he follow my measurements?"

I exclaimed, completely perplexed. My wife helped me up on the stool where we both sat for a moment's silence.

Eventually she responded: "Sidik only works in inches!"

A day on the tiles

I had been invited to play golf on a Sunday morning. As I arrived at the course, a storm broke and down it came. I hadn't seen rain like it before. The road was soon flooded and now, being trapped, I did what any true-blooded Aussie would do, headed for the bar. The course was closed and after a couple of hours the water had subsided enough for me to get home.

We had not long moved into our apartment. When I opened the door there were buckets everywhere, carpets rolled up and furniture moved around. My wife explained what had happened. The water from the storm had come pouring through the ceiling in 2 rooms and she had been flat out emptying and replacing buckets and any container she could get her hands on.

First thing Monday I rang the landlady. She promised to get the tradesmen onto it straight away. Amazingly, they were there within 2 hours. I left my wife to deal with the 10 men from the roofing contactor as they crawled into the roof cavity and over the roof to find where the water came in.

Arriving home I asked whether they had found and fixed the leak. In a fairly good mimic of the supervisor my wife replied, "All fixed, lah". I asked what they did. "They replaced some broken tiles," she said, and with a grin continued: "They pinched them from the roof of the unit next door"

Bed and buried

I was going through a period when it was really hard for me to get a good night's sleep...just restless, and no matter how tired I was, I couldn't sleep.

Our bed at that time was a beautiful old Javanese bed we had bought in Bali. It was over 100 years old.

I consulted this guy who was into feng shui. He said someone had obviously died on the bed before, which was creating bad vibes.

No sooner did we stop using the bed, than I was sleeping like a baby again.

Next whore neighbour

My wife and I had just finished dinner at home with our housemate R, and his Singaporean girlfriend, L, a sweet, conservative type.

It was a typically sticky Singaporean night and the old ceiling fans of our black and white weren't having much effect, so R and L suggested we all go to a bar in Scotts Road, to soak up the air conditioning as well as the beer.

My wife, H, and I passed on the offer, saying we'd prefer an early night, but for them to go ahead without us. We retired to bed soon after they left and had no trouble falling asleep, despite the heat.

But by about 3:00 a.m. I was aroused again- "aroused" being the operative word- as what woke me was something like a soundtrack to a Savannah video. Erotic moaning sounds to be more specific. But the moans didn't last too long - they quickly crescendoed to high-pitched squeals and wild grunts. Savannah was now more like Razorback!

They seemed to be coming from R's bedroom. In my dazed state I tip-toed towards R's bedroom door down the long hallway. My curiosity got the better of me (or was it my voyeuristic tendencies?) and I had to investigate.

I put my ear against the louvre door and sure enough this was a "live" event. Definitely not a video.

I thought to myself, "Man, that L really goes off. You wouldn't have expected it," and "Good one, R!"

So with a smile on my face and a stirring sensation further below I retreated to my bedroom to unsuccessfully emulate R's performance. Alas, H was dead to the world.

It was a Sunday and we slept all the way to noon, when the phone rang.

"Hello", I answered.

"Hi, it's L."

"Well, hellooo..." I replied, trying not to laugh. "So you're home already."

"Sorry?" she asked with slight bewilderment.

"I thought you'd sleep in late here after your, ahem, late night. You two sounded like you had a good time." I giggled. There was a pause.

"But I *didn't* stay over..."

I immediately covered the mouthpiece, swearing to myself.

"Shit!"

Many happy returns

This guy in Singapore was celebrating finally paying off his mortgage. He bought his place for $300,000 and had diligently paid it off each month for 10 years.

Now he was finally free, and the house was valued at $3.6 million!

Levelled

I was at my girlfriend's apartment in Mid-Levels (Hong Kong) one night. We were doing the dishes after dinner, looking out the window onto the lights of the next block a few hundred metres away. It was pissing with rain.

We then sat down to watch telly and heard this major rumble, like a rolling thunder. But it seemed to build and go on for an unnaturally long time.

Going through to the kitchen, we looked out the window - all the lights on the next block were out.

In the morning we found out the truth...the whole apartment building was literally out...washed down the hill in a landslide.

Get a life

Three of us shared an apartment in Hong Kong in the late Eighties, and had a great flatmate thing going. Unfortunately, one girl decided to move on, so we searched for a replacement.

After screening a few candidates, we decided on Z. Nothing to look at (*my* main criteria!), but pleasant enough.

Day one after she moved in, I came home from a very gruelling day in the office - an advertising agency. She started making small talk, which inevitably got around to "So what do you do for a living?"

No sooner had the words "advertising" left my lips than she was off like a rabid dog on the subject... all the ills of materialism...what about those poor people in Papua New Guinea that were spoiled by watching Dynasty...on and on she went. I was personally responsible for all of this.

I tried to counter by talking about "it's only tv...it's good to have aspirations, and what about all the poor *Americans* that were spoiled by watching Dynasty...and, it's only a job." None of this appeased her.

After all, the lesbo-vegetarian-communist-greenie used to spend her Sundays checking Japanese supermarket fridges for whale meat.

Cold comfort

A guy I had done some work with asked if I could briefly accommodate his new engineer until he found his own place. No problem, I said.

After picking him up from the airport, the boss and his new engineer arrived - he was from Iceland of all places.

Not knowing much about Iceland, and wanting to break the ice (pun fully intended) I asked what life was like in Iceland.

"In summer, we fish and we f***," came his reply.

And winter?

"Oh, too cold for fishing!" he said.

Smell a rat

Our company was to take a young trainee from Australia for a month or more, so my secretary dutifully began the search for accommodation...not easy for short term, junior level postings that fall well below the budgets of the average business traveller.

Eventually she found a share-accommodation place. The address sounded familiar to me for some reason. I took the eager youngster there from the airport, arriving at about 1am. The apartment was old, but clean and spacious. No flatmates in sight.

Come Monday morning, I asked how the place was going.

"Good," he said tentatively. "The flatmates are really friendly. You know there are five of them all sharing the one room. From Thailand." He seemed naively bemused.

Then it dawned on me. The block was a notorious flop-house for Thai hookers staying in Singapore. Unfortunately he never threw a house-warming party.

Horror show

A friend of mine had purchased painted wooden masks from Indonesia, some of which were rather grotesque...wide eyes, big teeth, that sort of thing.

What he did for added security around his house, was to mount these on the outside walls with lights inside them. Then he attached the lights to motion sensor devices.

Anyone walking up to his house at night would suddenly be confronted by these horrible faces, suddenly lighting up, in the darkness. Sure to repel intruders.

Lucky door prize

My local secretary loved dating (to use a polite euphemism) white guys. After she left us, she joined a Danish company, and was soon warming the bed of this particular 6 foot, blue-eyed blonde-haired adonis on a regular basis.

She had no sooner moved all her things in to his place (supplied by the company), than he was posted back to Denmark.

This was pretty inconvenient to her, so she decided to stay in the flat anyway. A week later, the ex-boyfriend's replacement turned up and found an unexpected flatmate - her.

She never moved out, and started warming *his* bed on a regular basis, as if nothing had ever changed.

Green fees

An American friend of mine fell on hard times, and nothing worked out for him. He asked if he could stay at my place for a couple of weeks before he flew back to The States.

At the end of 2 weeks, just as he was due to go he called me.

"I've got a confession to make," he said. "I've been using your phone to tee things up in The States. The bill's about $600 but I don't have any money."

As I was going through a keen golf stage, I accepted his new bag of Wilson clubs as payment in kind.

What plants?

My flatmate was horribly drunk one night (just for a change) and coming through the fancy apartment lobby, decided the potted plant near the elevator would look really really good in our place upstairs.

As this plant was a good 8 or 9 feet tall and in a decorative concrete tub, he had quite a battle wrestling it into the elevator. Just trying to stand was probably hard enough for him!

Next morning I awoke to see a beautiful (and recognisable) pot gracing our entranceway. He explained its presence. We were both impressed and chuffed.

After lunch, there was a knock on the door - two policemen.

"Good afternoonstable, c*nt," he says to my horror, and notices the block security guard behind them, positively identifying the plant.

With some feeble mumbling about a silly schoolboy prank, it followed me home, and promises not to repeat such irresponsible behaviour, the plant was wheeled out of our apartment and back to its rightful position in the lobby.

Sinking feeling

On holiday in Borocay, Philippines before the days of electricity on the island, we checked into a charming resort. There was only 1 room available. We were shown it. It was fine apart from the slight matter of the bathroom sink lying squarely on the bathroom floor.

"Nebber mind about dut," said the manager. "De flummer will be pixing dut tomorrow."

We negotiated a discount and moved in.

The "flummer" never arrived for about a week. When they did turn up it was 3 guys. They worked all day, and at the end of the day we still had no sink to use. The next day, ditto. Eventually day 3 the sink was up and in place, but no water. Day 4 some strangely bent and twisted pipes joined it to the water system. Day 5 it was back on the floor again, pieces everywhere.

We checked out the next day, marvelling at the productivity and cost of that little plumbing job.

Things that go grrrrrr in the night
In Hong Kong I shared an apartment overlooking a park. I enjoyed the serenity of the balcony, but was sometimes disturbed by the old Chinese grannies doing their Tai Chi and cackling away early in the morning.
One night I was really tired so went to bed early. About 2 am I was awoken by a jackhammer, which sounded like it was in my room. Maybe my flatmate had the vibrator on 'high'? I heard loud voices and saw lights through the bedroom curtain.
Going on to the balcony, I couldn't believe my eyes...a work crew was hammering away at the base of our block - a residential building - at 2 in the morning.
"Shut the f*** up," I yelled. No response. Eventually my flatmate (young Chinese landlady actually) came out to see what the noise was about. By this time, I had gone to the fridge and got half a dozen eggs and some tomatoes out. I was not wearing a stitch. She called the Police (about the noise, not the lack of clothes) and they eventually turn up.
Unfortunately, I was not able to get any shots at these guys as the Police supervised their retreat. When they're all packed up, the Police zoom away.
Then I got lucky - the workers still had to come back and pack up their lights. I managed a couple of direct hits with the eggs, amidst much profanity from both sides.
Then all went dark and quiet again like nothing ever happened. Truly surreal.

Hotline
JH was a hotel manager in Bangkok that kept a pet gibbon monkey at home that he grew very attached to.
One day this animal managed to escape from its perch and completely fried itself when it swung onto to 2 electricity wires outside.
J was devastated and didn't come to work for 3 days afterwards.

Eaten out of house and home
S was an old friend of mine, so when he said he was coming to Singapore to find work we were more than happy to have him stay for a

month or so before he got sorted out.

After nearly 2 months, he showed no signs of moving out, so we took to dropping subtle hints like, "Have you found a place yet?" and, "Oh, this place in the classifieds looks perfect."
He still didn't get the hint. Eventually after *13 months*, as my girlfriend and I were to be married, she said, "Either he goes or I go".
So I packed up his stuff into his cases and boxes and put them outside the front door. When he came home he rang the bell.
"Yes?" I enquired from behind the door.
"What's going on?" he asked.
"You're moving out."
"Oh, Ok then. See ya."
And off he went. We remained friends.

What mosquitoes?
R, a friend of mine from Sydney, came to stay with me in Hong Kong en route to backpacking through China.
As I was sharing a flat, I told him the best thing to do was just lay his sleeping bag out on the floor of my room. Being a hot summer, I left the windows open to get a bit of breeze.
"Don't you have a problem with mozzies here?" he enquired before bedding down.
"No, I've been here over a year and not a bite that I can remember," I truthfully answered.
The next morning he awoke - covered from head to toe with huge mosquito bites. I was untouched as usual.

If you have a good story about homes, contractors or landlords in Asia, let us know. Email us at **hardship_posting@hotmail.com** *or fax The Editor at 612-9499-5908.*

"Sick puppies"
True tales about Doctors, Nurses, Hospitals... and Mystics.

Now, being a man of moderation, I don't suffer many ailments...well apart from the odd cirrhotic liver, inflamed kidneys, heart thrombosis...you know the usual everyday kind of things. But the only times I've been what you'd call really "sick" (in that sense of the word) has been with these dashed mosquito-borne tropical diseases.

Malaria and dengue, mainly. But then there's the lucky door prize of Japanese encephalitis just waiting to be taken home by one lucky winner. Flaming knocks you round like a cement mixer to the back of the head. Not only does the cement mixer hit you from behind, fully loaded, but it also backs up and runs over you a few times just to make sure every single bone in your body is completely pulped. With the driver sneering maniacally as he watches you writhe in pain. Reminds me of my first wife. Really not a good feeling, and not recommended if you can help it.

But if you have a choice, go for dengue. You're clinically dead for a couple of weeks, but you can get back on the piss sooner. And there's no relapse. Whereas malaria is less debilitating but hangs around you like a whore waiting for her bar-fine to be paid, according to my mate Pete. Or as Somerset Maugham put it slightly less eloquently in Before The Party, "Pulls you down dreadfully this confounded malaria." Either way, you're gonna look like you just got released from Auschwitz.

Of course, there are precautions you can take, but I've found wearing a condom has not reduced my incidence of getting bit by mozzies at all. Instead, I just drink a dam-full of gin and tonic. Breakfast, lunch, afternoon tea, that sort of thing, just to be on the safe side...it's the quinine in the tonic water, you see. That's the secret. I don't know exactly what it does, but after five or six belts of G&T I always feel much much better.

Funnily enough, one of the most revered figures in Asian expat history, my good friend Sir Stamford Raffles (we used to call him "Chook" at school - actually I just made that up) was not a well boy, according to Dave the know-it-all. He read me this bit from The Singapore Chronicles about the poor bugger: "Although he was 39, his health was deteriorating after 15 years in the East. He was ravaged by blinding headaches from what was called 'Brain Fever'." Shit, I think I must have that.

But I always look to Keith Richards for inspiration in matters of health. That bastard's the same age as me, has crevices on his face you could go mogul-skiing on, has turned his body into a mobile science laboratory and still frigging manages to wake up in the morning. How does he manage that??? Anyway, as long as he's still alive, I reckon there's half a chance for the rest of us.

I've actually enjoyed some of my little hospital stays...well not the bits when they call in the proctologist of course, but the other bits. You know, once you're feeling like you're back in the land of the living, getting a bit of colour back to those chubby cheeks, and you can start getting frisky with the nurses again. Oh, they love it. "C'mon, dear, just put this under your tongue for a few minutes and see if the mercury rises."

I especially love the Filipino nurses with their cute little accents: "How is your *beaver* today, Sir?" Well *you* should know, love!

And what about the time the nurse came in at breakfast time asking how I was feeling. "A little stiff," I replied truthfully. Oh yes, like a good military man I'm always at attention when an orifice enters the room.

Most folks have got it wrong...if they need a major op or something serious, they always fly back to Australia, UK, the States or Europe. And even within Asia, there's a sort of hierarchical pecking order in terms of hospitals. In Indochina, you fly to Bangkok. From Jakarta you might fly to Singapore. And so on. But where do have the most fun with nurses - in the emerging markets, of course!

Unless you happen to be caught in the midst of an organ-stealing scam in China or Thailand, whereby they whip out your major organs and give them to the highest bidder.

But, by way of compensation, the hospitals are much cheaper. *Sorry, Sir, we've looked everywhere for your kidneys and can't find them. We'll give you a 10% discount instead. Hope you feel better now.*

Anyway, Asia has its own little medical quirks and miracle cures. Especially all the herbal stuff like ginseng, and loads of dried things, which is catching on in a big way in the West now as well, apparently.

But the one thing expats need is a good dick doctor. Not knowing anything about that sort of thing, I've actually delegated this task to my dear friend, Captain K. This man has been in the trenches deep behind enemy lines with me on several occasions. Er, not in war, mind you.

* * *

Captain K's Boys Book of the Clap

"In the days before the Pope and the flagging rubber industry conspired to invent AIDS to spoil everyone's fun, playtime in Asia was jolly enjoyable for us expatriate types. A constant smorgasbord of parties, naughty bars, freelance disco queens and pretty office girls meant that the ferret not only regularly got let out for a run, it was often begging to get back into the cage for a bit of rest! As I remember writing to me old mum as the reality of the situation gradually dawned on me, "This Asia's a wonderful place, you can hire somebody to do absolutely anything: wash your clothes, clean your house, drive your car - why, you can even hire someone to wank for you!"

There was a downside. People in polite (and ignorant) western societies called it venereal disease or VD. We universally called it The Clap. Now, we'd all been brought up to believe that this was somewhat akin to Dante's version of hell, with fleeting images of little umbrellas that were poked up your penis, secret clinics with blue lights out the front to let everyone know that they weren't secret at all, and the stigma of being permanently ostracised from the rest of the human race if anyone found out you'd had "it".

Reality turned out to be somewhat different. In those heady

pre-AIDS days when a condom was just a large flat with a swimming pool and 24-hour security, we all contracted a dose of The Clap about once a week, and treated it with about as much seriousness as a sore throat (which, come to think of it, was often one of the side effects). Gonorrhea, Syphilis, the various strains of NSU - we knew them all. The fact was, if you recognized the symptoms early and did something about it pretty quickly, The Clap was easily treated and (as far as I know) left no permanent effects. The trick was to do something about it quickly.

A visit to the doctor's

Which meant that a visit to the clap doctor became a regular and important part of our social lives. There were two main doctors in Asia that were responsible for the well-being of expatriate organs: Dr. Dick the Dick Doctor in Bangkok, and Dr. Pete in Hong Kong. In fact, Dr. Pete was rumoured to have once stood up at a rather late hour in a Hong Kong yacht club and announced, "There isn't a bloke in this room whose dick I haven't held in my hand". (Apparently some of the wives present didn't think this was very funny.) He also had quite a large yacht, named after how the funds were accrued to pay for it. It was called "The Pristine Richard".

These guys were (and still are) world-class experts in their field. They were dedicated beyond belief, reportedly accompanying their guinea pig mates as far afield as the bars in Kuala Lumpur, Jakarta and Manila to acquire intimate knowledge of the countless varying strains that could be acquired in far-off places, in the name of science (I hope somebody from the Nobel committee reads this - formal recognition is long overdue). And, of course, we did our best to further the global body of knowledge on the subject by returning with an endless assortment of weird drips, warts, blotches and swellings for examination and treatment.

Monday morning in either of their surgeries was an opportunity to catch up with a bunch of old mates and tell outrageous tales of the weekend just past. "Jeez, Dave, where've you been all week - haven't seen ya since we bumped into each other here last week! Whaddya reckon you've got? Oooohhh, the ol' Saigon Blue, aw, mate, that's a real bugger to get rid of. Did it make the area around your groin turn purple like this?" And so the cheery banter continued in the waiting room until your name was called and it was your turn.

As mentioned earlier, rapid diagnosis and correct treatment was imperative if the old fella was to be ready to be pressed into cervix, er, service, at the earliest opportunity (later that day). This meant taking a swab of some kind, which was then smeared on a glass plate, examined under a microscope on the spot, and then the appropriate treatment administered either by injection or by prescription (you don't get service like that with your friggin' Medicare or NHS!). Dr. Dick, however, had a rather nasty twist (an unfortunate choice of words) on this process of taking a sample. He kept an evil device consisting of about eight inches of straight wire with a little loop on the end, and a wooden handle. As you were sitting facing him describing the symptoms, the eye was inexorably drawn to this instrument of torture (invented, I believe, during the Spanish Inquisition and later perfected by Hitler himself) sitting next to a bunsen burner on the shelf behind him. Eventually the moment came when he'd tell you to drop your trousers and he'd heat the wire loop up over the burner to sterilise it, while the very organ that had stood so erect and proud when it was getting you into trouble withered away to nothing and cunningly tried to disguise itself as a pubic hair. The good doc tried to ease the anxiety with a little well-rehearsed dialogue: "Well, son, you've been here three times in the last three weeks with the same problem so I know what you do for a hobby; tell me now, what do you do for a living?" Ha ha.

In retrospect, I think it was just his eccentric little way of letting you know that you'd been a Very Naughty Boy. It worked quite well. As a deterrent I swear that there's absolutely nothing that touches the sight of that little piece of wire on a stick and the thought of it being poked eight inches (okay, four inches) down your dick. I'll bet it even hurts just to read about it.

Self treatment

Once you've had twenty or thirty doses, you tend to become quite adept at recognizing the symptoms. In fact, to this day I believe that I know more about the subject than most GP's in western countries. (This was demonstrated some years later by a doctor in Italy who insisted on giving me a series of fourteen injections for a minor dose that would have been cured by a single administration of an easily procured antibiotic; needless to say, that very antibiotic is today included in my travelling pharmaceutical kit.)

The Clap is a bit like snowflakes, only stickier - no two doses are the same. But eventually one learns to differentiate between the broad symptoms, and how long they take to appear. Knob sticking to underpants, when you take a leak it feels like you're pissing razor blades - that's a wee dose of gonorrhea. Constant need to piss but when you go to the toilet bugger all happens, difficult to shake (not your dick, the disease) - probably NSU. Sunken eyeballs, yellow skin, sores all over the body, followed by a slow, lingering death - yup, you've got (or had) syphilis. And so on.

With this intricate scientific understanding of these various diseases, it occurs to you that maybe you should be treating yourself. After all, in many of these countries you don't need a prescription to buy simple little antibiotics from a pharmacy. The first trick is to recall the twelve syllable chemical name of the drug that your mate swears knocked his dose on the head. But in this modern age it's getting easier, because the international drug companies have given their products user-friendly names that roll off the tongue as easily as the young wench that infected you in the first place. Rifiden. Lexinor. Zovirax. Not too difficult to remember at all!

Self-medication has many tangible advantages. It obviously saves the time and cost of a visit to the doctor (if you miss all your buddies in the waiting room you'll probably bump into them in a bar somewhere anyway). You can start treatment right away. Maybe best of all, you can wash your medicine down with a good ol' Jack Daniels or beer because there's no-one to tell you that you're meant to stay off the booze, shouldn't operate vehicles or heavy machinery and that kind of shit. When you treat yourself, *you* get to make the rules!

If your drug of choice comes in a box with a piece of paper with lots of information printed in 4-pt type, throw the paper away immediately. Trust me, it contains information you really don't want to know. Rifiden, I've heard, is also used to treat tuberculosis and leprosy. At least you know your dick is unlikely to cough or fall off.

Be warned that some of these magical cures have interesting side-effects. We'll use Rifiden again as an example. It has been known to make your urine go deep orange, or even blood-red, depending on the concentration. I know this because the first time I used it I was taking a leak at one of those trough-type urinals, and the guys downstream of me were freakin' out. Sorry fellas.

After many years, and many doses, my advice is as follows. The Clap is no big deal. Just treat it quickly. Always carry Lexinor 100's whenever you travel, because they are your personal "clap doctor in a wallet". Drink gallons of water, or water-substitutes like Carlsberg or bourbon and soda because it helps to flush out the nasty germs. And if it ever gets you down, just remember this: the guys that don't get the clap don't get it because they spend their time mowing the lawns, attending Rotary club meetings, and listening to whining kids. You've got The Clap, mate, because you're living life to the full in Asia!"

* * *

Wonderful stuff - some real dishonourable discharges there, as we used to say in the Army! Thank you, Captain K. How about a dose of clap, sorry a round of applause, for those worm's eye-view insights. That should be published as a major medical thesis, not buried in the middle of some crappy book on anecdotes.

Speaking of anecdotes, here are some anec-doses...

Colonel Ke

Elic Crap-ton

Of course, to be a helicopter pilot in Asia in the first place, it helps to be nuts. You have to fly a complicated piece of machinery down low near the jungle. Sometimes there are people on the ground who fire weapons at you. Other times you're flying your machine among the trees with a couple of tons of large metal pipes swinging beneath you like the pendulum of a clock.

Fortunately, E was nuts. When he wasn't flying in the jungles of Borneo he was in Bangkok doing one of two things. He liked to spend the afternoons and evenings in Soi Cowboy drinking. When he got drunk, he then took two or three girls back to his small apartment in Yen Akart and bonked until he fell asleep. (I almost forgot - the third thing he used to like to do was to fly a 6-foot rotor-span radio controlled Huey helicopter down the street outside his apartment to try to knock noisy motorcyclists off their bikes at 4:00 in the morning, but that's another story.) He was popular with the girls (he possessed plenty of that old financial magnetism that bar girls find so attractive) and liked his bonking, and consequently acquired about three doses a week when he was in town.

On one occasion he had a particularly bad dose that just wouldn't go away. His dick was in real bad shape, so eventually he stumbled into one of the discretely marked (in 6 foot neon lights) VD clinics on Ploenchit. The lady doctor asked him to unzip for an examination, then her eyes went wide and she staggered back a yard or two. Because E's dick, even at the best of times, was a battle-scarred veteran of virtually every kind of venereal disease known to mankind, and a few that were yet to be identified. (Rumour has it that E was the creator of that well-known Asian sport of cockfighting, so scarred and mangled was his dick. The chickens got thrown into the ring later.)

Anyway, as this doctor stared at his dick in silence, E started to get a bit worried. She told him she'd be back in a few moments. He heard lots of whispering in the corridor, and next minute about five or six additional people in white coats all filed in, donned rubber gloves, and started prodding and poking his dick, all the while chattering away excitedly in Thai. E was getting more and more concerned, thinking the only cure this time was an amputation.

After more prodding and animated conversation, the group went silent and the original woman doctor turned to him and said, "Sir, we have something we'd like discuss with you". E went white. I mean, a bloke could lose a couple of fingers, or a toe or two, and somehow you'd manage... But your dick!

The doctor continued: "We're currently working on a scientific paper covering in detail the various strains of venereal disease that are common in this area, and in all the years we've been working in this clinic we've never seen a penis that even remotely approaches the shocking condition that yours is in.

HARDSHIP POSTING

You currently have about four different kinds of STD at once, and you'll need megadoses of antibiotics to get rid of them. Now, what we want to know is this - if we donate our services free, would you be prepared to allow us to photograph your penis throughout the treatment so that we can use the pictures to illustrate our paper when it's published?"

Needless to say E was delighted. At one stage he was thinking he'd be lucky to survive with his dick intact, now it turned out the old fella was going to become something of a celebrity in scientific circles. E of course was rather proud of this when he related the story to all his mates in Moonshine later that evening.

Medicine Balls

There was a film director in Hong Kong who planned a nice relaxing holiday in Puerto Gallero in the Philippines.

This was in the days when Puerto Gallero was not the highly-developed tourist haven that it is today, and getting there from Hong Kong was something of an ordeal. After the flight to Manila the trip involved all sorts of vehicles in a descending order of reliability and comfort, including buses, jeepneys, and creaky wooden boats. (Depending on who's telling the story, horses and/or donkeys were sometimes involved. And, whatever the vehicle, they were always driven by a bloke named Jesus.)

He was just about to embark on one of these epic journeys when he noticed the telltale drip of some nasty disease. Luckily he hadn't yet headed out to Kai Tak, so he jumped into a taxi for a quick visit to Dr. Pete. A cotton swab and a peek down the microscope later, the nasty little varmints had been identified and he was on his way to the airport with a little bag of bright blue capsules to purge Percy and restore him to throbbing good condition. Washing them down in the plane with a glass of chilled chardonnay, he looked forward to his holiday in the idyllic setting of a beachside bungalow while the old boy magically mended itself.

So a plane, a bus, a jeepney and a boat later he finally arrived at the house and decided to go for a dip in the ocean. A couple of hours later he noticed an irritating itch around the groin, and hour by hour it became more painful and unpleasant. Worse still, his nuts started to swell. Like most of us, he thought he might as well take another dose of the medication, have a good night's sleep, and all would be well in the morning.

This was not to be. By morning, the irritation was worse than ever, and his balls had continued to swell - "just like medicine balls, only bright red and uglier". By now the pain was becoming unbearable, and he was walking around bow-legged in a pair of loose-fitting local fisherman's trousers, trying to relieve the pressure on his grossly distorted scrotum. The conclusion he had come to was that he was allergic to the medication prescribed, and the dip in the sea water had set the whole nasty reaction in motion.

Whatever the cause, no matter what a pain in the arse it was to have to head back to the city by boat and jeepney and bus, and even if they all were driven by Jesus, he was going to head back to Manila, find the very first clinic in Ermita with a "V.D. treated here" sign out front, and go and get it sorted out.

Putting on his loosest trousers, he hobbled out of the house and down to the wharf. Bouncing around on a hard wooden plank as the small boat crashed over the waves wasn't much fun, and the bench seat in the back of the jeepney and the trip on the crowded bus did not add to the comfort. But finally he made it in to Manila, manhandled his huge nuts into the cramped back seat of a taxi and headed for Ermita. As soon as they turned into the main street, his salvation stood out like a beacon: a big sign announcing "V.D. Clinic, First Floor".

The pain was excruciating as he mounted the steps one at a time, gripping the rail tightly for support. He finally reached the top, opened the door of the small clinic and nearly died when he looked over - sitting behind the desk in a starched white coat was a WOMAN! "Oh God, I've come all this way in agony and now I have to explain all this to a woman!"

However, he was in such pain by now that he just thought screw the embarrassment, I really don't give a shit, I just want to get this over and done with, so he blurted out the story: "It's like this - I was in Hong Kong and f***ed a whore from Wanchai on Tuesday night then I got a drip so I went to the doctor and he gave me some blue capsules so I took them but when I went for a swim my balls swelled up like medicine balls and went bright red and they look like this," at which point he dropped his trousers and flopped the whole sordid mess out into the open.

The woman stared at this horrible, sweaty apparition with the swollen, red testicles hanging out in front of her. A long moment of silence passed. Then she said, "Perhaps you'd like to tell the doctor this story. He's in the office next door. I'm just the receptionist".

Baby we were born to run

When our first child was born, we were not really financially prepared, to say the least. Doubly so when he ended up in the intensive care ward of Mount Elizabeth Hospital for the first week of his life.

When he was ready to go home, we had the awkward problem of dealing with the over-officious staff whom we knew would need to see cash before releasing him, officially.

Crazy as it seems, my wife and I decided to do a "runner", meaning make a dash for freedom and settle the massive hospital bill later.

I backed the car up nearer the entrance, then went upstairs to fetch my wife and child. Checking the coast was clear, we snuck out of her room, down the corridors, action-hero/spy style. Then into the lift. Down in reception, we whistled as we walked out, proud new parents. Then into the car and off.

We gradually settled the bill over the next few months without the baby being repossessed or stuffed back in.

No-Waiting room

My wife was booked to go into the hospital on Monday to deliver our first child. He had other ideas and made his presence felt at 3am on the Thursday before.

We rushed to the car, and drove like hell down Orchard Rd to Mount Elizabeth Hospital. Passing Orchard Towers on the way, I looked to see if anyone I knew was coming out.

At the hospital, we parked and looked for the entrance. There didn't seem to be any entrance for A&E at all.

"Hello, anybody there," I called out. Eventually, we found the entrance and they rushed my wife off in a wheelchair whilst I had to fill out reams and reams of forms. Once completed, I was taken upstairs just in time to see my wife put on a trolley bed and wheeled into the theatre. For months I had been thinking of ways of not being present in the theatre itself. But as this was now an emergency, it became academic - they slammed the theatre doors in my face.

I went back to the waiting room and found not a single magazine or newspaper to read. Even a 10 year old Readers' Digest would've sufficed.

With that I went back to the operating theatre, and opened the doors.

"You guys have any magazines around?" I asked the nurse.

"No," she said. "Please, Sir, wait outside."

"What kind of bloody show are you running here?" I ranted as she pushed me out of the theatre and back to the grey and empty waiting room.

Bearer of bad tidings

AD's father was visiting...an elderly Indian gent, who gave the impression of being a little loopy.

However, he professed to have all sorts of special mystic or psychic capabilities. After a short chat, he said he suspected I had two trouble spots...my forehead and my middle back. Sure enough, a couple of months later, I had a couple of cancerous growths removed...from my forehead and my middle back.

At our next meeting, he then turned his attention to my wife, N. He indicated she might have 'womens troubles'. Sure enough, a little later she was diagnosed with cancer of the uterus.

Religious practice

An ad by Kunming dentist:

"Teeth extracted by the latest methodists."

Alcoholic - moi???

F was admitted to hospital in Kuala Lumpur for an operation on her colon or intestine or some such organ, for which they needed to do invasive surgery by opening up her lower stomach.

HARDSHIP POSTING

After the operaration, the doctor said to her, "Everything looks Ok now, but I was a little concerned by your liver which had to go around. It was swollen to the size of what we usually only see in hard-core alcoholics."

"Really, Doc? That's strange."

She didn't dare mention the 11am marguerita parties with the girls!

If you have a good story about doctors, nurses or hospitals or mystics in Asia, let us know. Email us at **hardship_posting@hotmail.com** *or fax The Editor at 612-9499-5908.*

11

"Checking in, Sir?"

True tales of experiences in hotels in Asia.

Asia has more than its fair share of great dames when it comes to hotels. Dating back to...ooh...years ago. Dave tells me, for the record, the first hotel in Asia to boast electricity was Singapore's Raffles Hotel in 1899, the year I went off to fight in the Boer War. No, sorry, I don't think I fought in that one - I'll have to check the photo albums again.

The Oriental in Bangkok is one of my personal favourites...nestled on the banks of the mystical Chao Phraya River. Heck, I'm sounding like a travel brochure. My old mate Conrad used to stay there, you know. Writing literary classics...and probably nipping down to Patpong when the old creative juices weren't quite flowing.

And old Somerset Maugham...he spent more than the odd night with his head buried in the pillow of Asian hotels. The Oriental in Bangkok, The Raffles in Singapore. Must be something in those Singapore Slings. Wish I could write like him. They even had a place called The Writer's Bar back then...all dark and cobwebby and...see that's my point - I ran out of adjectives. And the Tiger Bar. Remember those dollies in the tiger skin outfits. Never mind the legendary tiger under the billiard table, I think I got a wild cat in the y-fronts. I often wonder what those little lassies are doing now. Either scrubbing Ah Beng's dunny in their housing board flat. Or shopping on hubby's card at Harrod's. Probably the latter.

And when you talk of grand old dames, you can't forget The Manila Hotel in, well, Manila funnily enough. What it lacks in originality of name, it compensates abundantly in good old-fashioned nostalgia. Oh, the names that have passed through its hallowed doors. The historical moments witnessed there with old Douggy Mac. The dusky maidens we have been able to sneak through past complacent doormen late at night. The laughs we have had waiting at the foyer for an early taxi and seeing all those ladies coming out of the lifts in their evening wear.

The Shilla in Seoul. Perched proudly atop the hill overlooking the haphazard sprawl of Seoul. The Peninsula in Hong Kong. More Rolls Royces there than at the assembly plant, I reckon. The salesman that signed that particular deal would be enjoying gin slings with very large umbrellas with his feet up in Spain, I reckon.

A good example of how it can really go to your head is the Amanpuri in Bali. Hell, my good friend Mick Jagger got so carried away there he *almost* married Jerry Hall! Phew, close shave, Mick.

And who could forget the "Five O'clock Follies" at the Rex Hotel in Saigon? The place is a heap now - on second thoughts it was a heap *then*- but golly they put on a good fireworks show every night. Mind you, the entertainment was lousy...never got the American sense of humour, especially when it was The Pentagon cracking the jokes!

Then you get the quirkier establishments. My very good friend Colonel Jack Foster, a rather eccentric British military chap, built his own little gin palace called The Lakehouse in the Cameron Highlands of Malaysia. Jack was a funny fellow. He got his little Chinese mistress to run the place for him, but had a sign out the front saying, "No dogs, no children, no Asians." True story. But I reckon the odd dog would've got through with enough make-up on.

But where else, I ask you, can you be served so graciously as you are in Asian hotels...those little butterflies floating from table to table in their cheongsams cut so high you can tell what brand of razor they shave their armpits with. And the little darlings kneeling on the ground as they lovingly pour your beer. The white Spanish long-sleeved shirts with puffed forearms and the short black skirts of the angels who dance floatingly in the foyer of the Peninsula in Manila.

God, it'll ruin Asia if women's lib ever catches on here.

Colonel Ke

The longest walk

It was my first trip to Manila and my boss was briefing me on where to go, where to stay, etc.

"The Holiday Inn, Roxas Boulevarde," he emphatically recommended. "Just round the corner from the Mabini strip (red light district) and they let you take birds back to your room."

Sounded perfect.

"But," he said, "you've got to be prepared for the longest walk."

"What's that?" I innocently inquired.

"That's the walk from the elevator to the taxi stand in the morning," he explained, "across this huge lobby past busloads of old folk holiday makers having their breakfast, with your 16 year old bargirl who is wearing a lime green miniskirt with tassles, and silver boots with 7" heels. That, my friend, is the longest walk."

Head waitress

After telling my brother about the nightlife of Asian cities, he finally visited me in Bangkok where he was booked at a well-known five star hotel. Prior to checking out the nightlife, we sat in the lobby bar where we both ordered beers.

The waitress came up with the beers, knelt down and asked by brother, "Would you like head?" Without batting an eye, my brother said: "Yes, at 10 PM. Room 646". The waitress smiled, set down his beer and walked away with a confused look on her face.

Stainless steal

I was in Jakarta preparing to shoot a television commercial. As the job was going to keep me there for several days, I requested they put me up in a somewhat better hotel than was their usual practice. I had a membership card for an international hotel chain that - with the discounted price - brought the room-rate to a level they were grudgingly willing to accept.

The shoot went smoothly enough, and we wrapped up on schedule. I was booked to fly back to Singapore early the next morning and had not had a chance to eat before arriving back to the hotel rather late in the evening. Too tired to clean up and go to a restaurant, I ordered a fairly substantial fare from room service. When the young man arrived with my meal, I was pleasantly surprised at the setting. Silverware, fine bone china, crystal, the works ...

I had a very enjoyable feast in the room, followed by coffee served out of a lovely silver pitcher; not one of those cheap thermos bottles, but real solid, silver-plated metal. *A fantastic finishing touch to a beautiful meal,* I thought to myself as I rolled the serving trolley out into the hall. I left it in a recessed door area where I'd seen many other trolleys parked. The next morning I headed for the lobby where a driver was supposed to be waiting to take me to the airport. I didn't have time for breakfast, so I went straight to the checkout counter to settle my account (and hopefully find the driver). I was in for a bit of a surprise however.

Instead of handing me my bill and thanking me for staying with them, I was accused of stealing the silver setting from the trolley. I tried to tell them I had left it in the hallway, but they wouldn't have any of it. They were convinced I had the stuff in my luggage. In order to avoid 'house arrest' and to get out of there in time to catch my flight, I had to allow the desk manager to search my suitcase and travel bag. Even though he never found so much as a bar of soap from the hotel, I'm sure he was still convinced I had somehow absconded with their precious coffeepot.

Needless to say, I've not paid them a visit since. And for anyone considering a heist at this hotel, let me just say I don't recommend putting the stuff up your rectum. It was hell getting through the metal detector at the airport - just kidding of course!

Bad Korea move

RC, MB and I went to North Korea. Our driver was a former soldier in the North Korean Infantry (I guess most males are). But the interesting part about him was that he fought in Uganda. He was a real womanizer and we all went drinking and got - as usual - hammered.

We sang Karaoke all night - the Koreans sang "Revolutionary Karaoke" while we sang Elvis - acappella, of course, because they had no English songs. The night deteriorated into ballroom-dancing with the bar maids (5 out of 10) and individual dances. Mr. Kim, our 50 year old ex-soldier-turned-driver got up and did a Ugandan war dance - at which we almost shat ourselves.

After way too many Soju's, it was off to bed in the darkened hotel - they had turned off the power to save money. I was falling asleep (passed out) when I heard a knock on the door. It was a very drunk Mr. Kim who dragged me down the hall - to get laid. Despite another few rounds of Soju, I didn't have enough to drink them pretty. I think it was more survival instinct - I didn't relish being thrown in a North Korean prison.

Wrong number

B had a great time at the Hyatt Hotel in Singapore many many moons ago. He went up to their pool area one Saturday afternoon, had a swim, enjoyed a few beers. Much to his surprise, the service person asked if he would like to sign it to his room. Living in Singapore, he wasn't a guest, but that didn't stop our intrepid B from signing it - Room 1306.

He told his friends about this wonderful free escapade, so next weekend a few of them went for a swim and a few beers. Same deal. Signed it all to Room 1306.

Over time, the group grew in size, and became a regular Saturday afternoon hangout. Always signing to Room 1306.

One weekend, he tried the same thing. The waiter went off, and then returned.

"Are you sure of your room number, Sir? "

"Yes, absolutely. 1306."

The waiter disappeared off again, a trifle puzzled, and reappeared momentarily with the hotel manager in tow.

"Good afternoon, Sir," the hotel manager did his hospitable best. "We'd like to confirm that you are a guest at the hotel," he continued.

"Yes. Room 1306," said B.

"Impossible, Sir, the 13th floor is closed for renovations."

He was made to pay up for that day's drinks, a little red-faced. But nobody put two and two together and realised that he had been doing it for months. No doubt there were fewer bill queries from the *real* guests in room 1306 after that!

Sleeping soundly

I had been summonsed by my client in Kuala Lumpur to attend an urgent meeting. So I packed my bag and hopped on the plane from

Singapore.

Arriving at their office, I asked his secretary to tee up overnight accommodation.

"Slight problem," she said. "There is a Commonwealth Heads of Government Meeting on at the moment. Everywhere seems to be full."

"Nevermind, anywhere will do," I said optimistically, knowing there would be one decent room somewhere.

At the end of the day, she announced there was a vacancy at The Emerald. Various staff in the vicinity sniggered. Not a good sign. So they drove me downtown to The Emerald, pulling up outside a very non-descript old building in not the best part of town.

I pushed open the frosted glass doors into the reception to find a billiard table and a bunch of heavy-smoking locals playing pool right in the middle of it. I went through check-in formalities and they give me a room key.

I opened the room door, and the place was a mess. All the furniture had cigarette burns on them. The door had 3 locks and chains. I subsequently discovered the sheets had little rips in them. It was disgusting.

I promptly went out, had far too much beer, a brilliant massage, and returned to the hotel, locked all three locks and slept soundly...meaning I could hear every sound in the entire neighbourhood...cars, bars, bands, people shouting.

I have subsequently driven past The Emerald a few times, and it always brings back wonderful memories of perhaps one of the worst nights in my life.

Very Invisible Person

I was going on a trip to Bangkok, and had already made my hotel reservations when I bumped into a friend of mine, the Sales Director of another hotel chain. Over a few beers, he said: "Fax me in the morning...we'll give you the best suite in the place, and an offer you can't refuse on the price." Which I did.

Everything was arranged, and I felt great about 'the deal,' with his personal assurances of red carpet treatment.

On arrival at Bangkok airport, I went across to the hotel representative holding the sign and introduced myself. "Mr Jones...hmmm, we don't seem to have any Mr Jones on the list." He made a phone call back to the hotel. No booking under that name, but I decided to turn up and sort it out at the hotel.

On arrival I was ushered upstairs to the executive floor check-in and pleaded my case, telling of the special personal arrangement. None of this registered anywhere.

"Perhaps we can check you in and you can call Singapore tomorrow, Sir," the receptionist offered.

"No, perhaps *you* can call Singapore tomorrow," I countered.

We then argued over the rates, but agreed that all would be sorted out in the fullness of time.

Feeling a bit disappointed and pissed off, we hit the town that night. It was a big night, ending up around the 5am mark knowing that I had no appointments the next day and could enjoy a good sleep in. At 7:30am, my bedside phone rings. *What the...?*

"Mr Jones, this is GR, the resident manager. I owe you an apology. I've just got to my office and seen this fax from JB in my tray about your reservation. Is there anything I can do to make up for it?" said the grovelling manager.

"Yes, don't wake me at 7:30 again," I barked and hung up.

Starry starry night

In the late 80's I was in Shanghai for the pre-opening of the new Sheraton Hotel. As we arrived, there were considerable crowds outside the hotel, milling around expectantly.

The Manager who welcomed us, explained they'd just had George Bush's presidential entourage through last week, and Steven Spielberg was currently an in-house guest. That would explain the crowds I thought.

Coming back to the hotel at night, the crowds had tripled. Amazing, I thought. All for a glimpse of Mr Spielberg (whom I bumped into in the Friendship Store - he didn't recognise me).

The next day, the manager explained the crowds. "Oh, they're here everyday...they watch the external elevators going up and down outside the building. At night, we switch on the coloured elevator lights, and that's a real crowd pleaser."

So there were hundreds of Chinese, watching these lifts go up and down outside the hotel day and night. Obviously the local TV wasn't much good!

Mirror image

The Sheraton Great Wall Hotel in Beijing was a masterpiece of architecture that was going to change the landscape and dominate the skyline in that area of town.

Which it would have done, had the local hotel chain directly across the road not copied it almost exactly brick for brick in design, creating a replica facing it.

What the fax going on?

Tired from a torrid day and night of business in Tokyo, I decided to watch a little TV in my room before crashing out.

Flipping the channels I came across an interesting show that had a bunch of suited Japanese men talking animatedly in front of a row of fax machines, whilst at the bottom of the screen there seemed to be a photo of a naked lady.

This seemed a bit strange, so I watched a bit more closely, and suddenly saw the nude figure move. Hmmm, a real live naked woman. After she changed position, all of a sudden this bank of fax machines came alive, spewing out pages and pages of pictures and images, which the guys collected and pinned to a board.

It turned out that viewers were supposed to draw their interpretations of this nude model, which some of them did quite well, and fax them in for appraisal. Others took a bit of artistic license and introduced other people (probably themselves!) into the scenario, and I swear even nuns and farm animals.

Beat the hell out of watching the weather channel!

Don't spill any

PJ and a buddy of his were in southern Thailand one trip. They ended up back in his hotel room, with a bottle of wine and a couple of dusky professional maidens.

They poured the wine, and things took their course. They sipped their wine and chatted whilst receiving tremendous blow-jobs from the tarts. Then, disaster struck - they ran out of wine!

Without missing a stroke, as it were, PJ called room service and ordered more wine. Room service duly arrived and poured the wine - whilst the action was still going thick and fast around him - and left as if it were the most normal thing in the world.

Save your document

I was required to go to Jakarta to address a seminar on shopping centres or somesuch, a topic I had addressed before. I had the perfect plan...just cut and paste my previous address, and update some of the figures. Easy.

Taking my Apple Mac powerbook, I did the cut and pasting on the plane.

Once at the hotel, I went down the business centre -carrying my powerbook- to print it out. The Indonesian guy on duty came back carrying some seriously oversized pin cables...they were never going to fit my small port.

"I need for Mac," I stressed. "Oh, no Mac," he said, "PC only." *Shit!*

Just then, an Australian lady, RC, popped her head over the partition, asking if I needed any help. She worked for the hotel, but Sunday was her off day. I explained the situation, but she could offer no solution with their equipment.

"Last resort," she said. "One of my girls from here has just moved across to The Shangri-La business centre. Let me try her."

Minutes later, we were in a taxi heading across town...me, my notebook and RC...to The Shangri-La. Yes, they had Mac equipment. I was saved.

Well, not quite because when I opened up the file to print, the girl said: "Your file is very old MacWrite...we only have Word, but we try." Sure enough, because I had cut-and-pasted an old document, it was a rather obsolete format.

We were then out of luck again...and I was thinking *this will be impressive in front of 200 people without a speech.*

Fortunately an Italian business guy overheard our conversation and came to my assistance. "No guarantee," he said," but we try something."

Minutes later, I was holding my precious printed speech in my hands. I could have kissed him!

RC then put us back into a cab, which she paid for, to our hotel. A classic hotel service story that you normally read about in those made-up ads.

Lift shaft

X was a legend. A huge rugby-playing guy, with an eye for the ladies. Whilst working in China, as a hotel F&B manager, he got lucky. Or so he thought.

The nightclub upstairs in his hotel was a notorious hotspot, and he took out a local Shanghainese lass from there one night. As soon as they got into the elevator, he pushed the "stop" button and they allegedly pleasured each other in the lift.

Completed, they straightened their attire and pushed the button to go down to the Lobby. As the doors opened, they were confronted by Security who whisked the overly amorous couple away.

The whole performance had been captured on Close Circuit TV by security! X was on a plane out of the country soon after.

Virtual relationship

When I was transferred to Singapore, the company put me into a hotel for a month while I sorted out accommodation. At check-in, I noticed a goddess behind the reception counter...your stereotypical exotic Singapore beauty, with almonds for eyes and a smile that lit up the whole hotel.

As the days and weeks unfolded, I occasionally saw her on duty and said "Hi" in passing, but never glimpsed her name badge.

At the same time, I was enjoying a great phone-only relationship with one of the hotel phone operators...she was in charge of wake-up calls, and my erratic hours were of great amusement to her. She would wake me up with dulcet calls of, "C'mon, sleepyhead, time to get to the office," etc. Our conversations on the phone grew increasingly lengthy and chatty. I ascertained her name was MC.

Then one day, the month's stay was up, so I told her I would miss her daily dose of morning wake-up calls and humour, and bid her farewell for the last time.

Going down to reception later to check out, I noticed the original goddess was on duty. Yes! I went up to the counter and noticed her name badge - *she was MC, the very same person I'd been having the phone relationship with!*

As it turned out, she said it was her birthday next week, and we should catch up for drinks. I eagerly called back the following week - MC had left the hotel. I wrote her a letter, asking the hotel to forward it, but never heard anything. Talk about the one that got away.

What a blast.

We were chatting to a guy in the hotel lobby in Sri Lanka. I think he was an American engineer. We got to chatting about the guerilla war and the recent bomb blasts.

Turns out he knew a thing or two about it...he was staying in one of the waterfront hotels that was blasted, and was extensively injured.

"You know that famous picture of the guy being carried out of the rubble in all the papers?" he said. "That was me."

Another couple was a little luckier...moments earlier they had been admiring the view from the large glass-fronted room, and had just climbed into bed when the bomb went off, spraying the room with deadly glass shards from waist-height upward. Lying down in bed, they were uninjured.

English spoken here - not

Hotels signs seen in China, taken from a widely circulated email.

In a Beijing hotel lobby:

"The lift is being fixed for next day. During that time we regret that you will be unbearable."

In a Shanghai hotel elevator:

"Please leave your values at the front desk."

In a Hangzhou hotel:

"The flattening of underwear with pleasure is the job of the chambermaid."

In a Jilin hotel:

"You are very invited to take advantage of the chambermaid."

In a Guilin hotel:
"Because of impropriety of entertaining guests of the opposite sex in the bedroom, it is suggested that the lobby be used for this purpose."

Something fishy

We had arrived late into Bangkok, checked into the hotel (quite well regarded) and ordered room service - 2 bowls of soup and 2 plates of Thai fishcakes. After what seemed forever, the bedside phone rang.

"Sir, fish cakes not so good..."

"Not so good?" I quizzed.

"It's rotten."

"Rotten?" I quizzed again.

"Would you still like it, Sir?"

"No, I think I just lost my appetite. 2 pieces of toast please."

Looking the part

TB was a notorious opportunist, and you could always count on him to wangle his way into (or out of) any situation. He's a fairly casual looking dude with scraggly blonde hair - a bit like Tom Petty. Once, we were all meeting in Bangkok. He arrived before us, and ends up in the suite of this hotel and he's only paying 1200Baht a night, whilst we're paying double that rate for a smaller room.

How did he do it? As he was checking in, so was the singer Robert Palmer's entourage. Naturally he said he was part of the group, and as he looked the part, they assigned him to the band suites at the special rates.

Special delivery

Leaving Hong Kong one afternoon I asked for a hotel car at 4pm to the airport. "Not a good time, Sir. Tunnel traffic too bad," I was informed, and they advised me instead to take the MRT across to Kowloon side and hop a cab from there.

Less than impressed, I hauled my bags to the station, boarded the train and got to Kowloon side. Coming out of the station, I realised I had left my passport in my room safe at the hotel.

I frantically called the hotel. They checked and sure enough, the passport was in the safe. They asked for my flight details and said they would try to get it to me at the check-in counter.

I immediately hopped into a taxi, and by the time I got to the airport, the hotel rep was already waiting with my passport. I was relieved. But so much for the tunnel traffic - how did he get there before I did?

If you have a good story about hotels or resorts anywhere in Asia, let us know. Email us at hardship_posting@hotmail.com or fax The Editor at 612-9499-5908.

"Solly, my England velly not good".
True tales of language problems and miscommunications in Asia.

Most people's first exposure to the Claymore-infested minefield of language barriers was probably when trying to follow the instruction manual of a Chinese, Japanese or Korean-made appliance back home. Blow me down! I did better following the flaming Greek or German instructions than the English ones.

In *Culture Shock*, Alfredo and Grace Roces put it better than anybody: "The Western visitor finds he is talking the same language but not communicating at all. With a sinking feeling he realises he is not in America, or England, or Canada but in an entirely different world."

Thank God, it's not just me then. In this case, they're talking about The Philippines, though it's equally applicable to other Asian countries as well. But the Filipinos do have the reputation of being the best and widest speakers of English, which only exacerbates the problem. (In fact I was nearly 20 before I learned that there's nothing wrong with exacerbation, and you can't go blind from it.)

Some made it easier for themselves. Dave the history-wallah says that Sir Stamford Raffles, to his credit, studied Malay, but also had Singapore's first linguist, Munshi Abdullah, at his elbow to bridge the gap between English and Malay speakers but when they changed Singapore's language to Chinese he was completely stuffed.

I admire people who take the time and effort to learn the local lingo, though. I do. Anyone with cheeks that can resist that much slapping deserves to be successful. I mean Cantonese has 9 inflections for each word, for crying out loud. Mandarin's a breeze - there are only 4. But you'll need to know about 3,000 of those squiggly words to be fluent.

Like anywhere, you always seem to learn the naughty words first. So of course I can get *in* to trouble in just about every Asian port I call on, but have barely enough of the local lingo to get *out* of trouble.

It's hard to explain that feeling to your friends or family who have only ever lived in Countryside England, or Boise Idaho, that feeling of sheer...sheer...aaaaaaaaaaaaarrrrrggghhhhhhh!!! when you've had an average morning and pop out to get a sandwich and a banana for lunch and you might as well be Marcel Marceau. The sounds don't help at all, no matter how you round your mouth, how clearly you enunciate it in the Queen's English, or how many times and HOW LOUD YOU RE-PEAT YOURSELF. So you end up gesticulating like some crazy circus animal until you end up with your sandwich and banana. Sometimes I think they do it on purpose...*let's see how weird I can get this white guy with the big nose in the loud shirt to act - How bad does he want this banana? Hmmm, pretty badly obviously.* Like making dolphins jump through flaming hoops for a measly morsel of sardine. Oh, I love Asia!

But if the heart attack doesn't get you, it's also one of the fun aspects of living abroad...bridging those little cultural chasms with a kind of mish-mash language hybrid that even a blue-collar pigeon, the dropout product of the government school system, would be ashamed of.

Makes you feel ready for the Diplomatic Corp. Which reminds me, I've not heard back on my recent application. I want to be the Australian High Commissioner to Koh Samui and I dare anyone to think they are more eminently qualified.

Or maybe if they don't need me in Koh Samui, somewhere like Cebu in The Philippines wouldn't be bad. All you got to do in The Philippines is say a three-letter word and everybody's happy. This word has about 11 different shades of it in that country, ranging from "absotively posilutely" to "maybe" to "dream on, Joe". The simple word is "yes".

No wonder my friends at The Lonely Planet Guide say English in The Philippines "Sometimes varies wildly from standard English."

And what about Japanese? Just to say "never mind" is *doozo ki-ni nasarazuni.* Or "that's too bad" is *Sore-wa okinodoku-desu-ne.* Even if it wasn't Ok you'd just say OK to get the matter over and done with. Especially with my Alzheimered mind...you've got to delete a word to add a new one in. And here's a phrase that I would have to purge an entire chapter for: *Motto yukkuri hanashite-itadajemasu-ka*, which means "could you speak more slowly". Now I don't know about you, but if I could say that, then I'd be probably bloody fluent already! Again with "We can't speak Japanese"...*Watashitachi-wa nihongo-ga hanasemasen.* What's wrong with "no speaka Japanesu"? After all, you do *chekku-auto* from your hotel after you have slept in your *beddo.*

It drove my good friend Dave Barry to despair. "I wanted to scream, HOW CAN YOU NOT UNDERSTAND ENGLISH WHEN ALL DAY LONG YOU LISTEN TO 'DO-WAH-DIDDY DIDDY DUM DIDDY DO?" he wrote in his masterly tome, Dave Barry Does Japan. (Note to editor: Hmmm, maybe we should call this book "Col. Ken Does Asia." What do you think? It worked for this Barry guy.)

I always love hearing conversations which rattle on in local lingo then all of a sudden there's an English word in there as if it's the most natural thing in the world. Like "*rinkydinkydadudinkdinkdink transfer interrupted, rinkydinkydadu modem connection*". Love it! Then you nod your head as if you're following the conversation and they say, "Oh, you understand?" and you say, "Sure, you're having a bit of problem with your computer," and they go, "Waaah, you understand velly good."

Bahasa Malayu is a bit like that too...well, not the formal language, but the way it has been adopted for modern usage. It's quite handy because now you can simply catch a *teksi* to the *kustoms kompleks* and get your visa stamped at *imigresen* there.

Speaking of catching cabs, did you know there's no Thai word for gonorrhea and syphilis? Pete the pornographer, sorry, photographer told me. But I've always loved the fact that the Thai word for "liver" is *tab*. It's like cause and effect...if you pick up the *tab* too often, you'll get liver damage.

That's what I like...practical languages. Unlike English.

Colonel Ke

Just what the doctor ordered
On a business trip to central Java I stayed overnight in a big 4 star hotel. Wanting to do some work, I called reception and asked for a power adapter for my computer.

Waited 20 minutes. Called again and was told the adapter was on its way.

Called 10 minutes later. Got a bit angry with the staff, but again, was told they had found the adapter and it was on the way to me.

Finally when the doorbell rang, I opened the door to discover the hotel general manager, duty manager, a nurse and *a doctor*, not an adapter!

© Captions of Industry Pty Ltd.   **www.hardshipposting.com**

Driving you crazy

This guy was sitting in a Manila Bar when this little damsel approached him. "You want to park with me, sir?"

"Park? No, I didn't drive."

"Not p-a-r-k, Sir...P-U-C-K!"

Learn Chinese in 5 Minutes

The following is from a popular email doing the rounds (origin unknown). It is designed to demystify the process of learning Chinese and give the expat a flying start in a hitherto difficult language.

HARDSHIP POSTING

[English phrase]	[Chinese Interpretation]
Are you harboring a fugitive?	Hu Yu Hai Ding?
See me A.S.A.P.	Kum Hia Nao
Stupid Man.	Dum Gai
Small Horse.	Tai Ni Po Ni
Did you go to the beach?	Wai Yu So Tan?
I bumped into a coffee table.	Ai Bang Mai Ni
I think you need a facelift.	Chin Tu Fat
It's very dark in here.	Wai So Dim?
Has your flight been delayed?	Hao Long Wei Ting?
That was an unauthorized execution.	Lin Ching
I thought you were on a diet.	Wai Yu Mun Ching?
This is a tow away zone.	No Pah King
Do you know the lyrics to the Macarena?	Wai Yu Sing Dum Song?
You are not very bright.	Yu So Dum
I got this for free.	Ai No Pei
I am not guilty.	Wai Hang Mi?
Please, stay a while longer.	Wai Go Nao?
Our meeting was scheduled for next week.	Wai Yu Kum Nao
They have arrived.	Hia Dei Kum
Stay out of sight.	Lei Lo
He's cleaning his automobile.	Wa Shing Ka
Your body odour is offensive.	Yu Stin Ki Pu

Sorry seems the hardest word

Like most expats in colonial Hong Kong in the 70's, I never bothered to learn Cantonese. The attitude of the time was: "It's a British Colony; 'they' should learn English!" Besides, how could anyone be expected to learn a language with nine tones and a change in tone gave a word a totally different meaning. Ridiculous.

About the only Cantonese I did learn was my address - necessary to get home in a taxi because taxi drivers at the time spoke little or no English. Not much different from today really.

Late one evening, with more than a few San Migs under my belt, I stumbled out of a Wanchai bar and hailed a taxi. I climbed in and told the driver my address, in my best Cantonese. When we arrived outside my apartment building I handed over $20 to pay for the fare which was around $15.

With this the driver started prattling on in Cantonese punctuated with "No changee! No changee!" The only thing I could understand was "no changee." I had been stung many times by the "no changee" ploy. But $5 on a $15 fare was a rip off. It was time to take a stand.

The conversation started to get pretty heated - with me shouting at the taxi driver in English and him shouting at me in Cantonese. Still, "no changee!" I decided the only thing to do was to tell him to drive to the nearest police station.

At this point the driver started waving his arms, shouting "Wanchai yun, Wanchai yun". Although my Cantonese was very limited I did know that "yun" meant "person". The little shit was calling me a "Wanchai person"! What an insult! I may have had slightly too much to drink on that particular night but I was no "Wanchai person"! (Wanchai: bar district of HKG)

Eventually the taxi driver drove to a nearby police box where there was a Chinese lady police officer on duty. "What's the problem?" she asked. I told her that the taxi driver had refused to give me my change, claiming "no changee" and on top of this had insulted me by calling me a "Wanchai yun". Then she and the taxi driver had a brief conversation in Cantonese.

She turned back to me. "Firstly," she said, "he really doesn't have change and he says he is very sorry. He was asking you give him the exact fare or wait while he went to the store on the corner to get change. Secondly, he didn't call you a 'Wanchai person'. What he said was: 'Wan chaai-yun', which means 'Let's look for a policeman'."

I apologised, told him to keep the $5, gave him another $10 for his trouble and stumbled into the night.

Boy oh boy!

My first month in Hong Kong was filled with new sights, new sounds and of course, a new language. I had moved there at roughly the same time as CM, a US expat who would become a good friend over the years. This actually meant learning two new languages - Cantonese and American.

During our first week we were invited to various client lunches and indoctrination programmes. CM and I began to pick up the local language. Starting out with the easy stuff like Taxi Cantonese, Restaurant Cantonese and of course, Wanchai Cantonese. Usually by 2am, in the Popeye Bar we were fluent - or so we thought.

A new client had invited us to the Mandarin Grill - a very posh restaurant in Hong Kong's Central business district.

After the meal, CM was keen to impress the assembled group with his linguistic skills.

He announced he would like to order a coffee, and that he would like to order it in Cantonese. One of the girls at the table carefully pronounced it for him, *"Yat bui ga fei tsai, m'goi."*

The waiter came and CM carefully enunciated exactly what he had just been taught.

The table erupted.

"You said the right words, but you got the tones all wrong", they said.

"So, what did I say?" asked CM.

"You've just ordered a young, fat boy!" they shrieked.

Fortunately for CM his sense of humour kicked in faster than his embarrassment, and he retorted, " Why of course I did. I just hope they're not out of them!"

Squeeze me?

English is the aspirational language of Taiwan. Many can clumsily speak a few words of English and most will take every opportunity to practice it. Fluency, or close to it, is a requisite for acceptance to American universities, so many study it with varying degrees of success.

A friend of ours was stopped by a motorcycle policeman for some minor traffic violation. The policeman must have been studying English, because as he strode up to her car and -in quite good English - advised her of her violation and asked to see her driver's license.

Our friend kept her head about her and, with a baffled expression on her face, said: "Is that supposed to be English?"

Suddenly unsure of his English, and apparently embarrassed by what must have been a major linguistic gaffe, he motioned for her to go on her way.

Blah blah blah

I was to speak at a seminar in Taiwan, and had been given a little bit of advance notice by the organisers that the audience's comprehension was probably not as good as I might hope or expect.

As I arrived at lunchtime, I headed into the restaurant where all the delegates were seated, eating.

"Is anyone sitting here?" I inquired.

"IBM," chirped a friendly Taiwanese lady seated opposite.

I sat down anyway.

"How was this morning's talk?" I continued optimistically.

"Yes, very cold," she said.

As it happened, the talk went fine (meaning no one nodded off, and a couple of people even nodded their heads as if I was making sense) and there were even a couple of questions.

Bloody hell

This German guy on business in Asia checks into his hotel, and is escorted up to his room by the butler.

Once the butler has unpacked his bags, he says: "Anything else, Sir?"

"Yes," says the hungry and thirsty German. "Bring me a cheese sandwich and a Bloody Caesar."

The Butler is a bit taken aback by the abruptness of the German, but turns on his heels and exits.

He appears a few minutes later...with a cheese sandwich and a pair of *scissors*!

Airhead

I was in a Tokyo department store and needed to buy a pair of shorts.

"I need a pair of shorts," I explained to the smiling Japanese shop assistant who asked to help.

"You are skydiving this weekend?" she asked. "We don't sell *parachute* here."

Monkey see, monkey do

It always amused me that when you want to get the attention of a waiter in Hong Kong, you use the Cantonese word, "M'goi"...which sounds exactly the same as the Tagalog word for "Monkey".

Size of contentment

My Belgian friend, D, arrived in Singapore for a visit a few years back. I set her up with another single friend of mine, an American from Houston who thought it would be hospitable on his part to invite her for a good old American BBQ on his deck.

When she arrived and saw the healthy-sized chicken legs grilling on the porch, she exclaimed in her broken French-English "I am so glad you invited me for Dinner, M. I haven't had a good big cock (*coq* is French for chicken of course) since I arrived in Asia last month. They are all so small around here!"

Michael never did tell us how the rest of the evening worked out.

If you have a good story about ranguage probrem or miscommulication in Asia, let us know. Email us at **hardship_posting@hotmail.com** *or fax The Editor at 612-9499-5908.*

"Work hard, pray hard."
True tales of goings on in the office and corporate world.

The motto in the developed parts of Asia is very much, "Live to work", not "Work to live." In the less developed parts it's more a case of, "If I get to live at all that's pretty hard work but quite a good thing."

All of us invariably move to Asia in the first place to work. We might have been here passing through as young and idealistic backpackers before, or young and idealistic soldiers before, but for most they come here to work, gain the international experience, and especially to gain the international salary.

Because as an expat you are invariably able to squirrel away more than you can at home. Well, that's the theory. Many of my good buddies (not mentioning Pete or Dave or Barry) just recycle it against the urinal wall...you've heard of investing in junk bonds, well this is more like piss-trough futures!

But, let's face it, that's a lot more value for money than some bug-eyed pin-striper telling you that sorry the market's a little bit bearish and you've made a paper loss. If I'm gonna lose money I want to damn well enjoy it. When I go down I go down in flames, as that French aviator bloke used to say. (Well, there's actually a couple of bars in Bangkok where you can see that.)

But there are other boring sods that actually do stick to their game plan and make a bucket of bucks. I've tried everything. Come Chinese New Year, you'll see me rolling oranges round my study floor on the 4th day. You'll see me tossing raw fish for prosperity, just in case. I hedge all my bets - pray to every money god there is, but there's obviously some sort of collective deafness thing going on with them.

I even tried reading Sun Tzu's "Art of War" to get the secret. Blow me down, how do those buggers ever get any work done if they're just fighting the whole time. How unproductive is that?

Anyway...there are a few little myths I want to explode here. People think of Asia as synonymous with industrious productivity. Not entirely true. My good friend John Naisbitt has this to say in his book Megatrends Asia: "In Japan the average work week has shrunk. Japanese workers now work an average of 1,800 hours a year, less than the 2,058 average in the US." But there are two flaws in the methodology...firstly, did they count the hours the Japanese spent on the golf course and in the karaoke bar as 'work,' which they should do because that's where all the serious stuff happens for them. Secondly, the American figure no doubt includes billions of hours filling out head office requests for useless information in triplicate, thereby inflating the figure without any corresponding increase in tangible output.

My modus operandi is rigorous discipline and application to the task. It's a case of working smarter, not harder. For instance, if I were ever late for work, I'd always make sure I left early to make up for it.

But by and large, though, most people in Asia, expat or otherwise, tend to revolve their life around work.

The key to success here is understanding what makes it tick. This will take you, oh, probably generations. Just when you think you've got it figured, the goalposts reappear in your peripheral vision like a fleeting illusion saying "nah-ne-nah-ne-nah".

And changes happen so fast - look at how 'doi moi' has opened up Vietnam economically. The Colonel's tried and trusted recipe - give 'em some Dong and they open up all right!

How many blokes have we seen trying to be the big corporate hero in Asia. He gets posted out here, and a couple of weeks later he calls his boss to report: "Yip, it's all making sense now." After a couple of months it's like, "Well, there are a few things I still need to understand." And after two years it's like, "I figured out I know *nothing* about this place!"

The funniest thing I see, and believe me I've seen a lot of funny shit in my time, is multinational companies rotating their expats out at the time when they just begin to be useful. Just when they're beginning to make amends for some righteous gaffes early on, and they've got a few useful phone numbers in the book, off they go. And the next green-horn comes in to be a hero.

And sometimes people end up as martyrs. Noel Barber, in *War of The Running Dogs*, describes Arthur Walker, manager of a Malayan rubber plantation, getting taken out at point blank range at 8am in his office. 8am? You've hardly had time to scratch your nuts and read the paper and your day's over. And that poor bugger Michael Wansley that was taken out in a drive-by assassination recently while auditing the Thai sugar mill. Just doing his job and calling it as he saw it. Well, he didn't see much of what happened that day, I assure you.

Maybe he didn't consult the feng shui expert. Maybe his kettle had the spout facing the wrong way. Or he didn't work in an impractical triangular cubicle where the good energy could flow in but the money couldn't flow out.

Anyway, on that note, I must dash off and resend a 'fux' to my mate in Manila. His secretary just called to say, "Can you fux me again, Sir.' Not the first time I've had that request!

But as my old man used to say: "Never dip your pen in company ink."

Colonel Ke

Bottom line

In Manila for a conference, we ended up down the Makati strip of clubs and bars. As there was a big group of us, we decided to hit as many bars as possible, and then one person would pick up the tab in each place, just to make it easier administratively.

In many places, especially seedier bars, the name that appears on your Corporate Card statement is usually something fairly discreet like XYZ Tailors or JoJo's Entertainment, or whatever, so I felt fine handing my credit card over for the huge bill we racked up.

I only noticed when I came to hand in my expenses back at the office that this slip for $1400 was from "Bottoms Club." Explain *that* to the finance lady!

© Captions of Industry Pty Ltd.   **www.hardshipposting.com**

The pressure's all mine

A year ago, a local Chinese colleague in our Hong Kong office resigned. Doing what she thought to be the right thing, she sent out a note to a large distribution list, thanking us for all the opportunities and wishing the company all the best.

"It's been a *pressure* working with all of you," was her unfortunate sign off line!

Ill wind blowing

We had a secretary who took care of 2 partners in a fairly small firm. One day after lunch, the two of us were discussing something when I felt the urgent need to 'let one rip'. No sooner had I released the most unpleasant of gaseous odours, than we heard footsteps coming up the stairs. It was the secretary! My partner dived for cover in his room, screaming with laughter and I was left to stand and field my secretary's question.

It was evident she sensed something's wrong but said nothing. I, meanwhile, was begin to feed off my partners laughter from the next room, and was caught somewhere between extreme embarrassment and amusement. She then left the room, with gaseous clouds still swirling, and I fell on the floor, tears of laughter running down my cheeks. She resigned soon after, but I don't think the incidents were related.

A bit fishy

We were sitting in this airline conference, and the speaker was delivering his market report on the new route...Tokyo to Guam. He then put up an overhead with a map of the area, including Saipan.

The guy next to me whispered "Oh, I always wondered where Saipan was, ever since the Saipan Trout Fishing Club sponsored the shaved pussy contest in Manila."

The morning laughter

Our office Christmas party was set and organised. Then a major prospective client called to say they needed us to present our proposal on, of course, the morning after our party. Despite our protestations, we couldn't move the date or the time.

Deciding to turn the negative into a positive, we came up with a game plan that required more than a little intestinal fortitude. We would make the presentation in our fancy dress clothes from the party - giving the impression that we had come straight from it, and were - therefore - great, dedicated and conscientious guys (and gals) to work with. After all, the client was in the tourism and vacation field.

All agreed on the plan. As the theme was "B", I was dressed as a basketballer...shorts, singlet, cap, boots. Next morning, I turned up to the office wearing this. Most of the others brought in their costume, but some backed out all together, meaning that all the others backed down as well and got changed into their work clothes.

With no time to make other arrangements, I had no option but to present in my basketball gear. And I was the Managing Director! The look on the face of the tie-wearing clients was priceless. We didn't get the business.

Annual General meeting

I was to meet the General and a few other high-ranking officers of the Sri Lankan army in Jaffna, stronghold of the Tamil Tigers of all places, to finalise some supply dealings.

The day before I left, I double-checked all the details and confirmed with the General's staff that all systems were go. I then headed to the airport and flew to Colombo, Sri Lanka.

On arrival, I was met by a driver who informed me that my meeting with the General was no longer "on".

"Yes, it is," I countered. "I spoke to his aide yesterday to confirm."

"No, Sir," he repeated. "You will not be meeting with the General."

"But," I steamed, "it was confirmed and I've just flown half way around the bloody world...don't tell me that the meeting with the General is not on."

"Sir," the driver explained calmly, " the General is dead."

The afternoon before, he and most of his top officers were taken out by landmines planted in the ceiling of the room they were meeting in.

We went up to the hills instead and spent a few maudlin days there before catching our scheduled flight out.

All singing, all dancing

We were to make a presentation of ad proposals to a major Japanese retail client. Part of this was coming up with a jingle that would get the whole town singing the brand name and feel good about the company's products.

For the grand finale of the presentation, my boss decided we should do a song and dance routine...wearing yellow t-shirts with the proposed slogan emblazoned across it, singing and dancing to their proposed new jingle.

As the big boss on the client side spoke virtually no English and was a bit inscrutable to say the least, I thought this was an ill-conceived plan, but went ahead with it anyway.

Come the big day, we rip off our suits to reveal the t-shirts, the music starts and off we go...soft-shoeing our way woefully through the jingle, building up to the big finish and...

Nothing!

The Japanese were absolutely quiet. No clapping, no smiles, no "not bad for beginners". Literally, nothing. All looked toward their boss for his reaction before committing themselves to an opinion.

The big honcho leaned over to his assistant, and whispered something in her ear.

"Now we talk about budget," she translated.

Out of the foyer, into the frying pan

This story always appealed to me, because I never had the guts to do it myself.

Some years ago, before global computer networks are what they are today, we worked together with this guy in Hong Kong as business partners to American Express. As a show of allegiance, we all had Amex cards.

He used his liberally, as we all did, but then got transferred from Hong Kong back to head office. He did a runner on his Amex bill in Hong Kong, and now heads up a very important business unit partnering them at a high level in New York. You've got to love the irony!

Absolutely routed

This company was opening offices in many parts of Asia Pacific, and even in the Middle East. Everytime I came back from these exhausting trips, RJ would say, "How was your holiday?" which used to piss me off a little. Actually, a lot.

So one day, I decided to sort him out.

"R, I've been thinking. It'd be a good idea if you went and met some of our clients in Pakistan, Sri Lanka and Dubai."

"You really think I could?" RJ said eagerly.

"Yip, absolutely. It'd be good for you. I'll set it all up for you," I said.

I then proceeded to make the travel arrangements as impractical as possible. Singapore to Colombo. Colombo to Karachi. Karachi to Dubai. Dubai to Karachi then back to Dubai. And so on. All at inconvenient departure times, on airlines such as Air Bangladesh, with massive amounts of time on the ground at each airport (like arriving just before midnight and having to wait for a 2pm departure time).

Of course, we sent him economy, so he didn't have access to airline lounges either. We had him arriving at 4:30am in places like Pakistan, with breakfast meetings set up at 7am, which of course no Pakistani would attend as they tend to be late starters.

3 days after he left, a call comes through to the office which I refused to take.

"Tell him I'm in a meeting," I said.

"But he needs to speak to you urgently," my secretary said.

"Tell him I'm not available," I ordered.

He obviously suspected something. But the final straw was on the final flight from Colombo. Eventually it looked like he might get some sleep, when at the last minute a Sri Lankan lady with a baby sat next to him. Just after take off, the baby threw up all over him.

RJ cracked."Those bastards in Singapore have sent you, haven't they!" he called out. The lady thought he was mad.

Finally, he got back to the office, worn and weary.

"How was your holiday?" I cheerfully asked. I think he got the point.

A ten-se discussion

An Englishman in Bangkok was to be delivered the bad news...the downturn in Thailand had finally taken its toll and he would unfortunately have to go.

The managing director, thinking of how to break it to him gently in the purest economic terms that he would understand, started off.

"Well basically *you* go or 10 of the locals go. That's the mathematics of it."

"Have you decided which 10?" was the expat's optimistic retort.

Executive washroom

An annual meeting had been arranged between us and the President of a major shipping company, based in Paris. Covering all the usual bases of budgets, markets, etc.

Unfortunately, there was a big cocktail function that I had been invited to the evening before, for something else altogether. As it often happens, the cocktail party spun out of control, and we ended up having a 5am finish on the Tequila shots.

I got up a little late, and a lot worse for wear, but determined to do a great job in the President's presentation. On the way to the office, I stopped to get something for my queasy and nauseous stomach...the 7-11 had nothing, but they did have Immodium (for diarrhea). I took a couple of those.

About an hour into the meeting, I felt my sugar levels going out of whack, and those first twinges of nausea make themselves felt. *Oh no!*

I excused myself, went to the bathroom, threw up and felt a million times better. Returning to the boardroom, I chugged some water.

"Are you OK?" everyone enquired. The presentation continued.

About 15 minutes later, that feeling again. "Excuse me again," I said.

Back once again, the client said they could re-schedule if I wasn't up to it. "No, no. Maybe just something I ate," I said.

5 minutes later I was in the bathroom throwing up again. That real turn-inside-out sensation.

I was by now pale as a ghost and trembling, but continued with the presentation. The client, especially the French President, thought I was a valiant hero.

"I heer many pipple get zis food poizonneeng in Asia," he sympathised, as I dashed out once more. With that the meeting was over. I declined to join them for lunch and went home to die.

Cheese and whine

I was desperately unhappy with the new management, and decided to bring this up to my regional boss. He suggested we meet and discuss over lunch at a nearby steakhouse.

He ordered a glass of red wine - I stuck to lemon juice, being lunch-time. Once our meals arrived and we started chatting, he said, "Are you sure you don't want to join me in some red?" I ordered a glass.

As we discussed the management problems further, we decided perhaps we should get a bottle of red between us. Before we knew it, that was finished and we ordered another.

"R, I'll cut to the bottom line...please fire me," I said.

"I can't fire you," he said, "DL (managing director) won't believe me."

"R, you are my boss. I'm asking you to do me a favour and fire me. I need the money," I said with some apparent logic.

With that he got up to use the public phone to speak with the managing director.

"Oh, heesh not there," he slurred. "Where ish he? ...Ok, I'll call him there. What'shh the number?"

The managing director was at a major client's office. He made the call anyway:

"D, it'shh R...yeshh, I know you're in a mmmeeting...Ok, I'll be quick - ish it alright if I fire B?...yip... yip...Ok." Click.

He came back to the table. "Congratulationshh, mate, you're fired!" he said, as we ordered another bottle of red. We finally ended lunch at 7:30 pm, staggered back to the office, packed up my stuff and was gone.

I received a fat cheque with 3 month's severance payment the following day.

Saved by the bell

I was in a cab in Colombo, Sri Lanka, on the way to a client's office. The front page news was a terrible bomb blast that killed umpteen people. On arriving at their office, they asked whether I heard about their terrible bomb blast?

"Somewhere up north was it?" I enquired, presuming it was in distant Jaffna.

"No, it was our downtown railway station, just here," they said.

In fact, the client continued, he was about to leave the office the day before when the phone rang. He decided whether to continue heading out or take the call. He took the call (one of the managers from our office, as it turns out) which delayed him. Otherwise he would have been passing the ill-fated station at exactly the time of the car-bomb blast.

The price of love

I was transferred from Auckland to the Hong Kong office, leaving behind a serious relationship in the New Zealand office.

We devised a plan to communicate regularly via phone and fax (this was before the days of email unfortunately) at the company's expense. This worked well for several months, as we invented projects and assignments for us to be working together on. As the faxes were public, we would sometimes use a short hand code for the mushier stuff.

However, when I resigned from the company, somebody must have had their nose put out, because I was presented with a bill from the finance department, itemising all the calls and faxes they suspected of being 'personal'.

After disputing a few of them, I ended up with something like a US$2000 bill. Ouch!

Fever pitch

I was booked in to make a presentation to about 75 business people at the Australian High Commission. That week, I was running an inexplicable fever of about 40 degrees.

The show must go on, I decided.

"Please forgive me if I spontaneously combust half way through," I said to the gathered audience.

Presentation completed, I decided to go home instead of back to the office, and collapsed. By 7pm that evening I was in hospital with dengue fever.

Thank God it's Friday

Usually in Kuala Lumpur I would try to schedule 4 meetings in a day, but would invariably have to cancel one of them due to overrun or unexpected (?) traffic delays.

My second meeting of this particular day was with a prominent Malay banker, at 11am. All was going well, when suddenly he looked at his watch, rose from his chair and said: "OK, I'll see you all back here at 2:30."

"What the f***'s going on?" I asked my counterpart.

"Friday prayers," she said.

With that, the room emptied out, leaving me to rejuggle my afternoon meetings and return flight.

Hard nut

One of the girls in our office was a real power bitch. Fun but hard. One day, returning to our office in Singapore, she had driven in the back way past a storm drain canal to park her car.

"I did a Good Samaritan act today," she beamed. "I almost ran this turtle over, so I stopped the car, picked him up and put him back into the water. But then he kind of went to the bottom."

"That's good," I said. "You're sure it was a turtle and not a tortoise?"

"What's the difference?" she asked. I grabbed an encyclopedia, and turned to an illustration. "That," I said "is a turtle, which is designed for water...this, is a tortoise designed for land."

Her jaw dropped as the thought dawned on her. "Oh no...it was a tortoise...I killed a tortoise...I put him in the water...no wonder he sunk to the bottom."

She burst into tears. So much for a Good Samaritan act!

Fantastic plastic

A film director was showing us his show reel. We shook hands and exchanged business cards. I noticed his were very distinctively designed, and made of plastic.

"No good for roaches," I said, referring to the common practice of tearing strips off business cards to put at the end of marijuana joints as a stopper so you did not burn your lips.

"We're obviously in a different league," he shot back, making dicing and scraping motions with his plastic card (like cocaine users do with razors and mirrors).

Getting nailed

The regional conference in Tokyo was about to start, but no sign of BS, coming via Manila.

He eventually turned up, with a typically great -but true- excuse...

He was having a few drinks with some good buddies (including the bar owner) in a Manila bar. This was during the "clean-up" of Manila phase, when they were trying to drive out and relocate the seedier bars of Mabini in the early 90s.

Suddenly, a truck pulled up outside the bar, a bunch of soldiers or police jumped out and proceeded to nail large planks across the doorway and windows. Effectively, everyone was locked in. The natural reaction was to panic.

Then B thought... *we're locked in a bar with bottles of Jack Daniels, umpteen eligible nubiles, and some good mates...things could be a lot worse!*

The party then got into full swing, and continued all night until they were released the next morning.

"And that's why I'm late," he explained.

Sleeping your way to the top

JP had just moved to Singapore from Hong Kong, and needed a place to stay. We had started a business, working from home, so the spare bed was our boardroom table.

A client wanted to meet. We said we were prepared to drive out to see him in Jurong (a long way out). He insisted that he meet in *our* office, much against our wishes, because we didn't have a 'proper' office, plus we had this hooligan friend staying over.

So we had to kick JP out of bed to make a presentation. Fortunately, the client was quite easygoing and liked the 'character' of our home office. He also liked the fact we had a fully-stocked fridge, and from then on insisted on making meetings at 4pm, always in our office. He'd then come around and drain our fridge of beers. He even once backed out of the driveway into our neighbour's car!

Un-real estate

My friend C was running a small business out of a shop-house on Boat Quay, in Singapore in the late 80s. Back then, Boat Quay was a ramshackle assortment of small trading businesses...sharks fin dealers, auto parts, etc. Not the Seine-like al fresco dining heaven it is today.

Because he had been renting for a while, his landlord approached him and asked if he wanted to buy the shophouse for S$450,000.

"Tell him to dream on," said E, his partner.

They moved out. Eighteen months later, the Boat Quay pub scene took off, and that place sold for S$4.5 million.

Expect the unexpected

I once got a call from one of our key prospects, and one of the most prestigious business partners you would wish to work with.

"We'd like you to come around for a chat," is all the operative cryptically told me.

I thought I'd prepare a credentials document anyway, and be prepared to talk about some of the areas we could offer them an improved service. We also had a polytechnic intern with us, so I thought I'd take her for the experience (plus she could carry the credentials documents).

It started off badly with us turning up on time, but at the wrong address (I was unaware they had several). We were then redirected to corporate HQ.

Arriving late, the receptionist said: "You're here for the presentation? Please go through they have started already." She opened the conference room door, and there was the full board of this listed company...a bunch of geriatric pinstriped Chinese stiffs...expecting obviously a major presentation on...who knows what.

"Shall we start?" the lady that called for 'the chat' said.

With that I turned to the intern to get the credential document to talk through...and...she had lost them! She had left them accidentally at the previous office we had come from.

Talk about tap dancing! Needless to say we never got a chance to work with them again.

Skirting the issue

Making a pitch to a major insurance company about our point of difference, I talked much about 'fewer, better people,' less bureaucracy and people that could really make a difference to their business. "For instance," I earnestly continued, "we won't have layers and layers of junior girls in short skirts acting as glorified note-takers on your account."

After we had wrapped up the formal credentials discussion, the client - a 30 something American guy- wanted a tour of our office (which was known internally and externally at one point as "Models Inc.").

"Wow," he said after we completed the tour, "I thought you said you didn't have junior girls in short skirts."

"Correct," I said. "These are very *senior* girls in short skirts!"

Co-pilot

I was waiting for an airline client to turn up one evening for a late meeting, when he called to say his flight was delayed. He couldn't re-schedule as he would be flying out elsewhere first thing in the morning. He proposed that he drop by my house later on in the evening to run through the design proposals.

Taking the work home, my 4-year-old son was intrigued by the designs, which I explained to him.

Duly around 9pm, my client arrived. We had a beer and a pre-amble chat about the designs, which he liked. Finding it difficult to make a decision, he turned to my son, and said: "Which one do you like?"

My son pointed to option C.

"Me too," the client said, approving it on the spot.

Save the mirth

DL had just started as Managing Director and was keen to make his mark straightaway. I remember , soon after he started, receiving a 3-line typed memo on crisp and freshly printed company letterhead.

The 3 lines?

Something to the effect of "In order to save paper and money, please utilise both sides of paper when photocopying, and use recycled paper where possible."

Burning ambition

J was a real character. An Australian film director, he would often make the most of free booze at production house parties, and then end the evening with a "burnoff".

The "burnoff" consisted of him taking off his shirt (usually a loud Hawaiian number) and revealing his ample gut, which was covered in a mass of body hair. He would then get a cigarette lighter, and set his body hair alight near his navel. The fire then would burn a strip all the way up his stomach, over his chest and up to his neck.

Of course, this always got other pissed guys enthusiastic to try it, resulting in "mass burnoffs" which invariably ended in tears and yells of "f********ck!" from those less experienced and less hairy.

Hang the expense

My friend R worked for one of the big French luxury brands. He would always complain how badly their company was doing in this part of the world, but would always fly First or Business Class, and stay at The Shangri-La. When his company decided to relocate him from Malaysia to Paris against his wishes, he decided to exact his revenge on the company.

Every time he came into Singapore, he'd call up and say: "Where eez ze most expenseeev place to drink in Singapore? And where eez ze most expenseeev restaurant?" He'd then take me out, all on his company credit card. This went on for a few months, of absolute excess each week or two, until he finally went back to Paris.

As soon as he got back to Paris, he joined a competitor who sent him back out to Asia again. But we never abused his new corporate card. Well not yet.

Breath of fresh air

I used to work at the Samsung shipyard in Korea, which was massive, so I sometimes gave guys a lift from our area to the front gate in my car.

Meaning no disrespect, I often had to drive with my head out of the window because the stench of their collective bulgogi-and-kimchee breaths was so overpowering.

A colleague of mine was a bit more prepared - he used to keep a bag of croissants in his car and offer them around to dampen the breath a little.

The ins and outs of courtesy

As anyone will tell you, when it comes to catching trains or elevators in Asia, there are no queues - as soon as the doors open, it's a mad rush for those outside to get in. And those that are in, have to struggle to push their way out though the incoming crowds.

One day, in Hong Kong, we were going down the elevator to lunch. It had been a bad morning and I was not in a good mood to put it mildly.

As we reached the lobby, all those on the outside rushed to get in as usual. I stood in the doorway of the elevator, my arms spread out.

"Alright, everybody out," I commanded. "We're going to try that again." They gave me more quizzical looks. "The concept is simple," I continued ranting. "Those who are now in the lift, please get out. And when everybody that's in is out, then those that are out can get in. Got it?"

My colleagues pissed themselves laughing, whilst the locals looked at me like I was from Mars. I felt better, but in no way feel that I changed their habits of a lifetime.

For richer or poorer

I did business in Singapore with 2 guys who were absolute classics. The first guy spent most of the first meeting impressing us with his wealth..."you see this shop, I bought this for only $300,000, now it's worth $1.3 million..." and so on. However, when it came to pay up a measly $750 bill, all of a sudden it was like "oh, business is bad, can we get a discount ," and so on. Real weasel behaviour.

The other guy was similar, but he drove a $450,000 Jaguar, but insisted on meeting after 10:30 so he could save the $3 daily CBD license to enter the restricted zone.

Title engineering

We worked with this hotel group, whose big boss was this Japanese upstart...a real livewire, and a bit of a character. His business card read "Chief Disorganiser."

Pooling our resources

We were doing some work with colleagues in Colombo, Sri Lanka. Very friendly and welcoming. Too much so, perhaps - they never gave us a minute to ourselves, despite the fact that we had other client meetings and deadlines to attend to. In desperation, we thought we would check out of the hotel they put us in, and check into a nicer resort hotel south of Colombo. We could then spend the next day, uninterrupted and actually get some work done.

Checking out sneakily, as we knew our hosts were expecting us in the lobby bar for yet more drinks, we made a dash for freedom out the door. As we did, we bumped into one of them coming into the hotel. "We're just...um...rushing to the airport. We decided to go home today," we fumbled feebly and probably unconvincingly. With apologies, we excused ourselves and rushed to the taxi stand, and headed to our resort down south.

We spent the next day working productively round the pool, noticing the surprising amount of lithesome blonde girls around the pool. One of the staff told us they were from the Moscow Ballet, performing at the hotel. That evening, we had the time of our lives, sipping cold beers whilst watching the sun going down over one of the most beautiful beaches you could ever imagine. Then, at sunset, we joined about 20 Russian ballerinas for a dip in the ocean. They were like mermaids, playing like dolphins in the waves.

Unfortunately we then had to take a shower (cold!) and head back to the airport. Darn!

World champion work ethic

This Eurasian guy HN ran a video production house in Kuala Lumpur, and was a mad soccer fanatic. Every World Cup, everyone knew not to call him for a job. He simply became nocturnal, bought a big Barco projector, stocked the fridge with beer, and became nocturnal. Everyone accepted this, and just worked around it. Way to go!

Thanks but no thanks

It is customary at Chinese New Year for bonuses to be dished out by the boss, although in our company it was not contractual. One year I thought I'd do it personally after the all-staff lunch.

After a sumptuous banquet, I lined up at the door with the "red packets" (envelopes containing money) to give to each as they went off on their holiday. The average was a month's salary for each.

Blow me down, but as I handed out the packets, I got no fewer than 3 resignation letters in return. A straight swap!

I have never felt so violated in my life.

"In that case, I'll take my money back," I said to one of the resigning ladies.

"Really?" she asked.

"No, just kidding," I said. But I could have killed her.

Ghosts of a chance

When I was managing an advertising agency in Jakarta, the official hours were 0800 - 1630, so I used to spend quite a bit of time in the evenings at the office with just the office boy guarding reception.

We moved office to a newly renovated building, and I noticed he wouldn't come to my room in the evenings, which began to piss me off. I questioned my secretary and she explained that no-one would come to that part of the office once it was dark as there was a ghost in the conference room (which was next to my office).

Apparently, a worker had hanged himself in that area during the renovation. I scoffed at this but the next evening I heard someone in the conference room. I was alone in my office. I went into the conference room but no-one was there. I thought I was being set up by the staff. Next evening, I heard the noise again. I crept up to the door, waited until the noise was there and opened the door quickly and looked in to see a body 'going' into a small, closed, cupboard in which we kept our video tapes.

As you might imagine, I never went into the conference room at night again, even though I regularly heard those noises. In fact it still sends shivers up and down my spine as I sit here writing about it!

The boss's big boss

I was working in an advertising agency in Jakarta. We had run up a considerable amount of debt to a number of local and international third party suppliers. We had not been paid by the client for about 8 months but were still running the account by running up huge totals with these suppliers.

We finally got a small sum in from the client but not nearly enough to go around. Having been the direct contact with all these suppliers, I felt it my responsibility to sit down and prioritize our Account Payables with my President, a Muslim Indonesian. We sat down and I proceeded to go through the top priorities one by one, explaining why I thought they deserved to be paid. One by one, my President was finding reasons why they should not be paid. I was not finding his arguments convincing and I was letting him know it.

Finally, after a rather heated exchange, my President stood up suddenly and, with uncharacteristic emotion, yelled at me that I was not in charge of Accounts Payable and neither was he. He said: "There is only one person who decides who gets paid and who doesn't....and that is Allah!"

I knew that I was beaten. There was nowhere to take an argument from there.

On company time

It was my first week with this Singapore ad agency. My managing director, a middle aged, strong-minded Chinese gentleman, suggested I accompany him to a meeting with a client who marketed several luxury watch brands from Switzerland.

We arrived around midday at the client's office ,where the Marketing Director's secretary ushered us into the small conference room. With a friendly smile she offered us tea and biscuits as we sat down, and informed us that Mr K would join us for the meeting in just a minute.

Soon, a jovial looking Mr K walked into the room, apologising for keeping us waiting.

"And who do we have here?" he asked my boss.

"Mr K, this is the new man on your account." he replied. "He's from Australia."

Mr K warmly shook my hand. "Ah, welcome, welcome"

I thought *what a nice friendly chap*.

Mr K then gestured to his secretary to bring something - a large wooden jewellery box, about 2 inches deep. She opened the lid in front of me to reveal a collection of beautiful mens and ladies watches.

"Very nice," I remarked.

"Take one," he said with that eternal smile.

I was taken by surprise with his offer and looked to my boss for reassurance. He nodded as if to say *it's okay, take one*.

Wow, I thought, what a great perk. A free watch. And expensive ones too! Not such a bad job after all.

So I took one I fancied from the box and tried it on. The band was a bit loose.

"And take one for your wife. You are married ?" Mr K asked.

Now I was really impressed. "Er...yes I am", I answered as I began to choose from the ladies' collection.

"Let my secretary adjust the band for you," he suggested. I handed her my stainless steel man's watch.

Just as I was about to pick a lady's watch from the box, Mr K began to scribble on a pad and suddenly asked, "To whom shall I make the invoice?"

"Invoice?" *Shit!* I quickly dropped the watch I had chosen for my wife back into the box, panicking that I would have to pay for that, too.

There was nothing I could do. It would look embarrassing for not only me, but also my boss if I were to hand back the other watch, just because I now had to pay for it. I thought what have I done?

To save face, I surrendered and told Mr K reluctantly. Mr K and my boss looked at each other with a knowing smile. It was a set up.

I did what???

We were to hold our regional conference in Phuket. I'd organised it, and one of our worldwide directors was coming out from New York. He had never been to Asia before, and wanted to experience it first hand.

On the second evening about seven of us wandered out of our hotel to a beach bar, run by four splendid Filipino ladies. With us was one female client and P, our New York director. Well the ladies at the bar soon got the hang of the situation. The female client (who we didn't want with us) had hit the deck with presumably a spiked drink and had to be carried back to the hotel by one of the lads.

The rest of us continued to drink. The evening wore on, the music got louder, as did our shouting and singing. P in particular seemed to be enjoying himself. After going through the usual ritual of stripping to his underpants and dancing on the bar's beer cooler, he declared, "This is the best time I've ever had in my life and I never want it to stop. So I'm going to buy this bar."

He slammed his gold American Express card on the bar proclaiming his eternal love for the barmaids and how much he was going to enjoy being their boss.

Of course all of this was forgotten the next day, when he was nursing a rather stroppy hangover and dealing with a mysterious loss of clothing (long thrown into the sea). Forgotten, that is, until about a month later, when back in New York he received his American Express bill, which came to US$78,000. He then received by post some documents in Thai which subsequently turned out to be the lease for one year to some bar on some beach in Phuket, Thailand.

Corporate vision

We used to have an office in old Boat Quay, Singapore. We had heard it was haunted, but I thought nothing of it until one day when I heard a noise and looked up, and there she was...

The ghost was this middle aged Chinese lady, wearing traditional apparel. I saw her in really clear detail, momentarily, then with the blink of an eye, she was gone.

We nicknamed her Ethel, and we always felt her around. Whenever the office was in a mess we'd blame her.

Sometime later, I bumped into SR who used to be a tenant in the same building. I told him about my episode, and he too had seen her and described her in exact detail- hairstyle, clothes and all.

Power lunch

In Hong Kong for a trade show, R and J bumped into E, who they knew and also felt could help them in various business ways as he was very established and liked to give the impression of being a real power broker. So they invited him out to lunch.

"Sorry, guys, I'd love to, but I'm booked out all week," said E, citing some of the biggest names in the business that he'd be lunching with that week.

Rejected, the guys headed off down the road and came across a Wendy's burger joint. Walking in, who did they see in there...E!

He was sitting in a corner munching on a burger. Alone!

Wheel funny

DC was a bit of a prankster who worked for our company in a neighbouring country, so we invited him down to our office Christmas party. As the party (around a hotel pool) was about to start, there was no sign of him, and then...the grand entrance.

The doors opened, and a wheelchair was pushed in by a 'nurse'. In the wheelchair was a figure dressed in a Superman outfit, looking stricken and paralysed. They wheeled him to his table, where he said not one word for two hours, drinking through a bunch of straws joined together up to his lips.

At the end of the evening, we awarded him the best costume prize, the Christopher Reeves incident being fresh in everyone's mind at the time. As he was being pushed up to receive his prize, VD our managing director grabbed hold of the wheelchair and pushed it toward the pool.

The chair and a still motionless DC ended up in the water, where it sunk a little before resurfacing. Still no movement from him. The crowd erupted in applause and cheers for a very good, but sick, performance. The hotel was less than impressed the next day to get their wheelchair returned in a soggy waterlogged mess.

Foreign affairs

I had just completed a business trip in South Korea, which got out of hand a little in the expenses department...we spent an absolute fortune on dinner, drinks, karaoke and sundries.

On the plane home I was sweating, knowing I could not possibly claim all of this, yet I could not personally afford to pay the bill either.

Back in the office, I thought the best thing to do was to leave all the items in Korean Won currency (the bills themselves were all in Korean - no English description), let the accounts department do the conversion mathematics, and see what happened.

Being a director of the company, we didn't have to have our expenses signed off, but sure enough, I was summoned to explain this. "Mr A, you have lodged expenses for $800,000. How can this possibly be? Please explain," said the distraught finance manager.

When I explained that it was in fact *only 800,000 Korean Won*, she breathed a sigh of relief, had a nervous giggle and I heard nothing more on the subject.

HARDSHIP POSTING

He, she, it

We were holding our regional conference in Singapore one year and after a heavy dinner a bunch of regional managing directors and VIP's decided to trundle up to Club 14 (euphemism for a club in Orchard Road) for an after-dinner cleansing ale or two.

One of the VIP's was our President for North Asia based in Japan. M was particularly taken with one young lady at the club, who was strutting her stuff. In fact he couldn't take his eyes off her.

Whilst the others in the group were chatting away and getting drunker and drunker, M kept staring at this beauty on the dance floor. Eventually he summonsed up enough courage to go and ask her for a dance, to which (of course) she agreed. After a while, one of my colleagues dug me in the ribs and said, "Look at that girl M is dancing with, there's something not quite right about her."

I looked and for the first time recognized he was correct. "You're right," I said, "she is a bloke, a man!"

We all knew that M was an out-and-out homophobe, so were laughing about this, when one of our number thought that we'd better tell him. I went over to the dance floor and told him, but he shoved me aside, told me to get lost and that I was only jealous that he'd "got the only beauty in the place".

After a while another of our party went over to tell him the same thing, but got the same reaction. Then a third person from our group went and told him what we thought, but to no avail, he thought we were winding him up and told this person that he "was in love".

Finally our big boss, down from Paris, went up to M and told him that he also thought that perhaps he should be aware of what the "local boys" thought. Exasperated, M turned to all of us (he and his 'girl' were the only ones still dancing) and shouted at us all, "You're all just jealous and I'm going to prove to you that this young lady is female". At this point he grabbed the skirt of his dancing partner and lifted it right up to under 'her' armpits.

And there for the whole world to see was a glorious jockstrap bulging with male accoutrements and a falsie bra!

M turned white as a sheet and ran from the club to applause all around. The following morning, I had to be in early and arrived at our office just after 8.00am. On the steps outside sat M looking dejected. He looked at me sadly and said, "Please don't tell anyone".

Hirsute of excellence

Malaysia is known for its intolerance of long-haired individuals. S was the managing director of an advertising agency in Kuala Lumpur, which handled Telekom Malaysia as one of its major clients. He thought he was dead trendy with his greying ponytail tied back.

One day he received a letter from the client, on official letterhead voicing their concern about his personal grooming, and it was not a comfortable thing for a government body to be dealing with him. So, could he please cut his hair if he wished to retain the multi-million dollar business relationship?

He then noticed the date of the letter - April Fools Day!

Bum deal

R, C and I travelled to Subic Bay from Singapore on the insistence of our Manila office to attend a so-called important industry function.

After the first day, we realised we had wasted our time coming and wanted to depart, but could not as transport wasn't available until the event was over in two days time. Luckily we had bought 5 bottles of scotch at the airport. It would keep us busy at night and the place had a golf course, so we weren't bored during the day.

The first night we got stuck into the booze, getting pretty written off, and R passed out on an ice-covered bed. C and I decided to have a little fun with him. We filled a condom with toothpaste with the idea of sticking it up R's bum, so he would wake up the next day thinking either myself or C (who happened to be our boss) had rodgered him.

Luckily R was on his stomach so we had no problem getting his pants off with rear end facing up - not an attractive sight! C and I had an argument while standing over R on who was to do the stuffing. I end up looking away while my hands pushed R's buttocks apart while C fitted the rubber up his rear end. R in his sleep must have felt something wrong, and woke up.

The rather perplexed look of "what the f***?" on his face brings tears to my eyes whenever I think of this episode. After all, it's not every day you wake up to see your boss trying to shove something up your arse, with one of your senior colleagues helping him!

No show

L was to fly to New York for a conference. On arrival, he met a rather appealing American lass and spent the next 3 days solidly giving her a guided tour of his hotel room! He didn't manage to attend a single conference session, before flying home.

Terms of endearment

CB was on a business trip to Hong Kong. He called K, an old friend of his who had routinely spent nights on his couch in Singapore years before. But K was now filled with a sense of self-importance as managing director of a firm. He said he could not fit in any time for a beer or even a coffee.

As it happened, the other good friend CB had in Hong Kong worked at the same firm, so they arranged to meet at M's office and go for an early beer from there.

Waiting in reception, CB saw his killjoy friend K coming out of the conference room with a bunch of very serious Japanese clients, whom he's obviously hell-bent on impressing. He vaguely acknowledges CB's presence.

At the same time, M came down to reception and yelled out: "Oy, CB, YOU F***ING C***!" across the foyer at him.

Needless to say, K was not impressed.

If you have a good story about office or corporate goings on in Asia, let us know. Email us at **hardship_posting@hotmail.com** *or fax The Editor at 612-9499-5908.*

14

"Red tape treatment"
True stories of battles with Immigration,
Customs, and other officialdom.

My good friend, the ever-cynical and paranoid Pete the Pony-tailed Portrait Photographer, once said there was nothing more dangerous than an Asian with a rule-book.

But I think all these officials are wonderful people doing a very admirable job.

(Any notions I said that just to appease the publisher's lawyers are absolutely false.)

Well, that was easy. Now I can have a nap even before my regular scheduled morning nap.

Colonel Ken

Rolling stones gather no animosity

We were all descending on Ho Chi Minh City for a farewell party. It had been planned well ahead, so we were all sorted for visas, and looking forward to 3 days on the piss in Vietnam.

HCM airport is still a relic from the war...old hangars and dark...with thousands of people queuing everywhere, but all the signs were in squiggly Vietnamese. Which queue to join? We eventually chose one, for no particular reason, and stood in it for 45 minutes before getting to the front. The Immigration guy asked for the 7 forms we had filled out on the plane, plus the photo and form 8, which nobody had.

We were sent to a little area on the side where for US$2, we had our Polaroids taken and then had to re-queue. A nice little revenue earner.

Getting to the front of the line again, I got straight through, but my buddie NF got stopped - no visa. "F*** this," he said. "I'd rather be in

Bangkok anyway." He explained to the officer that the hotel had said they would sort it out for him. He was not allowed to call the hotel.

I volunteered to call the hotel once I was through. As N was obviously in for a bit of a wait, I passed him a Rolling Stone magazine to read.

I got through, and explained to the others that N had a bit of a visa problem. We decided to call the hotel but then to leave ahead of him, as he could be hours anyway. Just then, we see N striding through the Immigration, beaming triumphantly.

"How did you get through?" we enquired incredulously.

"Went up to the front of the queue and offered them the Rolling Stone, of course," he winked.

His visa was stamped on the spot!

www.hardshipposting.com

Smelling as-saults

A group of young and enthusiastic expats left Hong Kong early on a Saturday morning ferry to Macau. After arriving at Macau, approximately 4 or 5 cans away, we were picked up in a couple of Mercedes limousines to cross the border into China to the golf resort.

At the Chinese immigration, I filled in a form stating my most prized possessions, an el cheapo walkman, a six pack for the road, and so forth. The immigration guy gave back my passport all duly stamped, but without a precious piece of paper...

Returning to cross the border from China back into Macau, the immigration fellow asked for that dreaded piece of paper that should have been with my passport. Well, when in doubt, behave *ignorant* (this is something that comes all too naturally). That didn't work- his face got sterner and blacker, and I was thinking he was such a tiresome bore.

He kept asking for that piece of paper and I kept telling him that his fellow officer did not give it back to me. Wrong excuse!!! This made him all the more officious. Time to try another tack.

"It's back at the hotel."

"Which room?"

Difficult question after a whole weekend's destruction of the brain cells. I made up a room number hoping he would not call the hotel to check. He made me sign a form to that effect. He then told me to wait, and went away to talk to another officer. In the meantime a fellow traveller from our alcoholic golf tour who had already been cleared through Customs & Immigration held up and waved his British passport.

"You need a *real* passport," he yelled, in typical smug British fashion.

Now me, with an itsy bitsy antipodean passport, was ducking for cover at this point. *For goodness sake don't give this officer another excuse to get so excitable.*

Then the officer came back and asked me to open my weekend bag. Well this bag had all my weekend clothes from playing golf in an incredibly hot and humid locality. The clothing absolutely reeked of natural eau de cologne, stale beer odours, and of course, alcohol and bad-Chinese-food-induced farts. My bag probably weighed another 2-3 kgs from how much they were drenched with sweat.

I just gave the bag to him, not risking to open it myself. He opened it and stuck his hand right into the middle of my clothing- then the barrage of *gweilo* smells hit him. The expression on his face was priceless. No words can describe the look of disgust while he was trying not to pass out from the intoxicating *gweilo* fumes.

He pushed the bag back to me immediately and told me to hurry through, as he quickly handed back my passport.

Dirty old...dad

We arrived at immigration at Bali airport- my two pre-teen boys (both Caucasian) and my petite Chinese girlfriend who was wearing a baseball cap.

We queued up, and when we got to the front the boys were quite boisterous. Even though I had put three British and one non-British passport on his desk, the officer looked at me and said, irritably, "You stay here (in front of the desk) - your three children, they go through!"

Rugby Mild 7's

Japan, 1985, at Narita airport a plane had landed with a load of visiting Rugby players from Hong Kong. They were to play a University side in Tokyo and then visit Kobe (my home in Japan at the time) the following week to play Kobe Seiko.

They began to file through immigration, and one young player had lost his passport and another for some reason had no visa. How did they depart from Hong Kong? Nobody seemed to know.

I was one of the welcoming committee and standing at the end of customs I was informed of the mishap and the instructions that both lads must depart Narita on the next flight out. They were both key members and I thought it would be a shame not to try to test the system.

I had already been living in Japan for five years, and had learnt enough Japanese to be referred to as "henna gaijin"...strange foreigner! I had also been able to master the Japanese art of talking all round the subject, patience, and trying to find a compromise or two. I also acknowledged the Japanese appreciation and respect for authority, people in 'high places' and the importance of position and names, etc. Finally I also realised the admiration most Japanese had for the game and its players.

I managed to convince the airport authorities it was important that we try to assist these famous gentlemen from Oxford University but coming from Hong Kong- most were HK policeman! We had an initial four hour meeting with more than twenty various immigration officials coming and going, about twenty packets of Mild Seven cigarettes were consumed, and more when a few duty-free B&H's were handed out by one of the Hong Hong officials on tour. A copious quantity of green tea was also slurped. Rugby was discussed, and more rugby. The Japanese listening skills were honed and I explained the importance of the tour. Namely to boost the sales of Kirin beer, eat lots of sushi and to entertain the lovely young Japanese ladies who adored the game of Rugby.

Finally a solution and decision started to emerge after six hours. The first break came after a call from the Chairman from Kobe Steel. His call helped convince the officials some 'special treatment' would be appreciated. A second call from the host's Tokyo Hotel whose President was an ex Japanese national player (and very well connected) started an interesting compromise to the situation...

On condition a new passport was issued from the lad's Consulate the next morning in Tokyo he could remain in Japan to play the games. He would then, after receiving a valid passport, come back to the airport to have the passport stamped. The lad without visa was given a temporary stay visa for the period of the tour.

That was harder than any game of rugby I have ever played.

Inside job

When I first came to work in Thailand about 15 years ago, getting a work permit and long-term visa was a nightmare. Typically it took about 3 months to get approvals. Like most newcomers, I worked during the approval process - technically against the law, but the authorities, knowing that it was their system at fault, generally turned a blind eye to the practice.

Unfortunately I was the exception. Somebody shopped me. The international company I worked for had just taken over a local company and a few feathers had been ruffled. One Friday afternoon, a couple of Labour Department officials turned up in the office and asked me to accompany them the local police station.

I telephoned our company lawyer who told me that there was nothing to worry about. Easy for him to say! He told me to go with the officers to the police station and said he would send his assistant with cash to pay bail. He added that "under no circumstances" should I allow the police to put me in the station lock-up because, being a Friday afternoon, he probably would not be able to get me released until Monday morning. He emphasised a weekend in the police station lock-up could be very unpleasant.

At the police station, after making a statement confessing my "crime", I was charged, fingerprinted and photographed. What would my Mum say? I was to be released on 50,000 Baht bail. Fortunately my lawyer's assistant had just arrived with the cash. It was at this point the head police honcho announced that, as a formality, I had to be put in the lock-up before I could be released on bail. The logic of this escaped me but my main concern at the time was my lawyer's advice and warning.

I said the first thing that came into my head: "Is your gaol air-conditioned?" The policeman looked at me like I was an idiot. "No", he said. "Then I don't want to go in," I said with a straight face.

Realising this was some kind of *farang* joke, the policeman added, "And we have a lot of mosquitoes too". "In that case I definitely don't want to go in," I said.

Now smiling, the policeman said, "OK, this time *mai pen rai* ('forget it') but next time you must go in". Lovely people, the Thais.

Footnote: Eventually the case came to court and I was fined 50,000 Baht.

Life in the fast lane

The queues at Jakarta's international airport are notorious. However there was a quicker solution.

At Arrivals, there was an Immigration Office to the right of the long incoming lanes.

The trick was to slip $10 into your passport, and go up to the office and say, "I think I have a problem with my visa, Sir." The officer would open your passport, pocket the bucks, stamp you in, and you were on your merry way, much to the annoyance of those still standing in line!

Hold that plane

We were doing a lot of business in Sri Lanka, and the locals loved taking us to watering holes to relax at the end of the business day.

The head of the guys we dealt with was very connected, and one of his main drinking buddies, whom I got to know very well, was one of the heads of the Customs Department.

One night, we'd had a rather enjoyable meal and more than enough drinks, but I had an eye on my watch as I had a plane to catch.

"Why are you worried about time?" they enquired. "This is Sri Lanka."

"My plane leaves in less than 2 hours," I explained.

"Don't worry," said the Customs head. "No plane leaves this island without my personal blessing."

He then called the airport and directed the plane to be held until I arrived. He also instructed them to give me red carpet treatment at the airport.

"Now have one more for the road," he ordered.

Coming or going?

One of the popular pastimes in Singapore is to drive up to Malaysia for lunch on a Sunday. One weekend, we checked out of Singapore and drove over the Causeway to find long jams at the Malaysian entry points.

Except for the bus lanes.

So, naturally, I scooted up the bus lane. First stop was a window to collect a $1 toll. Paid. Next window was Immigration proper. "You're not a bus," the officer acutely observed. "Er, no, but...," I tried to explain in vain.

"You cannot enter here," he sternly admonished us. "I will keep your passports, now you must make a U-turn up ahead and come back out again," he explained.

Now we were in Malaysia, driving around Johor Bahru without passports, toying with the idea of going for lunch first anyway as we were already here. However, we decided we had better play by the rules, went round the big roundabout and returned to the outbound Immigration lane.

"Passports please," asked the Officer. A lengthy explanation then ensued about how we didn't actually have our passports, and the other officer was summoned. We eventually located him and our passports, which were returned and we were waved through. Phew!

Going back into Singapore, the Officer looked at our passport, furrowed his brow and asked:

"Which way are you going?" We said we had just left Malaysia and were now coming back into Singapore.

"No, no," he corrected us. "You have left Singapore but have not entered Malaysia yet." We told him of our ordeal. He then directed us to turn around and to get stamped out of Malaysia first, which we hadn't been because we hadn't officially entered.

Deciding it was too hard, we parked the car in Woodlands (the Singapore side) and walked over the bridge with our passports. When we got to the other side, the four of us lined up as if we were sitting in a car and, with the appropriate steering wheel movements and car sound effects, pulled up to the car entry lane.

A bemused Malaysian officer stamped us in, we then chugged over to the exit lane, got stamped out, then back to Singapore, where everything was fine this time.

So much for saving a bit of time by going into the bus lane!

Taxing my patience

In leaving Hong Kong, the admin department at work informed Immigration of my imminent departure as they were required to do. Not long after, I received a tax assessment form to complete and submit ASAP.

I dilly-dallied a little with the computations, and a couple of days later another one arrived - filled in by the tax department. Good news...their assessment was a lot lower than mine, so I hurriedly wrote out a cheque and sent it to them via my office despatch guy.

Getting home that evening, a slip of paper awaited me under my door. It was a notice from Immigration saying that I was barred from exiting Hong Kong until my tax matters were cleared up.

First thing next day I called them - they had not received my payment. I grilled the despatch guy. Yes he had delivered it to ground floor reception.

Back on the phone to the tax officer I advised them I had paid. "It's in your building somewhere, that makes it *your* problem," I said a little foolishly.

"We suggest you come down and make payment immediately in person," the officer instructed.

I was fuming. I went to meet the officer and repeated the story, hoping that by the time I was there my original cheque would have turned up. It hadn't. They requested a cash payment of HK$40,000.

I patted my pockets. I did not make a habit of carrying 40,000 dollars around with me. As the scene escalated (with my voice reverberating wonderfully in the crowded lobby area) they eventually backed down and agreed to accept cheque payment. They issued a receipt and I was out of there, much poorer in many ways for the experience.

Playing the blues

A mate of mine used to play in a jamming band in various pubs around Bangkok. When he moved to Singapore, we jumped at the chance to play together, and set about forming a band.

About a year later, I left due to increasing travel and work commitments, but the guys continued playing the pubs and clubs, with a mixture of expats and locals in the band.

One night down at Boat Quay, the pub was raided, and M was busted in a real shit sandwich... performing in contravention to his employment pass conditions. If you are performing for money, it apparently becomes an Immigration issue. If you're just playing for fun and beer, it apparently becomes a CID issue.

Well, M had a tough job pleading his case, and eventually his multinational company employer had to weigh in to get him off the hook and keep him in the country.

That really had him singing the blues. It was not long after however, that the rules on 'jamming' were relaxed and he can now rock to his heart's content after hours.

Green card, red faces

Life as an expat revolves around your green card, employment pass or whatever piece of paper is necessary to allow you residency in a particular country.

Leaving one company, with an uncertain future, I had negotiated with my ex-employer to keep the permit open for the time being (ie, not to notify Immigration) whilst I sorted out my options. They were reluctanctly agreeable, and we shook on this understanding.

Imagine my surprise then when I had a new passport issued, and went to get my permit and visa transferred across to the new passport.

"According to our records, you have overstayed by eighteen months, a very serious offence," said the duty officer.

"Impossible," I countered. "I have been in and out so many times, it's not like I've been hiding from you." I continued to explain that if my permit had already been cancelled 18 months prior, how come I was very publicly serving on all manner of committees, had permits and licenses issued to operate certain financial services (which required rigorous screening processes) and so on. The official looked a bit red-faced and sheepish. I decided to go on the front foot.

" I thought this country was very advanced," I continued. "I thought you had all the latest technology, and everything was databased, and all your government departments were cross-linked..."

He immediately backed down, and issued the new 3 year visa there and then. "Please don't tell anyone," he said.

Permission to leave

I had resigned from my job in Hong Kong and was due to leave the country so I had to go and do the clearance rounds at immigration, tax department, etc.

At Immigration, the officious officer noted that my Visa had actually expired a week earlier. I said that as I was leaving anyway, I didn't see the point in renewing. Wrong answer!

With that, he made me take a ticket to queue for an application for renewal of Visa. When my number was called, the officer asked how long I intended to stay.

"Actually I want to leave," I explained. He was a bit confused by this.

"I'm trying to leave Hong Kong but they said I must renew my visa in order to leave."

"So how long do you want?" he reiterated.

"I'm leaving tomorrow."

"No. Minimum is 3 months for work permit," he explained.

"Ok, give me 3 months."

"Ok, give me HK$165," he said in that polite Hong Kong official fashion.

I very gladly left the next day.

If you have a good story about dealing with officialdom and red tape in Asia, let us know. Email us at **hardship_posting@hotmail.com** *or fax The Editor at 612-9499-5908.*

"The finest money can buy."
True tales of dealing with Police and Traffic Police.

Expats and foreigners falling foul of the law in Asia are not a new thing according to my mate Dave. Somerset Maugham's story, The Letter, was based on a true case in Malaya in 1911 when Ethel Proudlock shot a planter, William Steward. She was sentenced to the gallows, but later pardoned by the Sultan of Selangor and sailed on the first ship to England.

And Barlow and Chambers certainly learned their lesson in Malaysia years ago- they'll never traffic drugs again. Nor will the hundreds of other more anonymous cases languishing in the region's salubrious penitentiaries on drugs charges.

A man of my integrity and standing, of course, has had no dealings with the Police, nor indeed wishes to. It just eats into my drinking time all that bureaucratic kerfuffle. And I'd much sooner spend my money on gin and tonics than parking fines.

There again, I wouldn't mind getting into a bit of trouble with those lady policewomen on scooters...you know the ones...the reflective sunglasses, the real S&M blue tights disappearing into knee-length black boots, and perfectly tailored white tunic tops that make their batons and handcuffs on their black belt standout. Makes *my* baton stand out, that's for sure. *Oh yes, officer, I've been a naughty naughty boy. I changed lane without using my indicator...use the nightstick, handcuff me, call me names.*

The problem with that scenario is that changing lanes without using your indicator - or your rear vision mirror - is pretty much compulsory on the roads of Asia.

But overall, my friends, it does not pay to mess around with the boys (and girls) in blue, or brown as they wear in Thailand and Indonesia. You've heard of good cop / bad cop combinations...well these guys often have bad cop / worse cop combinations. And those soaring peaked caps they wear just add to the draconian spectre. Designed by Hitler's own couturier, I've heard, and now widely available from second hand stores throughout Russia.

But you do get a bit of levity...the famous singing traffic cop in Manila is a classic, waving his arms around furiously as he directs the traffic. And I find it endlessly funny (albeit ironic) that in The Philippines so many gunfights are caused by macho off-duty policemen and soldiers enjoying a drink after work...with their weapons! *Sorry, Sir, you'll have to leave the grenade launcher outside. M16s are fine but we can't allow grenade launchers at happy hour. And your friend will have to park his tank outside as well.* Funny, that is, till you're looking down the wrong end of the barrel. Because the only barrel I like to stare down is one full of beer.

But where they should bring in the tanks is for little pricks like that guy, Michael Fay. A right little monster he was apparently. Fancy spray-painting graffiti on all those cars...doesn't he know that's what train carriages are for? A classic case of living out of America for too long.

And the only bank Nick Leeson will be breaking from now on is his own piggy bank ...and I hear it's quite a full little piggy bank, too.

As I can't think of a good way to wrap up this little section, I'll leave you with a little pearl of wisdom from my good friend, Confucius. He say: "If you use laws to direct people and punishments to control them, they will only evade the laws and develop no conscience."

Talking of punishment, I've just had a great idea. Lolita - bring Sir's handcuffs please.

Colonel Ken

Should be banned

These guys were in Jakarta for business on a Friday, and decided to go down with the guys from the local office to Anchol, a resort area down south, for the weekend.

Hopping into the ubiquitous Kijang jeep with tinted windows, they set off merrily, cracking a few beers as they went.

Nearing the resort, they noticed the incredible amount of traffic on the road south, putting it down to people escaping for the weekend. This seemed plausible until they noticed hundreds of people walking on the footpaths, and then - a roadblock up ahead.

"Shit, now I remember. It's that Air Supply concert on this weekend," said CF. He told the driver to keep going, until stopped by a soldier with machine gun at the road-block.

"Cannot pass here. Must park," ordered the soldier.

"Um,... band," explained CF, thinking quick. "Band in back."

With that, the guard peered disbelievingly in the window to see two guys, one big and blonde the other sort of darkish, in the backseat. They broke out into an ear-piercing chorus of "I'm All Out Of Love," the Air Supply song. The guard called out to his colleagues, looked at his watch and said: "Very early."

Oh shit! Now we're done for.

The guard nodded, and waved them on, as barricades were moved aside for them. They drove, pissing themselves with laughter, and parked

www.hardshipposting.com

beside the stage where there was a pool hall, dreading to think what was going to happen when the *real* band turned up.

Air Supply were actually held up at the gate - told the band had already arrived- and had to wait while papers were checked, etc. The concert started almost 1 1/2 hours late, almost causing the restless Indonesian crowd to riot!

License - what license?

I had lived and worked in Singapore for more than four years when I finally crossed paths with the law, an experience I don't care to repeat. I had just pulled out from my office and was turning onto the main road when a 'robocop' (the little white clad ones on the white scooters) pulled up beside me at the light. She looked at me and I nodded at her with a smile.

She signalled for me to pull over when we crossed the intersection. I was driving without a seatbelt, she informed me. She also discovered that I was driving without a valid license. I had never bothered to get a Singapore license on the advice of some friends who said it was better not to have one. Bad advice guys.

First, I had to explain what I'd been doing driving here for four years without a valid Singapore license. Then we turned our attention to my Canadian license, where we soon discovered it had expired - just two days prior on my birthday. I thought she was going to crucify me, but instead found her to be very polite - almost friendly - dare I say, flirtatious? I was sure I had this thing under control as she handed me my particulars back. No fault, no foul.

All ready to jump back in the car and thanking her for her understanding, I promised to go straight to the traffic police station nearby and get my license sorted out. She agreed that that was indeed the course of action, but informed me that I'd have to do it on foot - she was impounding the car. I argued and pleaded, finally getting her to agree to my business partner walking down from the office to take over driving duties. Relieved, I got my butt over to the cop shop straight away and found they were quite helpful in getting me suited up with a brand spanking new Drivers License. I found out about one month later why.

I was served notice by mail that I was to meet with a Sergeant 'something-or-other' on such and such a date (and don't be late). I knew it was related to the license thing, but had no idea what was in store for me.

Upon arriving at the station, they made me wait outdoors for about a half-hour in the sweltering heat. By the time I got in to see the case officer, I was a dripping, sweaty mess. I was not in a good mood at that point and decided to tell her they really should do something about the poor conditions around there. She listened politely, asked me if I had anything else I wanted to suggest. Then she proceeded to throw the book at me, listing one charge after another.

By the time she'd finished, I was out of pocket over $300 and had several demerit points to go along with my shiny new Singapore license!

Give him some credit

CF was pulled over for speeding in the outskirts of Jakarta. When the officer came over to book him, he acted all indignant.

"What the hell," he said, "I was chasing someone, now they get away," he explained to the Police Officer. "Me Interpol," he explained. With that he pulled out his wallet, and flashed his "police badge".

What the officer did not know was that this badge was nothing more than a plastic card issued to members of the Sydney Police Club gymnasium, where he occasionally worked out. But it did have the New South Wales Police logo on it, at least.

"You imbecile...wait till Central hears about this. What is your name?" he continued his offensive rant.

The Police officer apologised profusely, and offered him an escort into town to help with 'the chase'. With that, the Policeman remounted his bike, lights flashing, siren wailing and CF followed him at top speed, waiting for an opportune moment to turn off and disappear from sight.

Hard-headed

It had been a big night. Started off at a pub in River Valley Road, then moved on to Anywhere in Tanglin Rd. By the end I was hopelessly smashed, and did the right thing - caught a cab... back to the pub where I had parked my motorbike at the start of the evening!

Getting on the bike, I notice that my helmets have been stolen from the d-ring I usually locked them on. Full of Dutch courage, I decided to ride home anyway, and roared off up the road. I made sure I had some Polo mints in my pocket in case I got pulled over by the cops.

Along the way, several cars hooted and indicated that I didn't have a helmet on. "Get a life!" I yelled back.

Coming up to Alexandria Rd, the lights turned red. A Police van went through the intersection, but thankfully continued going. I breathed a sigh of relief - until I noticed a Police car on the other side of the intersection. As the lights turned green, he turned his red and blues on, and pulled me over.

I was so pissed, I forgot completely about the mints, and walked over to their car.

"Good evening Sir, you have no helmet," said one of two officers. I related the story of how it was stolen. "I'm the first to agree with your excellent helmet laws," I grovelled, "but if I had left my bike there, maybe they would've stolen that too."

The second officer went to the bike, taking the keys out of the ignition. "Your bike?"

Yes, I slurred. "What's your phone number?" he asked looking at the back of the keychain. I rattled it off. "Drivers license?"

I patted my pockets. "Er, that must be at home, I think," I said, knowing full well I never possessed a license to ride *any* bike in *any* country.

"Registration papers?" the officer continued.

The bike's registration had long since expired.

"Insurance papers?" he probed.

"Yes, everything all together in my file at home," I bullshitted.

"Where do you live?"

"Oh, just here. Very close, that's why I think it should be Ok to ride," I said.

"Where?"

"Pasir Panjang," I conceded, a good 15 minutes up the road.

The officers conferred for a while, shaking their heads. I thought I was doomed.

"Ok, you leave your bike here, and take taxi home," they finally said.

I think this case of the expat pissed out of his mind, with no helmet, no license, no registration and no insurance was just too much for them to deal with.

Unhappy Valley

We had been drinking copiously at Joe Banana's in Hong Kong, and decided it would be a great idea to ride to our boss's place up behind Happy Valley to have a few nightcaps with him, and perhaps have a few smokes on his bong as well. As you do.

We roared off on our bikes around Wanchai, then onto the road passing Causeway Bay. We rounded a corner at breakneck speed, only to find a Police Officer standing next to his bike at an intersection. We sped up to evade him in case he decided to come after us. At the Happy Valley exit we planned to take, there were temporary barricades blocking the side road.

We stopped briefly to discuss the situation, then thought *what the hell*, and eased our bikes through the barricades, looking behind us for the bike copper, before roaring off down the exit road.

Our smugness was shortlived for, at the bottom, the lights were red. Not only were they red, they stayed red, and the intersection was crawling with Traffic Police. It was horse race night at Happy Valley!

An officer came over to us to enquire what the f*** we thought we were doing. Trying to contain the alcohol fumes in our helmets, we explained that we lived "just here" in these apartments and we didn't know any other way of getting to them. Besides, we bullshitted, the officer at the top of the exit had given us special permission to come down.

A look of disbelief came across his face, and we were shitting ourselves as we knew that any minute now the original bike cop would be onto us from behind, compounding our sins.

After a bit of a conference, he came across and waved us through and on our way. We roared off in a cloud of blue smoke and alcohol fumes.

Breadbasket

Coming round the back of the big tourist lake and volcano in Bali in a minibus, we saw a couple of Policemen in a farm lane stopping vehicles.

The truck in front of us had baskets of fruit on it. As it drove through, the policeman helped himself to a handful of fruit. We were next.

"Don't look," said our guide as the driver stepped out. He went behind the bus and forked over US$5 to the Police, then we were on our way again.

"Much worse before Soeharto riots," he said. "Every intersection have this. Can cost you $25 just to go across town one day."

Chain reaction

I had probably received reminders in the mail to the effect that I had not paid my road tax, and then got a phone call requesting my presence at the Department of Motor Vehicles.

It was a bit inconvenient, but I thought I may as well get it over and done with early in the morning before coming to work...

Arriving at the department I was directed upstairs to The Enforcement Division. It transpired that I could no longer pay a fine and compound the case - I had to go to court! I couldn't believe it. "I'm supposed to handcuff you as you are under arrest," said the officer, "but never mind, we just put you in the back of the van." Now I really couldn't believe it.

Next thing, we arrived at the downtown subordinate court. I was taken downstairs to the holding cells. I was quite violently frisked as I entered, and was taken into an empty cell where the door was slammed behind me. There were traces where someone had taken a dump in the corner. The other local inmates looked at me like a tourist attraction from their cells. Fortunately I had a Newsweek magazine with me, and read this while I waited.

I heard my name being called, and was pulled out of the cell and daisy-chained with two other 'prisoners' and frog-marched upstairs into the court. God knows what their offences were.

The court session started. They won, I lost. I paid a several-thousand dollar fine, and walked out the back into daylight. Like a very bad dream.

Reverse racism

To get into my friend's driveway, right on a t-intersection, we had to turn into the street opposite, and back into his garage. One day, as we were preparing to reverse into the garage, a car came up behind us. My friend, who was driving, signalled it to pass with a hand motion out the window. The car stayed put, but started honking its horn. My friend again signalled for it to pass.

Eventually the car went around us, honking, gesticulating and unimpressed, and parked a few doors up. My friend parked his car, and ran up to the house where the people had parked.

"Excuse me!" he shouted. They almost jumped out of their skin. "What exactly is your problem?" he demanded.

"Don't trespass on my property," said the driver, a local gent.

"White pig...white pig," taunted his ugly wife from behind the car.

My friend delivered a short sharp lecture on courtesy, and left.

Half an hour later, there was a knock on our door. It was the police, and behind them, 'the couple'. "That's the one," said the ugly wife. We had to explain our side of the story to the two cops, and how difficult it was to enter and exit this driveway. When we mentioned we were racially taunted and branded "white pigs," the tables turned. Eventually, the cops made them apologise to us, and the matter was settled.

The cops then got into their car, reversed and took out the opposite railing in the process. Poetic justice!

Soft cell

JL had a big night and ended up face-down on the sidewalk of Orchard Rd. It wasn't long before he was bundled off to the Tanglin Police station, where they put him in a cell overnight. He was in good hands, though.

The next morning, the kind and polite officers explained it was for his own good, popped across the road to fetch him a breakfast of Delifrance coffee and croissants, and let him go.

One way ticket

We were returning to Kuta / Legiaan one evening, and were hopelessly lost. However, as we had just passed a bunch of Police on traffic duty, thought we'd do a U-turn and get directions from them.

As it was only a dirt road (albeit a very busy one) I turned around, and went against the traffic up to the Police post.

"Which way to Kuta?" I innocently enquired.

"You go wrong way. This one way street," barked the Nazi-like Indonesian police officer. I tried to explain that I was coming to him specifically for help.

"You no do this your country. Why you do this our country?" he continued, asking for my license. I handed him my Australian license.

"This no international license," he barked.

"Sure it is...I've used it all over Asia," I added a touch arrogantly.

He then asked for registration papers, which I didn't have as it was a rented vehicle. He shakes his head once again, implying I'm in big trouble this time.

"Is there any other way to settle this?" I enquired, subtly opening my wallet, hoping to see a tell-tale flicker of forgiveness in his eyes. Nothing. I quickly put my wallet away in case he decided to bust me for bribery as well (knowing my luck!)

He then took my license, studied it further under the headlights, and said: "I keep. My name Amin. You come see me 11pm tonight Police Station."

Bollocks to that, I thought as I drove off (he still hadn't given me directions yet!) A little closer to Legiaan I pulled into the Police Station, and explained to the Officer that this Amin bloke had kept my license and invited me to a private audience later.

A series of radio calls were made, lots of high-pitched indecipherable Bahasa exchanged and half an hour later, a guy on a motorbike arrived with my license. I was then ushered into an office in a scene which reminded me of Mexican jail scenes in B grade westerns.

Four policemen came into the room and stood behind me, while the officer positioned his heavy old manual typewriter on the desk in front of me, and scrolled his paper into position. He banged away on it, before pulling it out for me to read.

"Very serious. 3 offences," he says. "Wrong way up one-way street. No license. No registration papers. This very wrong." The officers behind murmur in agreement.

"How to make right?" I said. I try to plead my innocence, but they were not buying it. "Must come to Denpasar Court Saturday morning," the officer adds. I then explained that would be a little tricky as I would be flying out on Friday.

"Oh, then you pay the fine now, and I represent you in court," he said, at which point I realised which game he was playing.

"How much the fine?" I said.

"How much you have?" he countered.

He passed up on my playful gesture of a few new cassettes I had in my bag (obviously he wasn't a Bob Marley fan) before we settled on US$20. I paid him the money, and he passed me the typewritten sheet, all in Bahasa language, to sign.

"No way, I don't know what I'm signing for," I protested.

"Ok, nevermind," he said, and we bid each other a fond farewell, with all the officers beaming at the proceeds of the evening's little windfall.

Back at the hotel, I met my brother who had just been stopped in likewise fashion but got away with only US$10. Darn!

Trap for young players

Before the new North-South Highway was put in, the drive from Singapore to Kuala Lumpur was full of hazards...everything from logging trucks, busses on the wrong side of the road, errant chickens, but worst of all, Malaysian traffic cops.

This guy was stopped by a copper, who didn't seem to have any radar equipment, and told he was doing 145km.

"This is a spot fine of 300 Ringgit," the Policeman said. In the old days, this was a lot of money. "Three hundred? Are you sure?" my friend said, trying to bring it down to something a little more reasonable. But the officer was firm.

"Ok, I'll pay you 300," the driver said. "But this is a company car, so you must give me a receipt."

"Ok, 50 Ringgit," said the officer, pocketing the note and waving him on.

HARDSHIP POSTING

Long finger of the law

An English friend of mine, G, was driving along in Singapore one day, when this idiot cut him right off, narrowly missing his fender.

Obviously he reacted in the usual appropriate manner, gesticulating wildly and yelling. At the lights he pulled up next to local guy who had cut him off, and the verbal altercation continued with the Chinese bloke coming across and asking why my friend was making rude gestures at him.

"I will report you to the Police," the local guy ranted.

"Go ahead," said my friend, telling him his license number and name, certain that it was all bluff and bluster.

Sure enough, he was reported and charged for the use of a rude gesture, known in most circles as 'giving him the finger' or 'flipping the bird'. He had to go to the station and through the formalities. He told the officer this was a complete waste of time and effort. The officer agreed, but had to go through the formalities as a report was lodged.

Surprisingly, though, the case went further and he was expected to go to court to defend this charge. He asked for an explanation of the offending gesture he was being charged with. Extending the middle finger in a universally rude manner, he was told.

"But I don't know what that symbol is," he protested not very convincingly. "I'm English...if I'm going to offend somebody I would hold up 2 fingers in a V position."

Upon further interrogation, the local guy was then unsure of exactly what motion he had actually seen transpire. Case dismissed.

Red light, red tape

I had been zapped by a red light camera, and the summons indicated that it was a $150 dollar fine, 6 demerit points and I had to settle this personally down at the Traffic Police headquarters.

Queuing up with my cheque book to pay, I was asked if I had a current license. "If you don't have a license, then we cannot accept payment," said the bureaucrat behind the counter.

"Suits me fine if you don't want the money," I said.

"No, first you must go down the hall here and apply," she said.

The lady down the corridor explained that first I must get a license, then 6 points would be deducted. "Bad deal," I said.

She asked for my current international license - I produced my currently valid Australian license. "No, we must see your license that was valid when you first entered the country," she explained. "But I've been here about 5 years," I said. "I probably threw the old license away."

"Then you must get a transcript from your Motor Authority," she said, "proving that you had a valid license when you first came to Singapore."

"Ok," I added, reluctant to play international paper-chases, "but it might take some time: our government is a little bit like your department...very slow!"

Naturally, I never applied for the transcript, got the local license, nor paid the $150.

Sticky situation

K was an East Malaysian who carried an Aussie passport. One day he was coming in to Singapore, and was stopped by Customs. A quick inspection of his bag revealed some firecrackers and chewing gum. He ended up in the cells for 8 hours before being bailed out the next morning.

Do you take credit card?

I was visiting friends who lived in Kuala Lumpur, and was being driven around and shown the sights by his wife when we were stopped by a traffic policeman.

Although I wasn't driving, I was asked to get out of the car and follow the officer. He demanded a 'fine' of US$100 for some infringement we had allegedly committed.

Having just arrived in the country, and being a little naïve, I said I had no cash but could I pay in traveller's cheque. In frustration he told me to get back in the car and waved us on!

Gamekeeper turned poacher

I was in a bad part of Jakarta, the night before Ramadan, when I was pulled over. My local lady companion went hysterical when the cops got out their guns and asked for money.

I gave them the normal 'avoid the traffic fine' amount which was around Rp50,000 in those days (1982). But in this case (when everyone needs money for the holiday and my wallet is stuffed with cash) the big fat cop stuck his gun in my window and demanded my wallet.

My Bahasa was OK then, but it was difficult to hear with this young lady screaming and sobbing in my ear. Anyway, I gave him my wallet. He took all my cash and threw the wallet back in the car and told me to drive off.

Now who do you go and see when you get robbed by the cops?

If you have a good story about Police or Traffic Police in Asia let us know. Email us at hardship_posting@hotmail.com *or fax The Editor at 612- 9499-5908*

"Are you being serviced?"

*True stories about retail experiences
in shopper's paradise.*

I actually know diddly-squat about this whole retail thing, except for the feeling I get sometimes that places like Hong Kong and Singapore are just giant supermarkets and the cars are like trolleys trundling their way down their aisles.

Luckily, it was Dave to the rescue again. He's got a whole study, and several boxes under the stairs, full of books on Asian history. And for a jug of marguerita he let me into a few secrets. (A steal I thought.)

Asia was born on the back of retailing, although it probably wasn't called that back then. The Diaspora of Chinese traders spread in search of markets for their goods. Typically they went to wherever there were trading ports, with tin trunks full of goods. Some of Asia's biggest retail dynasties were started in this humble fashion. The service levels of many remains about the same, but not as personal. That's what I really, really hate. Still, there's a few little cuties in amongst them.

And Asia developed a wonderful reputation for being the shoppers' paradise. All manner of fabrics, jewels, trinkets, spices, cheap shaving kits - and the 24-hour suit. The 24-hour suit, for the uninitiated, is how long it lasts, not how long they take to make it. Travellers be warned.

I was in a Hong Kong tailor shop just last week, which I last visited about 20 years ago, and recognised the guy behind the counter even though he looked a lot older and decrepit, whereas I had stayed much the same - instead of being young and handsome I am now middle-aged and handsome. (Some people say I'm in denial but I've never been to Egypt.) Anyway, I said to him, "Can you make a suit one with one arm slightly shorter, a crotch that rips at the seam within a week and two legs of different material?" He replied, "Yes, of course, but why would you want that, Sir?" "Because that's how you made the last one, dickhead!" I said, and stormed out.

And Barry reliably informs me (well, as reliable as Barry can be) that there are also the pirated goods, "copies" as they are affectionately known, and "after midnight" merchandise. After midnight in this case doesn't refer to when they are sold; it refers to when they are produced at the factory without the boss knowing about it. Off the back of the truck, in other words. And the quality of the pirated stuff is invariably top-notch. It's got the fancy brandnames of this world really worried. Of course, I suggested why didn't they just hire these buggers. Like Sun Tzu said, "Know your enemy."

But if your enemy is a medical problem, you've got nothing to worry about in Asia. They've got cures for arthritis, rheumatism, hemorrhoids, baldness, cancer and Aids. Sometimes all in the one bottle! Just pop down the local herbal medicine hall. If the secret ever gets out, these guys could really make some serious dough. Or maybe the local consumers are just more gullible and pass away before they can make a claim against the company for making false claims?

And we should never forget status, which comes in many shapes and sizes throughout Asia, but mainly in the form of a mutated peace sign on the front of a German-made car. Additionally, the Chinese have adopted Rolex watches as their not-so-secret code of "I've made it," and the Filipinos have adopted, well, guns. I know this first hand, from having many an irate father draw a glistening Smith & Wesson on me when asking for his daughter's hand in marriage. "You've had every part of my daughter, so why not her hand as well?" one less-than-thrilled father-in-law-to-be had said to me, before putting a couple of shots into the ceiling.

Not so much one-upmanship as one-upyoursmanship.

I therefore decided it might be safer to marry a Chinese lass, but there again, they're all pretty handy with the martial arts and chainsaws, too. I've seen those Bruce Lee movies.

Anyway, we seemed to have swerved beautifully away from the topic at hand...shopping. Oh no, perfect accidental segue - Chinese ladies and shopping! Absolutely synonymous.

Quick joke: what's an Asian girl's favourite sexual position? Facing CK Tangs / Landmark / Chanel / Louis Vuitton, etc. (Delete as applicable to your city).

And you couldn't possibly talk about the Asian retail boom without reference to the "m" word, materialism.

But how times have changed. Dave told me (for another jug of marguerita, mind you) that Japan and Korea did their very best to avoid merchants in the 19th century, earning themselves the "Hermit Kingdom" tags. And now, with their fluctuating economies, they're doing pretty much the same again, unofficially at least, causing major hemorrhages and heart attacks in the corridors of the wanky European fashion houses.

Which reminds me of that great money changer joke of the Japanese guy changing some Yen in London. First day he gets a good rate, second day a little worse, and third day really bad. He asks the man why it's different every day: "Oh, fluctuations...," the changer simply explains. "Well, fluck you Europeans too!" says the Japanese businessman.

In Eat The Rich, the venerable P.J O'Rourke sums up Hong Kong beautifully: "All the opulent goods of mankind are on display in an air of shit and Chanel." But, more surprisingly is the rate at which China has embraced, well, not wearing the green Mao suit on Monday, Wednesday and Fridays, and the blue Mao suit on the other days for a bit of added spice.

My good friend, Michael Palin, noted this on his travels through China in Full Circle: "On streets which saw the violent birth of Chinese communism you can now buy a suit at Harvey Nichols, a coat at Ralph Lauren, a shirt at Gieves and Hawkes, and a pair of shoes at Charles Jourdan."

Gee, it doesn't seem that long ago that The Friendship Store was the only place to shop for anything other than the latest in peasant wear, with little polyester-trousered men sidling up to you and whispering out the side of their mouths, "Change money, change money." In fact, they looked a lot like little Oriental versions of Austin Powers, stuck in some God-forsaken fashion era but no one dared tell them. After all, in the land of the blind the one-eyed man is king. And when you're dressed in a Mao suit, who are you to tell someone, "White shoes with flared polyester trousers aren't a good look, Comrade."

But take it from me...snakeskin shoes and flowery shirts are an evergreen fashion statement. Like those little black dresses for the ladies - you just can't go wrong. The rest of you are just needlessly spending your money being fashion victims, following tenuous fads and keeping shopkeepers in custom.

God, I almost forgot. We've got the Anzac Day Ball on this weekend, and I haven't got my sequined suit back from the dry-cleaners yet. Got to go...

Colonel Ke

Running out of money

One of the longest standing 'hashers' in Hong Kong is BOF (Boring Old Fart). He turned 60 a few years ago but still regularly ran marathons on Sunday mornings before running with the Wanchai Hash in the afternoon. He drank lots too; especially after exercise.

One Saturday BOF had been up since 5.00 am to walk the Lantau Trail (50 km of ups and downs). He finished just before dark, got the ferry back to Hong Kong and joined his hash mates in The Wanch for a few beers. The beers kept on flowing until his mates withdrew towards midnight, but BOF was still game so he moved on to Joe Banana's where the *gweilo* totty hangs out. A few cocktails later, it was 2 am and he decided to call it a day and crawled into a waiting taxi.

Halfway home, BOF realised he had no cash left, so he asked the taxi driver to stop by a convenient ATM machine. Realising BOF was in a bit of a state, the taxi driver kindly helped him out of the taxi and over to the machine. BOF was fumbling away and could not get the card into the machine, so the taxi driver helped him. BOF could not key in his number, so he asked the taxi driver to do it for him. At last the cash was dispensed; BOF took it and tried to get his card out, too. He dropped it, but the helpful taxi driver picked it up and put it back in BOF's wallet for him. He got home, paid the taxi driver, and fell asleep before getting his clothes off.

The next day he happened to be in the shops looking for some new shoes. After trying on half a dozen pairs, he took out his payment card and handed it to the assistant. There followed much fumbling and farting by the shop staff as they tried to get authorisation for the purchase. After a few minutes, a couple of policemen wander in to the shop, and the assistant announced that BOF had presented them with a stolen card! Vaguely recalling the events of the previous evening, it all began to add up - the taxi driver switched cards on him - but the Police took quite a while to convince.

It turned out the taxi driver had immediately taken out the maximum cash allowed from BOF's account, and even moved cash between accounts to try to squeeze out as much as possible. He'd then purchased a gold ring to this value, before the card was cancelled. Quite a pro apparently.

The bottom line? HK$ 55,000 (US$7,000) and almost a criminal record for a 7 km trip home in the back of a taxi.

Own worst enemy

I was in Bali not too long after the demise of the Indonesian economy. Everything was really really cheap, so I went on a shopping spree.

Picking out a nice leather belt, the shop assistant said: "25,000 rupiah."

I countered with 20,000, hoping to get her down a bit.

"18,000 last price," she said. Sold!

Faking it

In Bangkok markets, I came across some interesting products...leather boots, with the distinctive yellow triangle and black industrial typeface logo of that well-known earthmoving company, Carterbilly. Also, some sweatshirts by that famous American designer, Timmy Hillfinger.

Taking a dim view

I had a friend, R, in Hong Kong, and one of his favourite pastimes was annoying uptight shop staff - by picking things off the shelf, and consuming them before he'd paid for them. He would always pay. But just at the point when they were foaming at the mouth and threatening police action.

In general, they did not have a reputation for being either helpful or polite, so this was his answer to that.

In one particular case, he wandered in about midnight, having sunk a few pints in Wanchai, and proceeded to grab a few items of dim sum from the cold cabinet. He then proceeded to start microwaving them, which did not escape the eye of an alert and extremely serious-about-his-job shop manager.

"You must pay for food before eat," protested the manager.

"Keep your trousers on, I'm going to pay," replied the antagonist (in a strong Yorkshire accent).

"You must pay. Now." This was ignored. "If you don't pay now, I call police," continued the manager.

"Call the police then," my friend said, sinking his teeth into the dim sum.

The police were called. In they stormed. It wasn't a SWAT team, but they obviously aspired to it.

"Excuse me. This man has reported that you are stealing food."

"I'm not stealing it. I'm just eating it."

"Yes, but you must pay before eating it."

"I'm going to pay."

"You live in Hong Kong?"

"Yes."

"Show me your I.D. card."

"I haven't got one."

"Why not?"

"Don't want one."

This flummoxed the Chow Yun Fat wannabe for a second, as normally he would be met with some snivelling lie about how the maid had accidentally put the I.D. card in with the washing, bullshit...

"You must pay for this food," said the officer firmly.

"Oh, bloody hell, if it makes you happy."

R then reaches into the pockets of his jeans only to discover, much to his surprise, and brief horror, that they were empty. *Oh shit. What now?*

Just then, a Filipino guy he knew from one of the nearby restaurants wandered in having just finished work.

"Hey Jesse, could you lend me $10?" he called out.

End of story.

In a Wuxi dry cleaner:
"Please drop your trousers here for best results."

Outside a Tianjin clothing shop:
"Order your summer suits quick. Because of
big rush we will execute customers in strict rotation."

In a Xian tailor shop:
"Ladies may have a fit upstairs."

Daisy Does Donald
A friend of mine was running a part of the Disney operation in Asia. As I'd just returned from Bangkok, I asked him about the extent of counterfeit and piracy.

It was rife, he admitted, but they were doing their best to stamp it out and deal harshly with anyone caught infringing Disney copyrights or using their characters unlawfully.

"I presume the t-shirts in Patunam Market with Daisy giving Donald Duck a blow-job are not real then?"

Cut price
In the shopping centre one lunchtime, I saw a hairdressing salon, and decided to get a haircut even though it wasn't my regular place. The sign said "Gents $10." About standard, in Singapore.

Haircut completed, the lady asked for $15. I pointed to the sign saying $10.

"Chinese New Year bonus," she added rather gruffly.

I pleaded ignorance to this particular practice, and pleaded for exemption given I was expat and therefore not really keen on playing this particular game. She pushed the point more forthrightly.

"OK, I've only got $10 in my wallet. I need to go to bank to get more money to pay you," I lied, hoping at this point she would waive the excess premium.

"Yes, OK you go come back," she said, pleased that she had seemingly won.

"Yes, yes," I said, and walked out, never to be seen again.

I subsequently learned that 'the bonus' is indeed a traditional practice amongst hairdressers at Chinese New Year. But no-one seems to know where it stemmed from. *Greed* would be my guess!

Absolutely jenuine

My visiting brother had gone shopping in a street market in Kuala Lumpur in the late 80's. A rack of jeans caught his eye, but he thought the price was too good to be true.

"Real ones or fake?" he asked the stallkeeper.

"All real. 100% I guarantee you," the Indian vendor replied.

On closer inspection, the jeans label in the familiar logotype read: "Live's 501".

"If you have a good story about retail experiences in Asia, let us know. Email us at hardship_posting@hotmail.com or fax The Editor at 612-9499-5908."

"Going nowhere in a hurry."
True tales of adventures in taxis, public transport and assorted traffic incidents.

Let's face it...it's gonna be quite some time before we have an Asian Formula 1 driving champion.

In China, blow me down if something like 42,000 folks don't lose their lives on the road each year. That's like a major stadium football crowd. Cheering no more. Full-time score: cars, trucks and assorted horse-drawn vehicles 1, Chinese folks 0. Even more scary considering that the average punter (and they are very average after years of Communism) is only tootling along on a push-bike. How far wrong can you go? Very, obviously.

If your brakes fail in Singapore, you end up in Malaysia! However even in a country where it's hard to get out of second gear, the fatality rate is about twice that of major western countries. Maybe it's got something to do with their unofficial "decimated drivers" program for big nights out...scary to see the world's most expensive cars piloted by someone that's just nailed three bottles of brandy celebrating a big contract. And he's on the handphone at the same time.

In Korea, traffic police report a record number of drivers claiming faulty accelerators for causing accidents. "Ah, solly sir...this model onry have blakes as optional extla...but accerelator come flee".

Michael Schumaker, don't look in your rear-vision mirror...there are no Asian drivers about to overtake you. But look out for them pulling out from sidestreets ahead of you!

However, Asian traffic takes on its own lunatic rhythm...just try crossing the road on Nguyen Hue Boulevarde in Saigon (sorry, Ho Chi

HARDSHIP POSTING

Minh City as they now like us to call it since Uncle Ho's pajama brigade won the last match) around six in the evening.

And then there's Bangkok and Manila, where the rhythm is more *rheumatic*. Like the cars have zimmer frames, it moves so slow. Still it's a bloody good chance to catch up on your reading (I always take a couple of good books -or at least a young lady who's read a couple of good books- with me for on the road entertainment).

And Kuala Lumpur around lunchtime on a Friday. Always ensure you are going the opposite direction from the mosque...er, unless you're going to it like a good Muslim should be.

Then, there's that special breed of human being...the taxi driver. When I shuffle off this mortal coil, I will come back and mess with these guys in every ghostly way possible. Turn on his "not for hire" sign just as he approaches a group that's been waiting for an hour in the rain, make nasty farting sounds (and emit appropriate odours) without an apology, and put my foot on and off the accelerator so the car lurches forward in an ungainly manner, precipitating motion sickness...oh, sorry, they do this already. I'll have to think of other forms of revenge.

It's funny, but have you ever noticed there's a distinct power struggle going on in different cities between the cabbies and the customers on the roadside? And it's all related to relative wealth. (No, not how many bucks their uncles have, but their country's overall fiscal health).

Let me explain, because I know some of you slower readers are not quite with me here. In Tokyo, they drive straight past you. In Singapore, they'll stop to see where you're going before driving off without you. But in Hanoi they'll be following you down the road yelling, "Hey you!" to get your attention. There it is...laws of economics in a microcosmic nutshell. I saved you the cost of doing that MBA you were considering, so if you'd like to put the difference in the mail to me, that'd be just nice. Just a little conscience payment to keep your old mate Col. Ken in gin and tonics.

And have you ever noticed that every cab driver has a cousin living in *your* hometown? You could be from Kansas City (hey, someone has to be) and sure enough, the guy in the driver's seat will be like, "Oh, my cousin Lee rivving in Kansas. Do carpet creaning busiless. Velly enjoy. Kansas City number one, ha ha."

HARDSHIP POSTING

And before I take you through the joys of Asian public transport, a little taxi joke to finish off with. The headline in the Bombay Times reads: "Taxi crashes: 43 dead." Think about it.

Anyway a nice cue, or perhaps *queue* would be more appropriate, to talk about some quintessential Asian sights and experiences: overcrowded modes of transport. The got-to-be-done peak hour trains in Tokyo...the carriage is already showing signs of the rivets popping, but you've got some official looking guy in a smart blue suit and white gloves shoving you in. I could have sworn I saw him put his foot on the side of train to get more leverage and actually use a giant shoehorn to get me in.

And then there are the little bite-sized public buses called *mini bas* (surprisingly translates as 'mini bus') in Malaysia, with faces and arms and unidentifiable body parts and clothing protruding from every pore of the vehicle as it struggles up a long hill, lopsided on the door side, belching dark diesel clouds on an express pass to the ozone layer.

Do the Guinness Book of Records still run the vehicle cramming records, or did that die out with the free love era? Because these guys would win hands down. But there again, it's hard to tell exactly where the hands are in such a crowd.

Then in more remote (or less developed) parts, the game to play is obviously "How many people and objects can we fit on this bicycle?" The answer? Hundreds. Or entire 4-generation families at least. Or if the bike is used for business, how many brooms can we stack, or toys or computers. I've seen a wall of cardboard boxes hurtling towards me before, like a runaway warehouse, nearly bloody knocked me over, and it was only when the whole load had gone passed me I realised that somewhere in the middle of that was a bike and some clown riding it.

Didn't it occur to him that perhaps ringing a bell might be a neat way of drawing attention to the fact that he was heading your way like a juggernaut on full steam ahead.

There again, given the overall ambient noise level of Asian traffic, you couldn't hear a dinky little bell anyway. Have you noticed how noisy it is on the roads? One hand is always on the horn (hey, what I do in my own car is my own business!). Somebody does something stupid - horn. Somebody almost does something stupid - horn. Somebody does nothing - horn, just in case, because you know it's only a matter of time before they do something stupid. Traffic going nowhere; gridlock, back-up, total standstill - go the horn!

In fact, maybe that's why there are no Asian formula 1 drivers...the racing cars don't have horns.

Colonel Ke

Major investment

I went down into a bar one night, and bumped into a mate of mine, who used to be my boss. He was completely pissed as usual.

"Ah, mate," he said. "I've got to -hic- show you shumfing because I know you of all people would - hic- appreciate it."

We went up the stairs to the front entrance of The Hyatt. "Isshn't she a bewdy," he slurred, pointing at his brand new Porsche Cabrio, glistening in the moonlight outside. "Over four hundred thoushand f***ing bucksh of -hic- motor car," he said proudly. "Nearly half a million bucksh."

Just then, the valet guy came to attend to him. Our hero turned to his local girlfriend and said: "Have you got a couple of bucks for the parking, love?"

www.hardshipposting.com

Religious reasons

I had made the trip from Singapore to Colombo several times, and each time the drill was the same. Get to Colombo airport at about 10:40 pm (local time), and grab the hotel car to town. About 45 minutes.

However, I'd never done the trip with such a bad hangover before. My head was throbbing and I was suffering major sleep deprivation from the night before. I hopped into the car as usual and was just about asleep only minutes from the airport when I noticed some pretty lights. "That's nice, what's that for?" I asked the driver. Buddhist new year, he explained.

A little down the road, there were more lights. And roadside flags. And lots of people ambling down the roadside. It got thicker and thicker until suddenly we were almost at a standstill...throngs of people on the side of the road, and cars and trucks in lanes all round me.

I tried to ignore it and sleep. But the headache grew worse. The car went slower till we stopped altogether. Then we started doing that stop-start-go-one car-length-stop routine. Eventually we came to a road block. I thought, "Ok, here's our chance to cut straight through whilst all the festival traffic follows the crowd round the corner." No chance. We all had to detour round the corner. An adjacent truck was blasting diesel fumes into our car, making me totally nauseous. I fell asleep again.

The driver was stopping the engine, getting out of the car, looking, then getting back in again, moving forward about one space, and stopping the engine. I felt like blowing up the entire country right there, right then. I did not need this shit.

We eventually cleared the mob, and got to the hotel. What was usually a 45 minute run took us 4 and a half hours!!!

It was by now nearly 5am in my normal time zone. My wife had called only to find out I'd not checked in yet (funny, she's always nervous about me travelling in war-zones) and ended up in a total panic. Plus I had a breakfast meeting scheduled in about 3 hours' time. The whole thing was a complete disaster and I vowed never to return without checking the religious calendar first.

Stopped in my tracks

I was at a party one night in Hong Kong, and the topic came around to cars. I asked if anyone had seen a very strange sight that morning on the road around Causeway Bay...a brand spanking new white Mercedes Benz had mounted the road divider railings, almost like a tram, and slid along it for a good 50 yards before hitting a street light pole, stopping in its tracks and coming to rest in a mangled heap.

"What kind of f***ing idiot could possibly do that," I said.

"Er, it was me actually," said our host.

Oops!

Bottoming out

My boss had always longed for a Porsche, and on his 30th birthday he went out and bought a beautiful shiny red number that we all drooled over. Unfortunately, in Hong Kong, it was impossible to get it much past 3rd gear (legally), it bottomed out in every carpark, and he eventually wrote it off less than a year later after a spectacularly long lunch.

Bruised ego

The rental shop had given me one of those little scooters with a basket on the front as they had run out of trail bikes. Embarassing, but at least it got me around Phuket.

I had made arrangements to meet a Thai girl off the cruise boat when she finished work at 6pm. As it happened, I was otherwise unexpectedly detained by another damsel from the night before.

By the time I had politely sent her packing at 5:30, I was horribly late to meet girl No 1. I revved up the beast and went flat out from my Patong Beach hotel, up the windy road to Phuket Town.

I was flying along and lost it on a corner outside the cement factory. With a cement mixer coming the other way, I decided to head full throttle into the sand on the other side of the road. I just made it. The truck roared past, and I caught my breath. *That was f***ing stupid*, I said to myself.

Once I had regained my composure, I went flying off again, taking that little scooter up to past 100kmh. No helmet, of course. Just then, I came around a corner and saw a bus stopped in my lane. I overtook it only to see an oncoming car, and as I pulled back into my lane I realised why that bus was stopped where it was... it had gone up the slope, obviously lost engine power and slid backwards down the road leaving a trail of oil in its wake.

I hit the oil slick, and was on my arse before I knew it. I went one way, the bike went spinning another. I remember thinking, *I hope the camera's Ok*. Then I noticed about 50 people, who had obviously gotten out of the broken down bus, clapping and cheering this idiot *farang* who had dropped his bike.

Miraculously with little more than a battered and bruised ego, I made it for my date. It was great- but not really worth it after all. In fact I got on better with the *chaperone* than with the tour guide I had my eye on!

Time to kill

My first time in Jakarta on business. I had been warned how woeful the traffic was, so allowed about 1 1/2 hours travelling time at peak hour to be at my meeting on time.

I hopped into the hotel car. Not even 15 minutes later, the driver said: "Here you are, Sir." It was just behind the hotel. I felt a complete idiot.

Lost for words

I lived in an apartment in Hong Kong, but didn't own a car although I was made to understand that there was a parking space allocated for me...a most prized benefit. One day I bought a car, and proudly drove up to the apartment gate.

The worst security guy, who reminded me of Chairman Mao, was on duty. He spoke no English and thought his uniform was his ticket to throw his considerable weight around.

I motioned for him to let me in. He gave me the universal sign language for "no can do." I tried again, with a combination of gestures and broken English. No can do. More shaking of head and waving of hand. "Me, penthouse, 21st floor. My space here. Ok!" I pleaded.

"*Moa*," (no) he responded in Cantonese.

I upped the ante a bit. He started motioning for me to reverse out. With that I said "Well f*** you!" and this old Chinese gent turns to me and says "Fook you too!"

HARDSHIP POSTING

I dropped the clutch and reversed in a cloud of blue smoke. A lost battle.

Taking a back seat

On holiday in Boracay, we had gone to Kalibo for some revelry. Early the next morning we wanted to take the first bus out of this shithole. We wandered across to the post office - the next bus was in 10 minutes. Next was to get some coffee and breakfast. A tall order in a one-horse town, but we at least got something to help our hangovers and messed-up sugarlevels from the night before.

Then, with a rumble, screech of brakes and a cloud of dust, our bus arrived. It was already full, but that did not stop another 20 people from hopping in and *on* it. The suitcases were piled high, and one guy was busy tying a live pig to the back...suspended on some ropes at the back.

We got on and found a seat in the back row. It was hot. The B.O. was crippling. The bus headed off on its bumpy ride. Within minutes, I was feeling distinctly unwell. I asked if I could sit near the door. The fellow I asked did not quite understand until I did a quick mime act of the consequences. At least then I was getting some fresh air. But I could not hold on for long.

I stood up and leaned out the open door, losing the entire contents of my stomach, and a little more I suspected, in a wonderful wind-swept arc. The guys hanging on the door thought this was hilarious!

I then spent the next 45 minutes throwing up every bit of gastric acid my body could produce as the bus bumped its way through the countryside, stopping only to let a soldier in red rubber thongs off into the bush (he was on the roof with his M16 all the way) and also to let the guy re-tie his pig, which had fallen off with much squealing and pande-monium all round.

Off the beaten track

Back in '85 the year in which I first arrived in Hong Kong, the social life started quite quickly in an atmosphere of many newcomers. Soon someone had the idea of a tram party on a double-decker tram. I was informed to bring a water pistol.

We all met at the tram depot in Causeway Bay. On board were

about 30 people, mainly young expatriates and a handful of Hong Kongers, each with their water pistol, and in some cases "water rifles". There was free flowing beer and wine which heightened the excitement. Soon the tram started rattling down the tracks on a route that would take us out of Causeway Bay, through Wanchai (infamously called the "Wanch") and to the farthest end of Central and then to return over the same route back to the depot. When the water supplies had run out, the beer and wine came in handy as ammo. The shooting of fellow partygoers also changed - the tram had open windows which allowed complete freedom to fire outside the tram.

On this hot and balmy night, the next targets became unsuspecting travellers in other trams passing in the opposite direction. Often the targets were totally surprised and could not fathom why they suddenly had got wet in the face, or in their hair or on their clothing, as we had already passed by. Worst still they were wearing sticky and smelly alcohol. Those who realised quickly enough soon waved fists and hurled abuse at us. This only added to our alcohol-inspired merriment.

Other targets were pedestrians, people waiting at tram stops and taxi drivers with open windows. Sometimes, an angry taximan would scramble out of his car and chase after us waving his fists and shouting incomprehensible Cantonese abuse. We would watch the next set of traffic lights to check the red or green lights to estimate whether the retaliating assailant could catch us or would run out of breath before he caught us.

We couldn't understand why most did not appreciate our warped sense of fun.

All parties come to an end, and we arrived back at the tram depot about 2 hours later. Entering the gates of the depot, we saw about 30 uniformed Hong Kong policemen waiting for us. Our highs descended to extreme lows. My first thoughts were that I had only been in Hong Kong a few short weeks and was about to get deported. There was a panic- where did we hide our water pistols?! There was nowhere. After stopping we were told to get off one by one. Sheepishly we had to walk down past a line of policemen.

The last two guys getting off the tram were nabbed by the policemen and taken to one side. After a talking to, they had their details taken, and had to apologise to a woman who had a whole glassful of wine splashed in her face at a tram stop.

Close quarters

My colleague JM was showing all the classic signs of having been in Hong Kong too long. He had become very irritable and short-tempered and he talked a lot about "punching peoples' lights out".

One morning driving down Cotton Tree Drive towards Central a sports car driven by a young Jardine Johnnie-type tried to cut in front of JM's car. On edge since he had got out of bed, JM aggressively closed the gap between his car and the car in front so as not to let the sports car in. He gave the JJ-type the finger and mouthed a few choice expletives at him through his car window.

Undeterred, the JJ-type continued to barge in until the two cars met with a crunch. Now *extremely* pissed off and with the adrenaline flowing freely, JM put his car into first gear and floored the accelerator with a view to pushing the sports car out of the way.

The JJ-type did the same ... and the two cars proceeded fully 100 yards down Cotton Tree Drive with their bumpers locked together, accompanied by the sound of screeching tires and metal-on-metal, surrounded by smoke and the smell of burning rubber. JM and the JJ-type shouted and gesticulated at each other as their cars crabbed down Cotton Tree Drive, much to the amusement of the Chinese drivers and commuters. Here was *proof* that *gwailos* were crazy.

Eventually JM forced the sports car against the curb opposite the old Hilton Hotel and the two cars came to a grinding halt. JM leapt out of his car, fist clenched, poised to king-hit Jardine Johnnie.

As he approached the sports car JJ looked at JM pathetically and said: "I'm terribly sorry, old chap. I'm afraid that Hong Kong is getting to me. I guess I got carried away." Totally disarmed, JM said, "I know exactly what you mean, mate. I'm the same way myself. I suggest we forget the whole thing."

With this, they shook hands, prised the two cars apart and continued on to their respective offices.

Coup goes there?

There were two serious coups d'etat while I was working in

HARDSHIP POSTING

Bangkok. The first soon petered out as the generals came out of their camps with all the military vehicles, heading towards parliament, on a Monday morning - during rush hour. They all got stuck in the notorious Bangkok traffic and couldn't get anywhere! The second time they set off before the rush hour and made it to their designated positions. It was announced on television and radio for everyone to stay at home. In those days there were no English stations, so I go off to work unaware of what had happened. But I got to the office in 10 minutes instead of the usual one-hour plus, so I knew something was up.

I opened the office but no one else turned up. Eventually, my finance director called me and explained what was going on and said I should not leave the office as there was quite a bit of trouble downtown. Our office was just round the corner from Patpong, so I wasn't going to stay on my own all day. I walked round to our favorite lunchtime bar and spent all day watching developments on the television, having Thai politics and royalty explained to me while events ran their course. I was the only *farang* in Patpong that day!

Eventually, much to my disappointment, by late evening it was all over and I was able to go home.

Lost cars

The newly-arrived expat in Kuala Lumpur left the company-provided car for his wife to familiarise herself with the surrounding neighborhood. She drove around for a couple of hours before getting completely lost. Then, horror of horrors, the car broke down.

She decided to lock the car up, get a 'teksi' back to their apartment, and tell her husband when he returned from his hard day at the office.

When he arrived home, she informed him of her little adventure, but reassured him that she had written the street name down so they could go and retrieve the car.

"Here it is..." she said producing the piece of paper, *"Jalan Sehala."*

There are lots of *Jalans* in Malaysia as it means 'street.' But there are also plenty of *Jalan Sehala's*, as it means 'One Way Street'.

Legend has it they found the car a few weeks later.

Can opener

Our advertising agency was doing work for the BMW distributor. Because of this we decided to buy one of the first new 3 series (1984) to be assembled in Thailand.

It was three weeks old when I decided to give four working girls (three of whom were sisters) a lift to their home at bar closing time. As one does. Don't ask me why but it seemed a good idea at the time.

Bangkok is one of the few capital cities in the world with train lines crossing main streets without bridges or gates, only bars lowered down when trains cross the road. These bars have red flashing lights on them when they are lowered. On this night, either I didn't see them or someone had forgotten to turn the lights on. Our car hit the bar at over 100km - luckily it swung up, but still managed to take the roof clean off! Lucky, too, the train hadn't arrived yet.

Somehow, we all managed to keep our heads (literally) although the girls lost theirs completely with shock. And that is how I ended up the owner of the *only* 3 Series convertible in town.

Road Rage

In Jakarta my driver was driving us down a small street and a pedestrian, without looking, walked out in front of the car. We had no problem missing him due to the slow speed we were travelling.

Suddenly my driver stopped the car, got out, confronted the pedestrian and then proceeded to beat him up!

After, I asked why he did this. His explanation? "Our car had right of way and not him, so I beat him up for making me stop".

Head-on accident

Driving a car in Taiwan was a maddening experience. The locals completely ignored all rules of the road and they would go to seemingly any length to get ahead of the cars in front of them. They could always be counted on to ignore traffic lanes.

They also seemed to ignore any consequences of their pursuit of one-upmanship. One day a train stalled while crossing a major road in Taipei. Traffic quickly backed up and before too long, drivers began to use the opposing lane in their attempt to get around the cars stopped in front of them. Soon both lanes of traffic were filled with cars headed in the same direction, with the stalled train blocking their path.

After many minutes the train restarted and began to move on its way. As it cleared the crossing, it revealed that drivers on the opposite side of the train had been trying the same maneuver! It took quite a while to clear the bedlam.

Riding high on the hog

I was the slightly less than proud owner of a 175cc Yamaha motorbike in Hong Kong, but used it more than my car because it got through traffic much better.

One weekend, I had collected my Filipina girlfriend to go to a friend's wedding. She forgot to tell me it was their custom to take a *lechon* (make that a spit-roasted pig - whole!) to such festivities, so we had to find a suitable butchery.

We found a butcher near Causeway Bay who sold lechon, and headed for the party feeling a little conspicuous. Just me, my girl, and a whole roasted pig glistening in the sun with an apple in its mouth!

My fare share

My first trip to Korea, I decided to head into Seoul to catch some nightlife. I hopped into a cab at the hotel. The driver spoke no English, but off we went.

Imagine my surprise and delight and mystification when we stopped about a kilometre down the road, and two dainty young things hopped from the dark roadside into the cab beside me on the backseat. Hmmm, here was one for Letters to Penthouse, I thought.

I said Hello. They smiled. But it didn't seem to progress much from there as they gibbered away in Korean. A few kilometres later, with nary a goodbye, the door opened and they disappeared into the darkness, robbing me of several fantasies.

It was only after a few days in Korea I realised that cab-sharing was a common and completely innocent practice. I hope they felt it was their loss too.

PS: Is there a Korean version of Penthouse?

HARDSHIP POSTING

It's not fare

Tired and grumpy after a hard day's work, I slumped into the back of a cab. "Con-Dat Doh," I said in my best Cantonese; Conduit Rd.

Next thing I notice we're round the back of Hong Kong Island, very much on the scenic route. Many windy kilometres later, we got to my place.

The driver stopped the meter and asked for his fare, at least triple what it normally was. I don't need this shit. I was fuming.

"Solly, Sir, I part time dwiver," explained the cabbie.

"Ok, I pay you a part time fare," I said, putting the usual fare amount into his hand and storming off.

Not for hire

A friend of mine in Singapore got by fine without a car. Being a big boozer it was probably a good thing. He had put a cabbie on re-tainer... a monthly stipend for this guy to pick him up from home each morning and take him to work.

I thought this was excellent, although illegal, but soon had my very own guy on call. For a fixed fee each month he'd pick me up and take me to work. I'd tell him my meeting times which he had to collect me for, and he even took our family to the zoo one weekend.

All for probably half of what it would cost to pay off a car of my own.

Then it went horribly wrong. "I'm going to Indonesia for a week," he announced. Ten days later he called to say he was extending 'for a week'. I never saw or heard from him again.

Then the monsoon season hit, and you couldn't get a cab for love nor money, and I was standing in the road up to my knees in flooding rainwater when the Japanese tennis mums from the next apartment stole my taxi. *F*** this,* I thought, and bought another car the very next day.

Save batteries, not lives

Shanghai 1987. We took a cab to dinner one night, and the taxi driver was very nattily dressed in grey jacket and white gloves...yes, a magician's white gloves.

We couldn't help notice that he didn't have his lights on, which we pointed out to him, making it very difficult to see all the people, objects and vehicles passing dangerously across us in every direction.

"No lights...save battery," he explained.

Just then, a bus roared across us through the intersection. Our hearts stopped, our bowels started.

"No problem," he said, waving his white gloved hands like the Queen Mum, and grinning manically.

Terminal velocity

We were looking forward to a relaxing weekend at our friends' place on Batam Island, a comfortable 45 minutes by ferry from Singapore, a trip we had done several times before.

Tickets booked, we headed down to the ferry terminal at the World Trade Centre, proud we were actually a little early for once in our lives. However after checking out all the boarding gates, I couldn't find one for Nongsa.

"Oh no, all ferries for Batam now go from Changi," the officer advised us.

Shit, it was leaving from the other end of Singapore. A quick call to the other ferry terminal. They couldn't hold it for us, but they knew we were on our way. We raced outside to the taxi rank and fortunately there were a few spare cabs.

"Tanah Merah Terminal," I said. "How fast does this taxi go?" I asked.

I negotiated with the cab driver...if we got a speeding ticket I would pay for it. That was all the encouragement he needed as we weaved and swerved our way up the East Coast Parkway all the way to Changi. My knuckles were white on the dashboard. Around us was the insistent "ding-ding-ding" of the device that tells all Singapore cab drivers when they're over the speed limit.

This guy was way out of his depth, but we got to Tanah Merah just in time to see them start casting the ropes. No time for duty-free shopping but we made it!

Cold as ice

Beijing late 80's. Returning from a business trip to Hong Kong, I got into the hotel car, and we were running late as usual.

The driver was a rather stately looking chap, very upright but completely expressionless. We ambled off down the driveway in a late model Volvo. Once the traffic (meaning horses and bicycles and army trucks) were clear, he pulled out into the main road going no more than 30 miles an hour.

His speed never increased. His expression never changed.

Looking at my watch, I decided we had better step on it. Not sure if he spoke English, I say to him "I very late. Must faster."

With no acknowledgment whatsoever, he floored it. He had the Volvo on the wrong side of the icy roads on blind corners as traffic whipped past in the opposite direction, millimetres away.

At the airport, still shaking with cold and fear, I thanked him and bode him farewell. He did not say a word, did not smile; just drove off. At 30 miles an hour.

Stop at nothing

I found Tokyo cabs infuriating - they would never ever stop for a *gaijin* (foreigner) because they knew you would only be travelling within the inner city hotel district. They were after the juicy fares to the far-flung outskirts of Tokyo by drunken Japanese businessmen at 3am in the morning instead.

However, this did not make it any easier to take. After a good night out with my friend who lived in Tokyo we needed a cab. They just kept driving by, despite our frantic waving (or maybe because of it!).

Eventually, fuelled by a crate of sake let's not forget, I walked into the middle of a three lane road with my arms outstretched. "Stop, you bastard!" I yelled at an oncoming cab.

He kept coming.

At the last minute he slowed, probably not because I was there, but because the light was red. I was yelling at him, but he wound his window up, and as he pulled away, I grabbed his aerial which left me with a cut hand.

"Japanese f***ers," I yelled into the darkness as I lay in the road, clutching my hand. Several cars swerved around me, and my friend just didn't want to know me.

HARDSHIP POSTING

To this day, I can't remember how we finally got home. But I know it wasn't by cab.

Time on your hands

I remembered Singapore in the late Eighties. You couldn't get into a cab after dark without the cab driver trying to talk you into a quick detour via some hostelry of a dubious nature, where he no doubt got a commission (in cash or kind) on services rendered.

One time I had been working my ass off to finish all my work before heading off to Australia for Christmas holiday. As usual, I had left myself just enough time to make the plane.

As I boarded the cab in the Beach Rd area, the cabbie predictably asked me where I was going (airport) and whether I would like a lady.

" I wouldn't mind, but I'm running late," I said, my watch showing just after 7pm.

"What time's your flight, sir?" the cabbie enquired. 8:15 I told him.

"Oh plenty of time. Geylang is just right here, Sir." He was really insistent till the very last minute.

I couldn't quite figure where there was 'plenty of time', given the trip to the airport was about half an hour and the plane left in about an hour and I still had to check in, etc.

Maybe he thought I was the original "one minute man" !

I brake for dinner

Returning from a resort in the south of Sri Lanka, we had ordered a taxi for 8:30pm, on the advice of the concierge, to get us to the airport on time.

For some unknown reason, we were packed and ready to go by 8:20 so went down to the lobby. We were off to a bad start - the driver came across and said; "I've been here since 7:45 o'clock, you know!"

"Well, we booked the cab for 8:30," I reminded him.

He sullenly packed our bags into his Toyota van, and we hopped in the back. Driving in Sri Lanka is interesting at the best of times, but at night time it's doubly exciting. He gunned it, weaving in and out of gaps that didn't exist, creating three lanes where only two existed. It was nailbiting. He tailgated cars, sat right on their rear fender waiting for his next overtaking maneouvre. We were terrified.

Eventually, when it seemed there was no end to his madness, he pulled over on the side of the road.

"I haven't had my dinner yet," he explained as he casually hopped out to have a leisurely sit-down meal of curry and rice at a roadside stall while we (paying customers) sat in the van and waited.

Colour bind

I had been invited to the opening of a new Italian restaurant, and knew that driving would be a bad idea as there was bound to be lashings of free wine and champagne. There was!

Catching a cab back, I told the slightly elderly driver my address and eased back into my seat for the ride. Coming down a major 3-lane road, I was surprised to see him stop at a set of green traffic lights.

"You can go, mate - it's green," I said.

He looked around a little dopily.

"You can go," I repeated. "It's the red ones you want to watch out for. Go...!!!"

Just then we got whacked by another taxi from behind, shunting us right through the intersection. I looked around to see a cloud of blue smoke, with bits of glass and rubber on the road.

"Told you," I said as I casually got out, slammed the door and walked to the side of the road and hailed another cab home.

The next morning I woke with the sorest stiffest neck you could imagine, from the whiplash.

Wake me up before you go-go

I once had this taxi driver who was obviously overworked. As we stopped at a red light, he dozed off and said, "Wake me when it's green."

Parking hell

A local lady who worked for us was the worst driver you could possibly imagine.

Every morning she would drive to work, stop in the busy 6 lane road outside our office, run upstairs and ask someone to park it properly for her. How did she get her license???

False hopes

I already owned a motorbike, but wanted a set of wheels for the rainy days. Being a 'back up' vehicle, all I needed was 4 wheels and a roof - just so long as it got me from A to B.

Looking through the classifieds, I spotted one: a van. A really, really cheap van.

I called the guy, and we agreed to meet in a central place. "Look out for a yellow van...I will park right out front the cinema," the local vendor said. "My name is Tommy."

Waiting at the meeting place, I was overjoyed to see a bright yellow van turn up. It looked in excellent shape, and as it drew up to the kerb I noticed the AA (Automobile Association) logo. *Excellent, it would've been impeccably maintained,* I thought.

As the driver got out, I said: "Hi, you must be Tommy." The guy looked at me strange and just walked past.

Just then, with a clanking and a screeching, a pale yellow rusty van pulls up behind him. This thing was a shitheap. Belching smoke, rust holes everywhere, brakes barely working.

"I'm Tommy," the guy with the brylcreemed hair and gold tooth said, optimistically.

Not geared for this

I put my car in for a service, and was frankly used to it always coming back worse than when I put it in, or else it developed an altogether new problem.

Collecting my car from the garage late one night, I paid the hefty bill and the night-shift guy gave me the keys and indicated that the car was "over in the corner".

Sure enough, my car was parked with its nose right up against the wall.

Got in. Started her up. Hear that engine purr. Put it in reverse and...the car wanted to go forward. "What the...?" Tried again. Put the gearstick into reverse...and it wanted to go forward - into the wall. Tried again, moving the gearstick carefully into the reverse position. Same again.

"These f***ing idiots," I fumed, as I stormed back to the guy. "What the f*** have you done to my car???"

He was a bit taken aback, and came over to check. I showed what I was doing and, as I did so, noticed that I was putting it into high gear...reverse was up the *other* side in this car. Doh! Having driven an Alfa for so many years I'd got used to where I thought reverse was *supposed* to be. Although this car was an old Mercedes, I hadn't had it that long.

I slipped it into reverse, sheepishly. "Er, it seems to be Ok now," I said, and drove off feeling like a complete idiot.

Looking like the back of a bus

We were driving one nice clear Tuesday afternoon, when all of a sudden a big and expensive car next to us does something really stupid (as they do).

I noticed the driver was a real *tai-tai* (rich housewife) looking Chinese lady but thought nothing more of it.

Next thing, we pulled into the main road and were travelling quite quickly and saw her coming up behind us, but on the inside kerb-side lane. Looking ahead, I saw a bus stopping at a bus stop (as they do).

This lady was still speeding up, and was right beside me on the inside lane when she impacted with the stationery bus at over 80kmh, pushing her head under the dashboard. I still see that expression at moment of impact today. The car ended up at least 3/4 of its length buried under the bus. She survived, I read in the paper, but what was going through her mind? (resist temptation to insert 'her asshole' joke here - ed.).

One way traffic

I was crossing the road with B, a long time Bangkok resident, when he said: "You know you've lived in Thailand too long when you look *both* ways crossing a one-way street!"

Uneasy rider

I was riding my motorbike out to see a friend in Sai Kung (Hong Kong New Territories) on a Saturday night. I had been out there before, but blowed if I could remember the exact route.

HARDSHIP POSTING

Coming through Shatin or somewhere on the Kowloon side, I took a turn off which fed me straight back into the main street I had just come from. I tried again, same result. I tried a different road, and back to the main street again.

Frustrated, I stopped at the lights. When they turned green, I was obviously over-revving as I dropped the clutch and all of a sudden I was doing this spectacular 'wheelie' for about 100 yards up the main street. Being a fairly new rider, I didn't know how to get the damn thing down, so was part dead-impressed and part shit-scared.

I eventually spotted some police on the side of a bus terminal exit. They must have been pretty bemused to see this motorbike zooming up this bus-only area, until I got up close and they realised it was another dumb *gweilo*.

I explained my predicament and asked for directions. "Simple," they said, motioning the direction and route I should've taken.

Fifteen minutes, and several laps later, I was back in the main street at the lights, cursing myself and most of mainland China, when who should pull up next to me and tap me on the shoulder? One of the cops who had given me directions earlier. With a knowing smile, he was kind enough to escort me through the town and up to the Sai Kung Rd.

Taxi race

Finding a taxi in Central in Hong Kong on a race day was a nightmare. One stinking hot Saturday race day, around mid day, I decided to climb Wyndham Street in the hope of flagging a cab before it reached Central.

After nearly an hour of frustration standing in the sweltering sun, *finally* a vacant taxi came down the hill. It came to a stop about 20 meters from me, which it had to do because of the queue of cars backed up from the traffic light at Queens Road.

As I made a sprint for the taxi, an Indian woman in her forties carrying several large shopping bags dashed out of the sari shop on the corner of On-lan Street and quickly jumped into *my* taxi. I opened the door of the taxi and said to her, firmly: *"Excuse me*, this is my taxi. I've been waiting here for almost an hour!"

She stared straight ahead, ignoring me. *"Excuse me!"* I said, more firmly and louder. She continued to ignore me. I was now angry ... very angry ... but not too sure what I could do. I could hardly drag her out of the taxi, could I? "You... you ... you ...," I stammered, having difficulty getting my tongue around an appropriate curse. Finally I blurted out: "You ... you'll be *Indian* for the rest of your life!"

To this day, she still is.

Lost cause

L was lost in Bangkok one night trying to find his way home, so pulled his car over to ask a tuk-tuk driver for directions.

"Lumpini Park where?" he said. "You drive, I follow, I pay you," he added. He then got back into his car, but the tuk-tuk driver didn't move. He got out and repeated the instruction before getting back into his car. Once again, the tuk-tuk didn't budge. This scene was repeated 8 times, until eventually the tuk-tuk moved off down the road.

He was following, when 300 yards down the road, the tuk-tuk stopped again. They were already at Lumpini Park all the time and L hadn't realised it!

Licensed to seat 450

D was on a bus to Baguio in the Philippines. It was already full to overflowing when they stopped at another stop outside Manila.

"They're picking up more people," his girlfriend L explained.

"But it's already full," he protested. "Where the hell are they gonna fit more people?"

With that, the conductor came down the aisle with a stack of plastic stools which were set up in the aisle of the bus for all the newcomers.

As they rose higher into the mountains, the air conditioning and colder air outside combined with the late hour meant that everyone was absolutely freezing. Several calls to turn the air-conditioner down were met with, "Cannot...it's controlled by thermostat."

So dressed only in t-shirts they froze their butts off all the way to Baguio, with some stranger sitting next to them on a little coloured plastic stool.

HARDSHIP POSTING

If you have a good story about taxis, public transport or mayhem on the roads in Asia, let us know. Email us at hardship_posting@hotmail.com *or fax The Editor at 612-9499-5908.*

"Trouble and strife in Paradise" or "I lub you, Sir, no shit."

True tales involving wives, girlfriends and concubines (sometimes all three simultaneously!).

When it comes to women, I divide them into 3 categories: she who must be *obeyed* (the wife), she who must be *laid* (the mistress) and she who must be *paid* (the short-time floozeys).

The Muslims have got it figured out...*polygamy* is probably the best way to go. A different wife for each day or occasion, or to match a certain outfit or mood, perhaps. The next step down is *bigamy*, in which you share two wives. And then there's the state of having just one wife - *monotony*!

The bored expat housewife stereotype actually does exist. Lonely and homesick while hubby is out sowing wild...sorry, while hubby is out working longer hours than ever, enjoying more challenging and exotic work experiences, and basically living a very fast-paced life. And she's left to scrub her toenails in readiness for that cocktail invitation that might be imminent. I know Dave's long-suffering wife Barb falls into this category (Hi, Barb, if you're reading this!)

But these days I notice these little expat dollies (or Whisky Tangos) are not taking it lying down as they used to, so to speak. They seem to have figured it out that unless they have a competitive offering, hubby is likely to develop "yellow fever"...and we're not talking jaundice here. The reality is that even if they do keep themselves in good shape, she might lose him to the exotic charms of the local lasses. The old "away game" in soccer parlance.

Many Asian cities have become known as "the graveyard of

marriages". I've discussed this at an intellectual level with a number of cultural and social anthropologists, and there seems to be a common consensus as to why Caucasian males prefer Oriental females: basically, your average sized dick looks so damned big in their tiny hands!

The problem, though, is that if you're out there merrily sowing the seeds, the handbrake gets a trifle suspicious when you can't quite fulfil her needs. Because she's human too, you know...well, ok I get your point. But anyway, here's a little tip from Colonel Ken's military days - always leave one shot in the barrel.

Alternatively, the other thing to do is not try and sneak in quietly when you get home really late. Make sure you make as much noise coming home possible. Bang the car door, jangle your keys, struggle with the lock, and make heavy footsteps throughout the house. Then when you finally get to your bedroom, make amorous advances to your wife with your beer breath and dribble - you can bet your bloody bottom dollar she'll pretend to be sound asleep! You're home and hosed, as it were.

It's funny to see not unattractive white girls that would be fending off dinner invitations left, right and centre in their home country begging to get a look in, meaning a bonk, in Asia (hilarious to me, not to them obviously).

Yet the Asian female has so much to prove. She is seen as demure and submissive, and needs to break these shackles behind closed doors. In other words, they go off! Oooooh, Lordy, yes!!! "They don't call them LBFM's for nothing," Pete says.

Look at who holds the world record for bonking...is it some big-hipped and big-lipped Texan broad? No, it's an otherwise sweet girl-next-door type originally from Singapore, Annabelle Chong. 250 guys in one night. That's approximately 17 football teams, depending on which shaped ball you play with. I believe the last few guys were wearing snorkels, flippers and full-length wet-suits. Now *that*'s the kind of girl we like to have living next door.

Having said that, there are two words which I find sum up some of the Oriental delights I've had the pleasure of mating, er, meeting: celibate and conniving. Yip, they sell-a-bit here, sell-a-bit there. And are always asking, "can-I-have this?" and "can-I-have that?"

HARDSHIP POSTING

My good friend Jim Aitchison has become somewhat of an expert in this field with his definitive works like The Official Guide to the Sarong Party Girl (or SPG for short). "And, of course she is the embodiment of the male Caucasian dream; the exotic, erotic Oriental girl, Suzie Wong in a sarong, complete with flashing eyes, a sexy figure and a sexually alert personality. She is the girl he dreamed of finding in the East."

Aah, I remember romance. In fact I'm already planning a little surprise for Mrs Col. Ken's big 50th birthday celebration next year - I'm going to trade the old trout in for a couple of twenty-five year olds!

But it's not like this consorting is a late 20th century phenomena, my mate Dave tells me. As far back as the 17th century, the fine men of the English East India Company were having their wicked way with the willing locals. According to the book, The Honourable Company, "In 1661 the ubiquitous Captain Hamilton maintained that the attraction of Ayuthai, the Siamese capital, had little to do with Siamese trade and a lot to do with Siamese hospitality. 'The Europeans who trade to Siam accommodate themselves with temporary wives who', the Captain reports with presumably, inside knowledge, 'generally prove the most obedient, loving and chaste.' They were also wonderfully understanding and raised no objection over their red-faced husbands 'continually carousing in drunkenness with wine and women'."

Perfect! And what a fine breed these fillies are. It's even pushed grown men to document their behaviour and whereabouts with a David Attenborough-like verve. The tome I refer to is called "The Daves' Encyclopedia of South East Asian Pussy." A true literary classic to rival the works of Conrad, Maugham and others, compiled by an august group of gentlemen that have collectively seen more Siamese pussy than the RSPCA.

And then there's the whole Mail Order Bride phenomenon. My favourite part is licking the stamp!

And you can't help noticing over in Tokyo, the phone boxes are plastered with colourful little stickers advertising their services. You don't have to be fluent in Japanese to work out what's for sale. Other places are a bit more reserved. In Korea and Taiwan you have 'barber shops'. It's amazing how many gentlemen with very presentable short hair suddenly develop the need for yet another haircut.

And, everywhere else, nearly every second shop it seems in some places, is the ubiquitous massage parlour. The 'chiropractor'. The rub and tug shop. The steam and cream joint.

To sum it up, in Asia, where there's a willy there's a way.

Colonel Ken

www.hardshipposting.com

Name dropper.
B had made several business trips to Bangkok and always enjoyed getting out and about at night.

One particular trip, his wife was accompanying him, and they decided to go for a late evening stroll through the Patpong bar area.

This one bar girl recognised him, and called out to him. He pretended not to recognise her or acknowledge her.

"I know you, I know you," she kept saying.

"No, no, no," he kept waving her away. "Never been here before," he said.

With that, she disappears into the bar, and re-emerges further up the street, with his business card! "This you, this you!" she says.

He was totally snookered on this one, and he had more than a little explaining to do. Why the bar-girl wanted to 'get' him remains unclear.

Chest thumping exercise
I had been living in Indonesia for a couple of years when a friend from The States came over to visit. It was his first time to Indonesia and I got him pretty fired up in advance telling him how easy it was going to be for him to get laid. My buddy fancied himself a bit of a stud, so he was pretty sure that he'd do well with the Indonesian ladies.

Once he arrived in Jakarta we set out on a road trip across Java. We spent 3 nights in various places like Bandung, and Yogyakarta. Each night we went out to the bars in search of ladies. Each night my buddy came up empty-handed. This is not easy to do but he managed it somehow. On the 4th night we were in a small town in East Java. I felt like I was letting him down after all my talk about how he was going to get laid all the time.

So I took it into my own hands (no, not that) and decided to pay to get a girl up for him. It was a small town, and not much around, but the doorman went off into the night to scare up some action. After about half an hour the doorman returned with a couple of girls. One was god-awful ugly so I had to send her packing. I brought the other girl into the room so my pal could see her and determine if he wanted her. My buddy was already in bed, bare-chested waiting in anticipation. I paraded the girl in and had my buddy size her up. He nodded in approval.

But then he watched in shock as the girl pointed at his bare chest, and shook her head in disgust.

"I don't want," she yelled, and ran for the door.

I will never again see an ego crash so hard. There was my horny buddy in a seedy hotel in a small, poor town in East Java and he had just been turned down by a prostitute who found his hairy chest too disgusting to be next to.

Taken to the cleaners

One of my clients in Taiwan was an American who happily adopted the expatriate habit of acquiring a local Chinese girlfriend. J met his at one of the hostess clubs in Taipei and she became a fixation in his life.

J would send his company-paid driver to pick her up for dates and he openly talked - actually, it was more like bragging - with me about her charms.

When his wife returned to The States for home leave, J invited his local interest to come live with him for the month. How much more convenient! His housekeeper might have been somewhat surprised by this guest, but her silence was assured as long as she wanted to remain employed.

He even provided his girlfriend with a key to his American style home. This was where he made his mistake. When J left for home leave his girlfriend returned and 'borrowed' most of his wife's clothes. Evening gowns to casual elegance befitting the expatriate spouse's life, they were gone!

J never mentioned this problem to me. I heard about it from my wife who had heard about it from J's grumbling wife.

And, no word on how he answered to his wife but I suspect it went something like: "Gee, honey, the dry-cleaners must have lost them."

Rub and tug

Walking back his Manila hotel one night, my friend P was accosted by this young girl looking for business out the front of the local church.

He said he'd already spent all his money and was going home. "You can pay by credit card," the little honey said.

He was amazed when she pulled out a pencil and 'rubbed' his Visa card under a piece of plain paper and got him to sign it. She then rendered the services in the church carpark.

On the cards

S had been in Hong Kong a little while, and his marriage was on the rocks. They had a big tussle over their marital property and belongings, coming to a mutually-agreeable arrangement. But his wife turned into a bitter and twisted so-and-so, and resented the fact that she was returning home to America alone.

S tried to get over this, and was painting the town red in Wanchai every night (possibly the cause of his break-up in the first place!)

Next thing, he received his Visa card bill...apart from the self-inflicted damage at Wanchai bars, he realised a fatal mistake - he had not cancelled his wife's supplementary card and she took cash advances to the maximum limit and cleaned him out big time.

Pull the other one

PS and I were in Penang buzzing around on motorbikes, and decided to stop at a "bathhouse" for a 'steam and cream', or 'rub and tug.'

We went in, discussed the options, selected the girls and, anticipating an enjoyable time, arranged to meet back at the same spot.

An hour later, we were both back at reception...clean as a whistle from head to toe, hair nicely done and smelling wonderful. Unfortunately, they didn't 'take the top off it' as we expected so, a little mystified, we hopped back onto our bikes and rode off into the sunset. Smelling wonderful.

Dirty young man

My Filipina wife and I had the blessing and problem in The Philippines of being able to understand the Tagalog conversations going on around us.

Often it was along the lines of "Shame, look at that poor little girl with that dirty old bastard."

Not a lot of good for my ego, given that my wife is one year older than me!

Dial-a-divorce

This guy was settling in for a rather big night down at the bars in Patpong. He did the right thing and called his wife, saying he was out with some important business colleagues and would be home rather late. Coming back into the bar, he then placed his mobile on the bar counter in front of him.

He then proceeded to chat up this particular bird in the bar, at length, over several drinks. A good night was had, but all hell broke loose when he got home.

Unfortunately, he had accidently pushed 'redial' on his mobile phone, and his wife had listened in on the whole conversation with this bar girl!

Lip Service

The dinner party was in full swing, when the topic came around to a case in the news which highlighted that blow-jobs were, by law, illegal at that time in Singapore. Even between consenting married adults, in the privacy of their own bedroom, with the blinds drawn.

One of the wives, a Chinese Singaporean, expressed surprise and shock at this. "Really?" she said, aghast at the discovery.

"I don't know why you're so concerned," said A, her English husband, "It's not like *we've* got much to worry about!"

Your place or mine

It was a classic scenario...a big night on the cocktails, ending up in Number 97 in Lan Kwai Fong, Hong Kong.

I was chatting up this hot little Malay bird, who had approached me and said, "You would look really good tied up". Always a good starting point, for a conversation. Finally, we got to the "your place or mine?" part of the evening, and she nominated her place. So off we went in a cab. She gave the cabby directions.

Pissed as I was, I was a little surprised when the cab pulled up outside of *my* place. *I could've sworn we were going to her place,* I thought.

Turned out we lived in the same block, a few floors apart!

This led to a few months of very tempestuous sex. She would turn up any time of day or night for a bonk. And she'd often leave notes in my car windscreen downstairs saying things like "You've got a great dick," with lipstick kiss-marks all over it.

Blue movies

It was my first date with C, a Hong Kong Chinese girl. Although she'd had a Caucasian boyfriend before, she was a fairly conservative type of lady in most respects.

We decided to go and see "Betty Blue" at the cinemas, a French movie that was sweeping all before it at the time. Neither of us knew what to expect, but bought two tickets anyway.

So we sit down, with the usual first date nerves and electricity and the movie starts. The first 5 minutes was this full-on French humping scene, even before the beginning credits rolled. A little embarrassed, I turned to her and whispered: "I think it's a comedy!"

Bum deal

X was keen on the "little boys". One night, after a few drinks and whatever they got up to in bed, he and his nightly prize were sleeping. However, he awoke to find this guy rummaging through his wallet.

Incensed, he allegedly threw the lad out of his house and crashed out again.

He was awoken a few hours later by the Police...they had found his companion near dead in a pool of blood outside his place. He remembered very little of this, of course, but it was to haunt him as the 'victim' remained in a coma for about 7 months, and the prosecution had to wait to see what the person's fate was before determining the degree of charges.

Fortunately, the guy pulled through, and he was eventually acquitted after several rounds of trials and appeals.

He later returned to his home country, where reportedly his new boyfriend (a junkie by all accounts) borrowed $10,000 bucks off him before cleaning out the house of all valuables and disappearing.

Blonde leading the blind

I was back in Australia for a break from Hong Kong, when I met this wonderful lady at a friend's party. She was highly attractive in the Gwyneth Paltrow / Sharon Stone mould, and mentioned she might be moving to Japan to become an English teacher. We chatted for hours. A few months later, I thought I'd write her a letter, beginning "Hi, you probably don't remember me, but I was the guy who..." and mailed it to her in Sydney. Not three days later, I received a letter from her saying "Hi, you probably don't remember me, but I was the gal who..." She was now based in Tokyo. Amazingly, our letters had crossed in the air.

We struck up a great pen-pal relationship (long before the days of email). Regular and fun correspondence. What's more, she began inviting me to stay with her and she'd show me Tokyo (and a lot more besides!)

As soon as I could, I made plans to go and visit her in her little Tokyo apartment...anticipating a short break with this wonderful warm, witty and downright sexy Scandinavian woman.

At the airport, I didn't recognise this dumpy lady with bad acne calling out to me. *Shit, I couldn't have been that pissed when I first met her!*

I spent the next 4 days trying *not* to get laid by her, I'm ashamed to say, as I tried to wrestle with the image I had in my head, and the person in front of me. "Don't tell me you're like all these guys that are just interested in the Asian girls," she said. *I am now*, I thought.

Getting back to Hong Kong, the first thing I did was pull out my photo albums and check...yes, she *was* that beautiful before. Oh, the disappointment!

Bizarre love quadrangle

In head office, I had gone out with this particular lady, B. After breaking up with her (her instigation) I had begun seeing another lady in the office, A. I was then transferred to Hong Kong.

I had heard that B was coming to town for a week, so thought this would be a good chance to perhaps revisit some previous romantic ground, so to speak.

When she arrived, she was very very distant towards me, which I thought odd. She was also completely against meeting up for lunch, dinner, drinks, whatever I suggested. *Strange*, I thought.

Only after she had left Hong Kong, did I learn why. She was now my boss's regular squeeze, and she had also found out about my relationship in the office with A.

Very messy indeed!

A matter of time

It had been a huge night out, and Mr X arrived home about 5:30 in the morning. Trying his best not to wake the wife, he tip-toed into the bedroom, and was doing his best to undress and slip into bed un-noticed. He removed his tie, and shirt. His pants were just about off when his wife awoke.

"What f***ing time do you call this, then?" she barked.

"Uh...uh...I'm up early...I've got a lot of stuff to finish up at the office," he said, creating the impression that he'd just got out of bed and was changing to go to work.

Of course, he had to go through with the charade. He pulled his pants back on, put on a new shirt and tie, had a coffee and had to go to the office. He felt like shit, but it was worse than the other possible consequences! They laugh about it now.

On-line sex

R was a bit of a legend in Hong Kong. The old Makati Inn was one of his favourite haunts, where he would pick up Filipina girls on a very regular basis (the small matter of his marriage and family didn't seem to restrict this).

The extent of his activities only became clear once he left the company, though. His replacement, P, requested for a new extension number after a few weeks of incoming calls on his direct line at work:

"Hellllooooo. Is Meesterrrrr Rob derrrrrr?" the string of Filipinas would enquire one after another.

Brotherly love

My brother was visiting us, and stayed with us in the apartment on the couch. One day we had been out playing cricket (me playing, him spectating) when he had met this 20-something English girl (whom I believe was attached to one of the other club's players). We ended up at Anywhere Bar if I remember correctly, and had all stumbled home from there, including this very presentable young English lass.

My wife and I said goodnight and crashed out, leaving my brother and this lass to their own devices outside.

About 4am, the door to our room opened, and it was this bird - stark naked - walking into our room. She disappeared into the bathroom. Moments later she reappeared and walked towards our double bed and flopped onto it - right between me and my wife!

She had a great body, and my wife and I were just flabbergasted, finding it wildly amusing. I was actually half wondering whether I should give her one or not, when she realised her mistake, said "Oops, sorry" and waltzed out through the door again.

Overheads

Overheard in Harry's Bar, Singapore: this guy was saying to his mate that he was doing a quick calculation and reckoned he spent more each month on massages than he did on his son's private school education.

Tri-cycle

B and I had gone out for a few beers, and having done that thought the next logical thing to do would be to take home one of the delightful Thai ladies we had been talking to in the bar.

As B did not drive, we all got onto my motorbike. The two of us, with the girlie sandwiched in the middle! B lived quite a way out of town, so we were very conspicuously riding for a good half an hour to his place.

Back at his place, not sure of how the arrangements were going to work out, I promptly fell asleep on his couch. B proceeded to have his wicked way with the girl right next to me (as he didn't have a bedroom per se). In the morning asked *me* to pay for her services as he had no cash!

Something was definitely wrong with this picture.

Life has its ups and downs

NM and I ended up back at my apartment with some Thai takeaway (not food) but were intent on doing some more drugs first. We pulled out the kitbag of uppers and downers, and proceeded to make a mixture of uppers to inhale.

The girl, either perturbed by the drug use, or feeling left out, stormed across the living room floor, grabbed a handful of downers, stuffed them down her throat then ran and locked herself in the bathroom.

N and I looked at each other horrified - it was a lethal dosage. *Shiiiiiiiiiiiiiiittttt!!!*

We banged on the door but she refused to come out. We knew if we did not get to her soon, she would be a gonner. We banged and yelled, but she still did not budge. We knew we could not call the police or the ambulance. What to do with the body?

After what seemed like an eternity, the door opened. She was slumped on the floor. We quickly grabbed her and held her face over the toilet bowl, and N stuck his finger down her throat. She emptied her stomach completely. Saved!

A wonderful end to a romantic evening. Not.

Pulls the birds

F was a sweet and rather naïve English girl who worked as a secretary in our office in Hong Kong. She wasn't the most attractive girl in the office it must be said, and wasn't inundated with invitations for dates.

But there was this middle-aged guy, rich as all hell, who fancied her. He called up, invited her out, and offered to pick her up from the office one evening.

He turned up in his gleeming Maserati, giving it a couple of extra bursts on the accelerator just for good effect.

F hops in and says: "Ooh, this is nice. Is it a Ford?"

Dipping the pen in company ink

A, a Hong Konger, was a real sweetie in our Hong Kong office. Hard working and cute, she caught everyone's eye, especially L's, one of the local guys. They ended up getting married.

No sooner had they returned from honeymoon, and still working in the same office together, than L was bonking C, another Chinese honey in the same office.

Obviously, the marriage fell apart in very short order. A ended up with one of the *gwailo* managers in the same office, but left soon after.

Love's a beach

NA and his girlfriend were stationed in Hong Kong, and holidayed often in Boracay. It was there, during a romantic beach stroll that N proposed. Three years later they decided to get married... in Boracay.

All the arrangements were being made to fly the families out when he got unexpectedly transferred to Paris. They decided to go ahead with Boracay as the location, and then things get interesting...

First on arrival in The Philippines, they were told their priest - the celebrant- had died. A replacement was found, but he insisted on doing it only if the rest of his family could fly to Boracay, too. Granted.

Then N's Mum was stranded at Manila Airport and could not get on a flight. She shared her plight with another guy in the queue who happened to work for Emergency Assist, who called back to head office. Within hours, she was being 'med-evacced' on a plane to Boracay. After all, you could not have a wedding without the groom's mum. They flew low over the beach on arrival, circling a few times, and dipped their wings to let everyone know Mum had arrived.

A chapel was specially built on the sand. A spectacular wedding was capped off by fireworks and Roman candles going off, with local village kids singing Tagalog songs in the background.

Burning question

M and P moved from Bangkok to Hong Kong. P was Thai, and had never really experienced a winter. She was puzzled when M announced one day he needed to go to the department store to buy a heater.

"Heater?" she asked, quizzically. "What is that?" Coming from the tropics, of course, there was no such thing as a device to *warm up* a room!

Get it in writing

My Asian girlfriend and I developed this great thing based on redeemable vouchers in our relationship. It started one day when she was having this terrible day at work and I faxed her a voucher for a neck massage which I proposed to administer that very evening to help her unwind from the day.

She was most grateful (in more ways than one) and soon we were regularly exchanging vouchers.

The piece de irresistable, though, was my birthday present one year. She presented me this beautiful pack of cards she had designed and printed. Each was a voucher with really creative wording, but offering a smorgasbord of wonderful options from "Picnic with basket of goodies and champagne" through to "Candlelit dinner at most expensive European restaurant in town" and so on.

My favourites though were the "This entitles bearer to rip off my lingerie with his teeth and tie me to the bedhead. Limit one expensive set of lingerie per session." And similarly raunchy ones.

Unfortunately we broke up just after I had redeemed the "This entitles bearer to a breakfast in bed, served with high heels, fishnet stockings and maple syrup" voucher.

She loves chocolates

My flatmate S enjoyed the local ladies very much, and being a tall quite good looking guy, had quite a bit of success.

One day, there was a large bowl of chocolate sauce in the fridge.

"What's this?" I asked. He explained it was a special dessert that D had whipped up. The next evening when I came home early, his door was slightly open and I noticed he and D naked on the bed...

They were both covered in chocolate sauce and eagerly lapping it up.

Written off

My wife and I had been invited to dinner with J and his wife Wendy. A pleasant dinner was had, and way too much wine for a Sunday night.

Instead of driving, I was thinking of cabbing home. J insisted we slept over at their place, and drive home in the morning instead. "Besides I'm always up at the crack of dawn to get to the office, anyway," J reassured me.

HARDSHIP POSTING

In the morning I awoke, feeling more than a little seedy, and looked at my watch. Nearly 8am! Jumping out of bed, the rest of the house was still dark and quiet - obviously the previous night's intake of wine had over-ruled J's otherwise reliable body-clock.

We decided to leave them a note and scarper. I grabbed a pen and paper and blearily wrote:

"Dear J and Wendy, thanks for a really great evening. See you soon. Love, Simon and *Wendy*."

My wife *Michelle* was not impressed! Monday mornings were never my strong suit.

Cat-astrophe

L and his family were great cat lovers, and had a cat they had owned for years. One night, L ran it over in his driveway (after a few drinks, more than likely). He distraughtly told the family its had died 'of old age' and promptly buried it.

However, the *real* story was known to his friends, and a few months later at a party his wife overheard someone relating the story of how he'd run this cat over. She was furious, and ran like an exocet missile across the room and thumped him in front of all his friends.

Licentious behaviour

My Thai wife had to go back to Surin province to apply for her driver's license, as everything in Thailand is dictated by the locality of your land title.

Surin is a long way North, so we reluctantly made the trip, only to find that there were various steps involved in getting the license and it could not be issued in a single day.

Pleading with the official, we said we could not come back any time soon so could we please do the practical test as well. "Sure," he said. "You know how to drive?" he asked my wife. "Yes," she replied, partly accurately. "Ok, you just drive around the *outside* of this track once," he instructed, telling her not to worry about the obstacle course, twists and turns in the track etc, which she did whilst he didn't so much as look across to see how she was doing.

When she came back, she was the proud owner of a Thai driving license, which probably explains a few things.

A marked man

On holiday in Bangkok, I stayed with my mate B. He had recently got divorced from his Thai wife and taken up with a new Thai girlfriend. One morning, I was sitting around having a coffee when I saw the ex-wife turn up to the house. I knew this was going to be ugly, so I introduced B's new girlfriend as *my* friend.

The ex-wife was not fooled, and produced this .38 handgun. I ducked for cover, and she stormed through the house threatening everybody, yelling and waving the gun around. I was sure it would end in bloodshed, so rushed out of the house, but fortunately no shots were fired.

If you have a good story about wives, girlfriends or concubines in Asia, let us know. Email us at **hardship_posting@hotmail.com** *or fax The Editor at 612-9499-5908.*

"Sayonara!"

*True tales of moving farewells
and moving companies.*

You know you've been in Asia too long when you're not surprised to see footprints on the toilet seat...and they're *yours*!

Even comments like Old Asia Hand and Fat White Bastard are heard behind my back frequently, and to my face even more frequently. But at least for me here, being a Fat White Bastard - something akin to Moby Dick on a bad hair day - is a novelty act.

A lot of expats never leave for that very fear of anonymity. Back home, they'd just blend in with the crowd at the suburban shopping mall. Just another fat ass in a fat ass world. Goodbye Great White God status.

But there are some to whom Asia really is a hardship posting (hope the publisher notices the gratuitous plug there) and they head back to Blighty or The States or Oz, or wherever 'home' is, as soon as their Tour of Duty is complete. Sometimes even before. Can't get out of the place quick enough. The fish and chips don't taste the same, can't go see my football team get thrashed every week, blah blah blah. Unbelievable. They want to turn the whole bloody world into a homogenous MacDonalds outlet. Not that I've got anything against that, mind you - some of my best friends are homogeniuses.

Granted, you've got to keep in touch with the real world. Which I do by flying to Bangkok once a month or so. Just to make sure that progress and technology is not leaving me behind. You'll be pleased to know I'm getting a computer next week so I can get on the email and swap lame jokes and log into AdultAsia.com. Of course, I won't operate it myself...I'll hire a young lass to do that for me, like most things. Don't worry about the Old Asia Hand, it's the Young Asian Hands that keep me here.

Some dare to leave, and we take bets on how long the bastards will be out there before running back with their tail between their legs. At least I think it's their tail; looks like it from here. Because their hometown has become a foreign place to them. Somehow strange and alien. Peopled by narrow mindsets and political correctness. Not the perfect world they saw through those rose-coloured glasses. And no chrome poles!

But for all its foibles, Asia is Asia. It wraps its invisible tentacles around you and sucks you in like a giant Japanese-made vacuum cleaner (I had a girlfriend like that once). Leaving strong men, like my good friend Douglas MacArthur in The Philippines, to say things like, " I shall return."

As I have never left Asia, I am ill equipped to comment on this area. But one of the guys that had a fair old tour is Lloydie. You probably noticed his name on the front of the book. I'll let *him* tell you about leaving then...wimp! Betcha he's back here before you know it.

* * *

A Letter from Changi Airport Departure Lounge

"Honey, we're moving!" These three simple words set in motion an epic saga, which still unfolds as we await our homebound flight to Sydney.

I had been an 'expat' for 12 1/2 action-packed years. In the intervening period, I had:

added a wife;

and a child;

gained several kilograms,

and lost my dashing young looks. Or so my wife told me.

First was breaking the news.

"Good, when are you leaving?" my *best* friends enquired. Others reeled in disbelief. "Austraaaaalia? What's there but all those fridge-sized sheilas? The lights go out about 9pm for God's sake- you'll be bored stupid," was the typical encouraging response.

HARDSHIP POSTING

Can I recall my resignation? Would my boss be agreeable to the rectal-exhumation of my job?

Too late. The moving companies were coming to quote the next day.

My time in Asia taught me to bargain ruthlessly and do deals till I could see eyes beginning to water. "We're the best, of course we're more expensive. Take it or leave it," moving company man number three said high-handedly and put down the phone.

So we decided to go with the over-caffeinated highly-strung man with all those beeping and buzzing telephonic devices that quoted the cheapest. By virtue of his bounding nature, and our onward destination, I dubbed him Captain Kangaroo.

Several attempts to get hold of him to confirm the order should have triggered the alarm. However, I was suffering the newly-discovered psychological syndrome of "homecoming stupefaction" which makes you exude bonhomie to all sorts of morons you'd be more than pleased never to see again in your life.

Time to notify the landlord. He had just renovated the house for us and taken a $1000 per month rental reduction. After a major withdrawal from my charm reservoir, the landlord was sorted. Not pleased, but we're off the hook at least. OK, we're done!

"What about school in Australia, and where are we going to stay until the tenants move out?" my wife enquired in that practical wife sort of tone.

Doh!

"And what are we doing about a farewell party, and where are we going to stay once the movers come in?"

Doh!!

"And you still need to sell your car."

Doh!!!

"What about my Australian residency visa?"

Doh!!!!

"And..."

A list of things to do was drawn up. Not only was the time-bomb ticking, but someone had lit the fuse, just to keep it interesting.

"Beep beep beep." The unmistakable sound of a moving truck backing into the driveway. Men dismounted like commandos storming an embassy. They turned the living room into a cardboard sculpture theme park. The tablecloth was practically swished away from beneath us, and the dining table turned into a bizarre-shaped origami before our Corn Flakes were digested.

Within three days our life was in 227 boxes, labeled helpfully with flowery descriptive monikers such as "wood piece," " papers," and "kitchen".

Now, to sell the car. My 1990 Toyota Corolla was a gleaming chariot that had to find a good home. Or the right price.

David The Dealer convinced me the car was a festering heap of crap and I should really be paying *him* to dispose of it. Bank orders and keys were exchanged, and he went powering into the sunset. Car sold. Tick.

Next was the Immigration Department. My number 988. "Bing," now serving 247. Twiddle my thumbs. Now serving 248. Read a paper. Now serving 249.Grab some *makan*. 251. Eventually I was officially "Cancelled". Next, on to the CPF Board. Ten years of savings that I hadn't been able to invest in honorary Brannigan's shares like the rest of my salary. I fairly skipped and whistled my way out, hardly feeling my feet touch the ground (much the same as Brannigan's on a good night!).

Empty house. Full pockets. Time for a party.

Saturday night was a flurry of caterers setting up their stainless steel temples for a right royal MSG-fest. The rent-a-dj going through his annoying "check 1,2" routine. I had a bar full of the finest nectars and spirits that had to be depleted before sunrise. The rest of the night was a blur of hospitality, joviality, and depravity. Then, around 3am, gravity.

Sunday morning. Why is that road construction crew drilling outside the window of my hotel? And now the CableVision team have joined in. Worse still, they're not outside at all. They're in my head. Nurse, Bloody Mary please!

Monday. D-Day. A final meeting with Captain Kangaroo. "Just need you to fill out this, this, this, sign here, here and here. A photocopy of every page of your passport. Plus a breakdown of the value of each the 227 boxes on the inventory list (yes, the ones listed as "lounge," "clothes," and "kitchen") for insurance purposes," Kangaroo requested. "So we'll have the stuff soon?" I inquired naively. "Yes, Mr Lloyd. One month maximum."

Good, I think, because these underpants and socks are going to be well past their use-by date by then.

I slumped into the armchair in the Raffles Class departure lounge. "Bloody Mary please!"

* * *

Good one, Lloydie. I think it's another reason I never left Asia - couldn't be bollocked going through all of that. Speaking to him the other day, he said it was nearly 4 months before they actually got their boxes, and luckily not much was broken. I tell you what - I'm gonna stay in my place in Koh Samui till the funeral director carries me out of there in my box. Too flaming hard!

Anyway, I'm going to have a cheeky little G&T now in remembrance of all my good friends that no longer live in Asia. But at least now I can keep in touch with them by female, I mean email. By the way, if you want to drop me a line, I'll be hooked up next week. My address is **ColonelKen@hotmail.com**. If I don't respond straight away, it probably just means my secretary's servicing my hard drive.

I love Asia. Cop you later!

Colonel Ke

Chest pains

Friends of ours returned home to the U.S. after 15 years as expatriates. During that time they had lived in Thailand, Puerto Rico, Holland and Hong Kong. They had also travelled extensively throughout Asia.

They collected some interesting art and furniture. One piece of furniture acquired in HK was a very large wood Chinese blanket chest appraised at US$25,000.

On packing day, the moving company very carefully placed all of their possessions in cardboard boxes. From clothes and shoes, to photo albums and art, everything was wrapped in paper and packed snuggly away. What could not be put in a cardboard box was protected with a wrapping of corrugated paper.

Their U.S.-based company had moved people all over the globe and found that they could save a few dollars by contracting with different companies for every step of a household move. So, in this move, the company that did the packing simply delivered the boxes to a pier in HK and a freight forwarder was contracted to pack the goods in a container. Unfortunately, their entire household sat in the cardboard boxes out on a pier during all that rain. Everything was soaked through.

The handover celebration over, the dock-workers resumed their duties and the wet cardboard boxes were packed in a large metal container and loaded on the deck of a freighter for the journey to New York.

Six weeks later the container arrived at their new home. Our friends were looking forward with great anticipation to having their possessions back. The door of the container swung open, and...MOULD! *Everything* was green. Even the insides of shoes were well coated with a heavy green layer of mould.

Most of the container's contents were a total loss. Only the blanket chest was salvageable.

Couldn't leave soon enough

For my farewell from the company, a dinner at a private room in a seafood restaurant was organised. Much beer was drunk, much fun had, speeches made, etc.

As we turfed out of the restaurant, it was time to kick on. Unfortunately, all the locals and some of the expats were going home (because it was a weeknight), leaving me to kick on with my boss (the real reason I was leaving) and the finance director (not a noted party animal, it must be said).

We had one drink downtown and then went our separate ways. Forever.

www.hardshipposting.com

Shooting through

It was time to bid farewell to Hong Kong, and there was really only one place that could possibly tolerate our antics...Casa Mexicana. (Is that still going?)

The usual night at Casa Mex involved dancing on tables, banging tambourines and canastas as the strolling minstrels belted out another Beatles favourite, and industrial quantities of marguerita.

Tonight was all of that and more. Someone had decided water pistols would be a good theme, so everyone came bearing arms. Toys 'R Us must have sold out that day...Super Soakers of every description were pressed into action in the restaurant.

Before long, we were all completely drenched. The floor of the restaurant was under about 6 inches of water. I remember some guy tipping an entire bucket of water on somebody...much more effective than a water pistol. And the management and other diners amazingly thought this was all wonderful fun - because it was.

Next day, I headed off for Bangkok, stuffing as many water pistols into my luggage as I could (as all my other cargo had already shipped). At the airport, I was stopped at the x-ray machines. The outline of several guns made them a little nervous! *Could they search my bags?*

A few officers pounced on my bags, unzipping them and pulling out the offending articles...bright plastic toy guns. Nervous and relieved grins all round when I tried to explain what a full-grown man was doing with these things. But they still insisted on packing and flying them separately- I could only get them back once we reached Bangkok.

Small token of esteem

It was my last day in the office, and a big send-off was planned. The Regional President was flying in, as were other regional directors. An all staff meeting was convened, the usual eulogies delivered.

Then came the big moment - the farewell present from the company.

The President proudly handed me this beautifully wrapped package. I began opening it, and inside is a beautiful velvet package. The staff 'ooh' and 'aah' in anticipation. I undo the cord of the bag and, tadaaaaaaaa!!!

I proudly hold aloft the tiniest silver beer mug you have ever seen. The President looked a little confused. The staff hushed.

"Oh, a bonsai beer mug," I exclaimed, slightly amused.

Anyway, after the meeting was adjourned, the President pulls me to one side and says, "Hey, look, I'm real sorry about that mug. My secretary faxed me the price to approve and it cost so much I assumed it was a full size one. I can change it if you like..."

"No, no," I said. "It'll always remind me of this company...small beer!"

A bad move

Moving from Singapore to Indonesia, RS had a lot of stuff broken, battered and otherwise rendered useless. He was furious, as much of it had been carefully collected over many years as an expat in many different parts of Asia.

The moving company offered him 40% of the shipment value as compensation, and was digging themselves in, firmly.

"No," he said. "I have worked in Asia for 16 years and if you don't ever want to move another expat in Asia again, fine. I will pay for an ad if necessary...," he threatened.

A check for the full amount arrived the next day.

If you have a good story about farewell parties or moving companies in Asia, let us know. Email us at hardship_posting@hotmail.com *or fax The Editor at 612-9499-5908.*

A few words about the Hardship Posting Team

Stuart Lloyd (Editor)

Stuart is a freelance writer/journalist who now lives in Sydney, Australia. He specialises in marketing, travel and music writing, having been published in Variety, Outbound Travel, HK Magazine, Australian Songwriter, Big O, Adweek Asia, B&T, Professional Marketing and Retail Asia, amongst others, and is the Editor (Oceania) of Orientation.Com.

He has a degree in Psychology and Mass Communication and spent over 16 years in advertising - during which he built and sold his agency to a major multinational. He has also been involved in radio broadcasting, documentary-making, and band management.

He has been married for 10 years to Michelle, a Filipina. They have one child, a dog, two budgies and three goldfish.

Stuart is also a performing songwriter, having received airplay on major Australian and American radio stations.

Colonel Ken Oathe (Narrator)

Col. Ken is an enigmatic expat who lives an idyllic existence on Koh Samui, Thailand. Born in 1946 in Australia, he was a military man for much of his life. His claims that he fought in both the Boer War and the Vietnam War are to be taken with a grain of salt, some lemon and a shot of tequila.

He is now a keen philanthropist and is a regular speaker on the corporate lunch and dinner circuit throughout Asia. A true bon vivant that pops up everywhere there is free booze. Or pretty ladies.

He has been married nearly 25 years to his Hong Kong-born wife, and believes "happily married" is an oxymoron.

Col. Ken is an avid rugby fan, and has never missed a single Hong Kong Rugby Sevens tournament since its inception. He was also a champion dragon-boater in his youth, but once again his medal claims don't tally with the record books.

For bookings, he can be contacted directly by email at ColonelKen@hotmail.com or through the publishers.

Larry Feign (Illustrations)
Larry is an American who spent 13 years in Hong Kong, honing his craft on the daily "World of Lily Wong" cartoon strip for The South China Morning Post. In addition, he has had several books of his own published. He currently works as a freelance humorist.
Larry recently relocated to London, where he lives with his wife Cathy and their two children.
To find out more about Larry and his work, check out www.humorist.net

Patrick Gauvain (Photography & Cover Design)
Shrimp, as he is usually called, has lived in Asia for three decades. In that time he has worked his way up to building Shrimp Studios, a major photographic, advertising, design, publishing and merchandising business.
He and his family live in Bangkok, Thailand.
His 'fame' is related to the exotic and erotic capturing of Asia's feminine charms. To check out more of Shrimp's fantastic catalogue, go to www.shrimpworld.com

Check out our website at
www.hardshipposting.com/hp
for new stories, expat links and more mayhem
and misadventure with Col. Ken

 **Ladies and gentlemen, bastards and bargirls, join our online expat community at www.hardshipposting.com/hp**

For more mayhem and misadventure, laughs, new stories, freebies, travel trials and tribulations, and over 200 useful and interesting links to expat sites.

Sign up for the "Friends of Colonel Ken" Club - it's free and you'll get:

* A regular "Debriefing Asia" newsletter, with my cynical observations of news items in Asia, jokes, relevant new web links, and sneak previews of the latest stories of misadventure
* special discounts on Hardship Posting books and merchandise such as calendars
* special offers from those in our club, such as bars, hotels, mobile phones, travel, moving companies or whatever dodgy goods or services they provide! (and free links to your homepage or relevant site)
* invitations to join the Colonel for some fun and games when he comes to your city/town/remote outpost
* and, mainly, a sense of belonging to a group of like-minded individuals that enjoy living life in Asia to the fullest

www.hardshipposting.com/hp

It's more than a website - it's a way of life!

Cop you later.

Colonel Ken

When's the last time you had 8" in front of you?*
Introducing Colonel Ken's 2001 Desktop Calendar!

Have you got yours yet? The Colonel and Shrimp have got together to produce this desktop calendar, full of practical features such as:
* 12 beautiful Thai ladies, exposing their ample charms each month.
* Important dates, such as the HK Rugby 7's, and obscure national holidays that you really should be toasting with champagne!
* 12 beautiful Thai ladies, exposing their ample charms each month.
* Lifestyle, fashion and health tips from The Colonel
* 12 beautiful Thai ladies, exposing their ample charms each month.
* Dates that bars might be closed for elections, or public holidays.
* 12 beautiful Thai ladies, exposing their ample charms each month.
* Did we mention 12 beautiful Thai ladies, exposing their ample charms each month, yet?

* Actual size: 8" x 6"

Get your name in print!
Contributor Guidelines for
"Hardship Posting"

Having read this book, you should have a pretty good idea of the sort of material we're after, in terms of topic and style. Note that you don't have to be an expert writer, because the Editor will edit and re-write submissions where necessary.

* word length: try and aim for 100-200 words
* make it short, sharp and to the point
* put the category and contributor's name in bold at the top
* there is no limit to how many submissions you make
* put your contact details (address, tel/fax and email) at the bottom of the page
* all published contributors will have their name printed in the acknowledgments section of the book, not alongside their individual stories, for anonymity
* all published contributors will receive an autographed copy of "Hardship Posting" as full and final compensation for their submission (at the Editor's discretion there may also be further incentives offered)
* **example of preferred submission format**:

Category: Hotel

Contributor: John Smith

"After telling my brother about the nightlife of Asian cities, he finally visited me in Bangkok where he was booked at a well-known five star hotel. Prior to checking out the nightlife, we sat in the lobby bar where we both ordered beers.

The waitress came up with the beers, knelt down and asked my brother, "Would you like head?" Without batting an eye, my brother said: "Yes, at 10 PM. Room 646". The waitress smiled, set down his beer and walked away with a confused look on her face."

Address: 69 Hardship St, Beijing, China.

Tel: 123-456 Fax: 234-567

Email: jsmith@hotmail.net

It's that simple! And if you know of others that have great true tales of expat misadventure in Asia, get them to contact us, or let us know who they are and we'll contact them.

Fax The Editor at 612-9499-5908 or
email it to hardship_posting@hotmail.com